CW01665205

JOHN PIPER

A Painter's Camera

JOHN PIPER

A Painter's Camera

Buildings and Landscapes in Britain

1935 - 1985

THE TATE GALLERY

front cover
Harvest Festival

ISBN 0 946590 81 8
Published by order of the Trustees 1987
Copyright © 1987 The Tate Gallery All rights reserved
Designed and published by Tate Gallery Publications,
Millbank, London SW1P 4RG
Printed in Great Britain by Westerham Press,
Westerham, Kent

This book is the first in
a new series to be based on material
in the Tate Gallery Archive.

Contents

Foreword

Photography has always played an important part in John Piper's working life. We showed a handful of outstanding examples of his landscape photographs in the 1983 retrospective exhibition at the Tate Gallery, and more recently the artist has deposited in the Tate Gallery Archive all the negatives still in his possession. This collection amounts to about 5,000 items, most of which have been identified by the artist and are now indexed topographically.

This activity began in the early 1930s, and there was an interesting moment of collaboration in 1937 with Paul Nash, another painter-photographer whose negatives are also held in the Tate Gallery Archive. Nash's famous photograph *Nest of Stones,* although meticulously arranged by Nash at his own window, was in fact viewed through John Piper's camera. Piper took the photographs and printed the negative, which Nash subsequently published. In the same year, 1937, Piper was commissioned by John Betjeman to write the *Shell Guide* to Oxfordshire, and a year later began to contribute to *Architectural Review* articles illustrated by his own photographs. Whereas the earlier photographs had often been of objects in a landscape, sometimes with surrealist overtones, now buildings in a landscape became Piper's particular theme. The primary purpose was to record topographical information, and certain series such as that devoted to the churches of G. E. Street have acquired a major historic significance in the revaluation of Victorian architecture.

There are sometimes close correspondences between paintings and photographs, but only rarely was a photograph used directly for a picture. Nevertheless it is of course the painter's sensibility which underlies all of John Piper's photographic work.

The selection of photographs published in this book was made with the advice of the artist from the original negatives, and all but a few were newly printed. The great majority were printed by the artist in his own darkroom, giving our reproductions a double authenticity since the quality of the image depends almost as much on the printing as on the original photographing. David Lambert from the Tate Gallery's Photographic Department worked with John Piper at his home during the printing, and he has used his experience of the artist's intentions when printing the remaining photographs later at the Tate Gallery.

Some of these prints will be on view at the Gallery at the time of the publication of this book, which has been edited by David Fraser Jenkins of the Gallery's Modern Collection who has contributed the introductory essay. Alun Grafton when working in the Tate Gallery Archive recorded and indexed all the photographic negatives.

We all owe a major debt to John Piper himself, who has given unstintingly his time in sorting the material for us and helping in the preparation of this book. We hope that it will give wider recognition to work that is surely one of the great British contributions to the art of photography.

ALAN BOWNESS *Director*

Introduction

A photograph is a record of an observation, but the record itself has to be set down. Squeezing the shutter is the half way stage. The material has been discovered and trapped, but the treatment is still to come. Piper has always worked primarily as a painter, even in all the variety of his printing techniques, and in the way the spotlights play onto his ballet sets, and in the hovering colour patches that radiate light from his stained glass windows in a church. Also with his photographs, it is as a painter that he finds the subjects that can be manoeuvred into an astonishing impact. He has sensitised his eye to be able to detect the effect that he looks for in a subject, not anywhere equally around him but in certain types of place and certain conditions. As a painter, although well ordered in terms of routine and procedure, he keeps the surface of his paper or canvas fluid and varied, encouraging to accident, and works it in an imagined space forward and backward, amongst an undergrowth of marks and colours. He has an attitude in common with Bacon and Sutherland, who read vitality into the touches of paint, applied with skill and bravura. Although the surface of the photographs is not touched, the method is more scientific only in degree. The discipline of his paintings is in the ordering of colour in patterns and intensity. The photographs, despite the lack of colour, are often extreme in range of tone, and it is the manipulation of chiaroscuro in the darkroom that is his chief means both of structuring the view and of pushing the particular idea.

The painter-photographer is distinct from the photographer (as is the painter-graver from the printmaker), and a way of looking is demanded at his completed work that is more critical in terms of content but may not be as perfect in technique. Many of Piper's photographs were taken for the original series of the Shell County Guides to Britain. One of Piper's colleagues, for example, in the series was Edwin Smith, whose work can be contrasted with his as almost the opposite in intention. The kind of subject that they chose was naturally much the same, except that Piper in his volumes was additionally the author and selected the places (and was responsible for the general attitude of the Guides, for which, from 1960, he was also editor). The similarity draws out the difference. Edwin Smith's are more professional: crisp throughout, unmarked, show the major interest in the place, and no doubt are afterwards archivally stored and identified. The effect of Piper's depends more than do Smith's on their printing, and go beyond the record, or the interesting contrast, to become one item in the range of a landscape painter with an original point of view. His subjects are more often unconventional, and are put across more directly. It is more evident that he is excited by a certain aspect of the subject and committed to his feeling for it, and is generous both in the extent to which everthing else is underplayed for this one aspect to be revealed, and in his own enthusiasm. It is possible to sense that he is about to take out pen and colours to make the subject again on paper, as happens with his photographs of life studies which are published as prints with the additions of overpainting and collage.

Piper's work is so attractive that he is sometimes thought of as an artist too easy on the eye. This criticism can be countered directly, and needs to be, since although the photographs have never been faulted, a disapproval of his vision applies as much to them as it does to the paintings. The complaint has been that this vision is not genuinely felt, and that it either omits too much of the contemporary reality (i.e. it is nostalgic), or else that it is an effect of the medium without content, and could be performed on any subject by juggling with the paint (i.e. that it is a spurious drama). The photographs provide the answer that what was created was indeed there. It is certainly a matter of experience to see it and technical skill to make it visible, as it has to be. Theatre is the most lifelike and also the most artificial of the arts, and moves the audience because of this paradox, from the knowledge that the representation is being done for a purpose which goes beyond the immediate thrill of enchantment. Landscape photographs, without a narrative and with no people, seem to have nothing to do with the effects of the theatre, and yet in some of these prints the natural illumination has the same appearance of surprise and contrast that Piper used also in stage design. Again, the evidence is here that it was the landscape itself that provided this effect. The range of subjects is controlled, and are not of just any landscape or any time of day. Like the incidents in a play, these are being brought to our notice for the interest that they have, singled out from other things seen before and afterwards. This criticism is in part a matter of misreading the politics of art. Piper's work is popular. He is able to work well with other people, and can work through their skill as artists in collaboration. This is a practical necessity for stained glass, not only because the work is done by the glass maker but because of the relation with the individual responsible for the commission. His style, although unique, is accessible, and just as his personality is given directly so also is he concerned to make work that is as available as possible. Piper's greatest popularity came from paintings of Venice exhibited first in 1960, and has been maintained by versions of later landscapes published as screenprints, made to be sold to a large public. This is a generosity of character which opposes, without deliberately intending to, the contrary view that the artist should restrict his appeal, whether to make a claim for artistic research or for the general good. Piper's work in both photography and painting makes advances on both these fronts by a more direct and popular means, as a consequence and not an aim of his career.

His admiration amongst his contemporaries in Britain went most to Paul Nash as a landscape painter and photographer, and to Bill Brandt as a photographer. His photographs slightly overlap both of theirs, and his career is a surprisingly close parallel to Brandt's. Both were born at the same time and in the same area and were profoundly attracted to the Paris avant-garde of the early 1930s. Both renounced the avant-garde for a more naturalistic style before the war, and were then employed to record war damage and conditions, and both men later pursued an isolated post-war style of landscape in extreme conditions, associated notably with life studies in distorted perspective. Brandt made portraits of famous people and not famous buildings, and, at their greatest difference, before the war documented social conditions and not the survival of the picturesque. But this comparison brings out how much Brandt's exposure of social class in Britain has obscured the continuity of his later work with his earlier, in the technical sense of tone and composition and in the surrealist feeling for the naturally bizarre, even in views of the slums in Bermondsey. Similarly the views of Brighton and Hafod House by Piper, although hardly an exposure of a current social outrage, are in the same language of human emotion that applies to his later landscapes. There is in them an element of physiognomic expression. This was perceived by Kenneth Clark when he wrote in the 1940s of the future of the pathetic fallacy, the reading in of emotions into a landscape, with implied reference to Piper and Sutherland. The photographs by Piper and Brandt share a dramatic chiaroscuro, sometimes to the extent of blackening out most of the image. Brandt's distortions of perspective are more extreme (and would not have been appropriate for the *Shell Guides*) but both of them often brought up the foreground close to the lens, whether paved street or field, to give a confusing base to the composition, flat and at the same time headlong. Since they were close to the pioneers of abstraction and surrealism, and in Britain were the pioneers themselves, it is not surprising that these qualities can be discovered in their prints: qualities of overall design, in line and mass, and a feeling for the anarchic vitality in observed natural objects. On prolonged study the human presence in these photographs becomes equivocal. They both exploited the deserted and lightless streets of London during the war, disturbing since lacking any inhabitants. Piper's towns and houses continued to be seen as if uninhabited. Brandt's blurred nudes on the pebbles of the Kent coast and the Grand Ailly at Dieppe are incorporated into this strange geology, where both landscape and oddly shaped fragments of bodies are as animate and pantheistic as a surrealist painting by Miró. Piper's portfolio 'Stones and Bones' (1978) of screenprints and photographs approaches the same animation from the other side: mountains and buildings are manipulated into expression as if parts of a live human body.

Piper very early in his career painted a few portraits, most of which remained unfinished, shortly after leaving the Royal College, and there is a connection between these and his first beach paintings. In all the thousands of his negatives there are absolutely no portraits. The photographs of Romanesque fonts and 'foliate heads' are at least figures, and the latter come near to being a metaphorical self portrait, and are not too unlike the lean features of his self portrait gouache on a black background painted in 1984. The human expression of the recent paintings of churches was pointed out by Moelwyn Merchant in his introduction to Piper's exhibition at Marlborough Fine Art

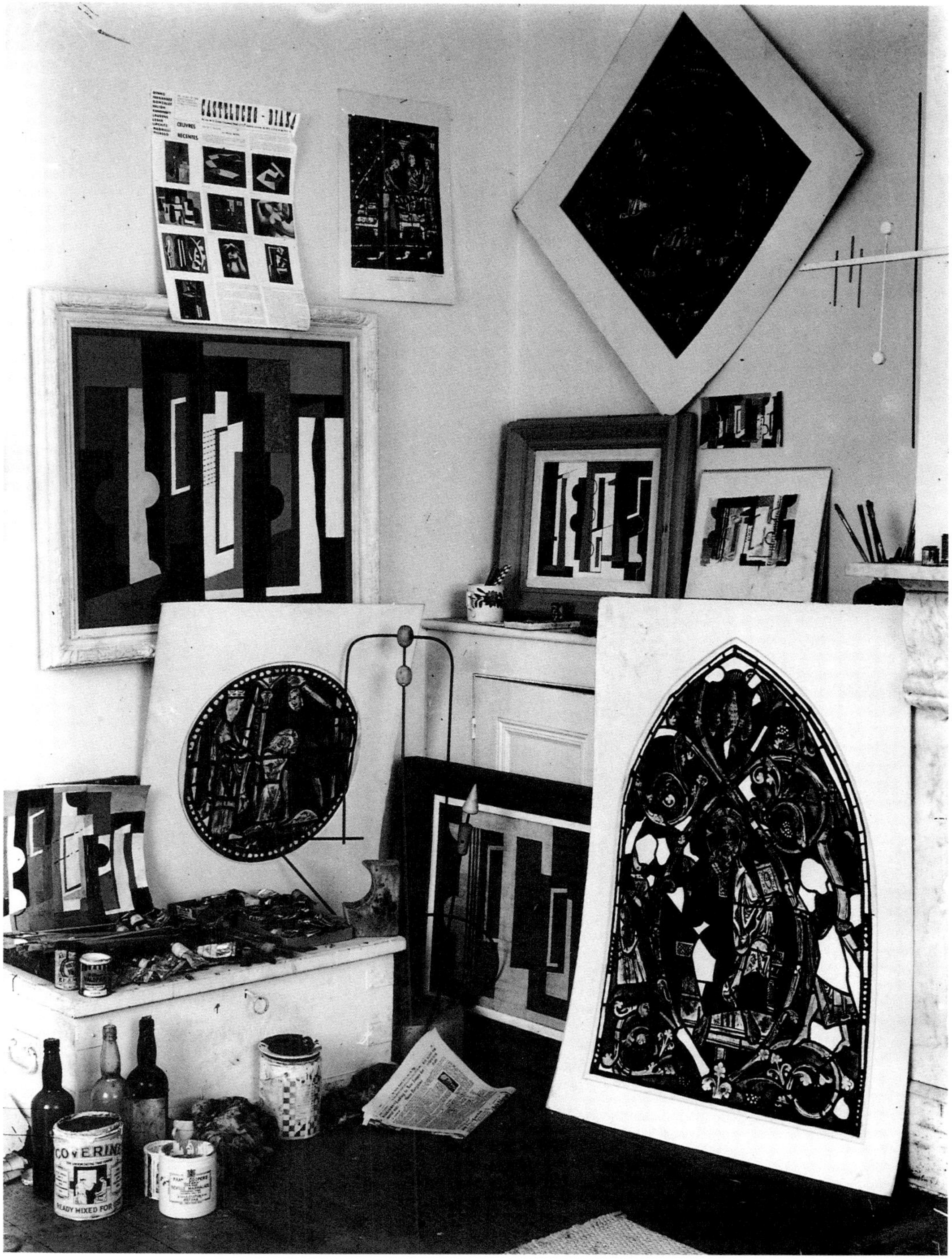

Studio of John Piper, about 1936

in 1985. This concealment is a vital part of the value of the photographs, and is not mere diffidence. Piper has always needed a technical constraint to fight against, and hence his frequent use of media new to him. He also seems to have needed to disguise his subject, in order to transfer, against the grain, felt emotion to something that is observed. The photographs of the 1940s show this most clearly, particularly those of Snowdonia, which share a public and private emotion due to the war. He had then been commissioned to record Windsor Castle in case it was bombed, and to draw in North Wales the underground store of the crown jewels and the National Gallery collection. In this way the mountain top photographs reflect his view of their patriotic resilience. The emotion in this case is not so much as concealed, for the images speak from their context in history. Later on there is a particular effect from the accumulation of certain types of place – which becomes a part of the artist's style, and of his retrospectively seen artistic personality – but beyond this there is visible in some of the photographs an alliance between a literal concealment in their subject – the ivy of the sculpture at Wotton, the dappled light on the Stowe 'Worthy', the flattening sunlight on the Stoke-by-Nayland door – and a technical concealment within the grain of the photographic paper. The subjects most obscured are sculptures of human figures. At its extreme, in the 'Eye and Camera' prints, the model is erotically charged and yet almost obscured by a difficult point of view and overpainting. The outstanding quality of the original prints is the way in which this blurred grain of the paper is used to simulate a radiance of light from the subject. It is an ironic effect, since it is achieved by feeling an expansiveness in the subject that can be set down by reducing the detail, so that by concealing some of what is there, the impact of the first sensation can be reproduced.

With Piper's photographs, as with his paintings, this kind of impact was based on training in Paris in the 1930s. His first photographs were for the local archaeological society which he organised as a youth. This function of recording details of architecture, served also by his topographical notebooks, has continued with the work for the Shell Guides, and it was for these that he took the greater number of them, which total about 5,000 now deposited at the Tate Gallery Archive. This topographical function was discarded in the mid 1930s when for two years his paintings were exclusively abstract.

The abstract paintings were studied by means of paper collages, at times expanded into constructions in space made from wire and coloured flats. Piper took photographs of these in order to see printed the result of lighting them like a stage, and subsequently used them as an example to his painting. These photographs of his own sculpture were followed during the period in which he went back to landscape by a series of articles for the Architectural Review on British art, which were illustrated with his own photographs: 'England's early sculptors' (1936) on Saxon carvings; 'The Nautical Style' (1938); 'London to Bath: a topographical and critical survey of the Bath Road' (1939); 'Fully Licensed: in praise of the ordinary public house' (1940) and 'Decrepit Glory: a tour of Hafod (1940). It was at this period just before the war that he was closest to Paul Nash, and printed for him some of his photographs. Nash had discovered on an Atlantic crossing in 1931 how photography could make a subject out of details of ships' equipment. Piper had been drawing masts and lighthouses on the south coast at the same time, but was now indebted to Nash for them as a photographic subject. There is some difference in style: Nash was the more surreal and showed these details out of context and hence close to the camera, whereas Piper was the more narrative and documentary. For a time the particular objects were isolated like a sculpture on a pedestal – and the surrealist painters often turned to sculpture and photography – but there is never a suggestion in Piper's work that these are dream landscapes.

Piper returned to certain places that he liked, and which he had more or less discovered (such as Portland, hardly painted before or since by anyone else), but the catalogues of his exhibitions show more than anything that he was for ever finding attractions in new places in Britain. In the 1940s he had made series of paintings of three great houses: Knole for Edward Sackville-West, Windsor Castle for the Queen and Renishaw for Osbert Sitwell. There are no photographs of these, and few at all during the war, when cameras were of course only used by spies. These houses are each an extravagant accumulation, asymmetrical as a whole and fascinating both in detail and as a composition. A love for the extravagant has persisted in Piper's photographs, especially for Harlaxton and the other great Victorian country houses. In the 1960s this was an attack on good taste, a position opposed to purist architecture and to architecture as an ideal rather than as an existing building. The Shell Guides similarly also took a position as an alternative to the exclusively historical and complete account of the buildings of Britain given by Nikolaus Pevsner, and were more concerned with an appreciation of the best buildings in each country and their character within a particular landscape.

For very many of his paintings and gouaches Piper also took photographs, which he placed beside his drawing board. Few of these are of the same view as the painting, and few of the photographs which he printed on a large exhibition size are repeated in the paintings. The studies used for paintings serve to clarify the detail, just as had the topographical notebooks, but the large photographs were selected as works that were already complete. They share with the paintings qualities of light, of presence and of composition, and like the paintings give a view for now of the places around us.

The recent photographs should not be undervalued in contrast to those taken fifty years ago since they necessarily lack the emotions appropriate to looking at pre-war Britain. When they were taken the older photographs drew attention to a tradition in rural and industrial landscape and architecture. The subjects even then were not often made in this century, and Piper has never been attracted to things (other than works of art) that are new, but nevertheless the subjects existed and their interest was a contemporary issue. A part of the avant garde (most notably in this context Picasso and Miró) had always recognised the primitive as an alternative to the everyday, and cast their work in the past. Piper's studio housed his abstract paintings and copies of medieval stained glass as equivalents. His photographs of the last fifteen years are the more arresting for being appreciated without misplaced love of the recent past, as were also the old ones when first taken, and the absence in them of the new continues to be a kind of primitivism, allied with his painterly skills in black and white.

DAVID FRASER JENKINS

A Note on Equipment

I started with a number 2 Brownie, but when I was about 18 I bought (in Brighton) a second-hand camera which I stuck to (with modifications and a certain amount of rebuilding) till I was sixty. My Brighton buy was called IDEAL, the name indented into its black leather. It was a 2¼ × 3¼ inches affair, with a Zeiss lens and rising front, which worked easily for horizontal and vertical exposures. When I had had it for ten years, I got it adapted to take film packs. Till then I had always used Kodak film, but Ferrania put film packs holding twelve on the market, and I used them for some time. One could use just one, or two, and close a slide on the rest of the pack. In about 1963 I bought a (new) Hasselblad, with a standard lens, and a little later acquired a wide-angle lens, and a telephoto. I took to using Ilford film and printing paper. I have two enlargers in the dark room, a rather clumsy upright one and modern Durst.

My wife and I live near Henley-on-Thames, and we were still without electricity through the war and later. Our house was on the fringe of the park of Stonor, and the owner was kind enough to house me and an enlarger in a room above stables, which was easily turned into a dark-room, and which had electricity laid on. I used this gratefully and happily for ten years or so, until modern services reached us.

I would add a note on the (mostly Romanesque) stone carvings in this book. When they were in a poor light, and not too far from the floor, I found the light of a tilly Paraffin pressure lamp of the greatest use. We travelled everywhere with it in the car, along with a sponge, with which one could wet outstanding parts of the design: often a great help in explaining a composition on a font or a capital.

JOHN PIPER

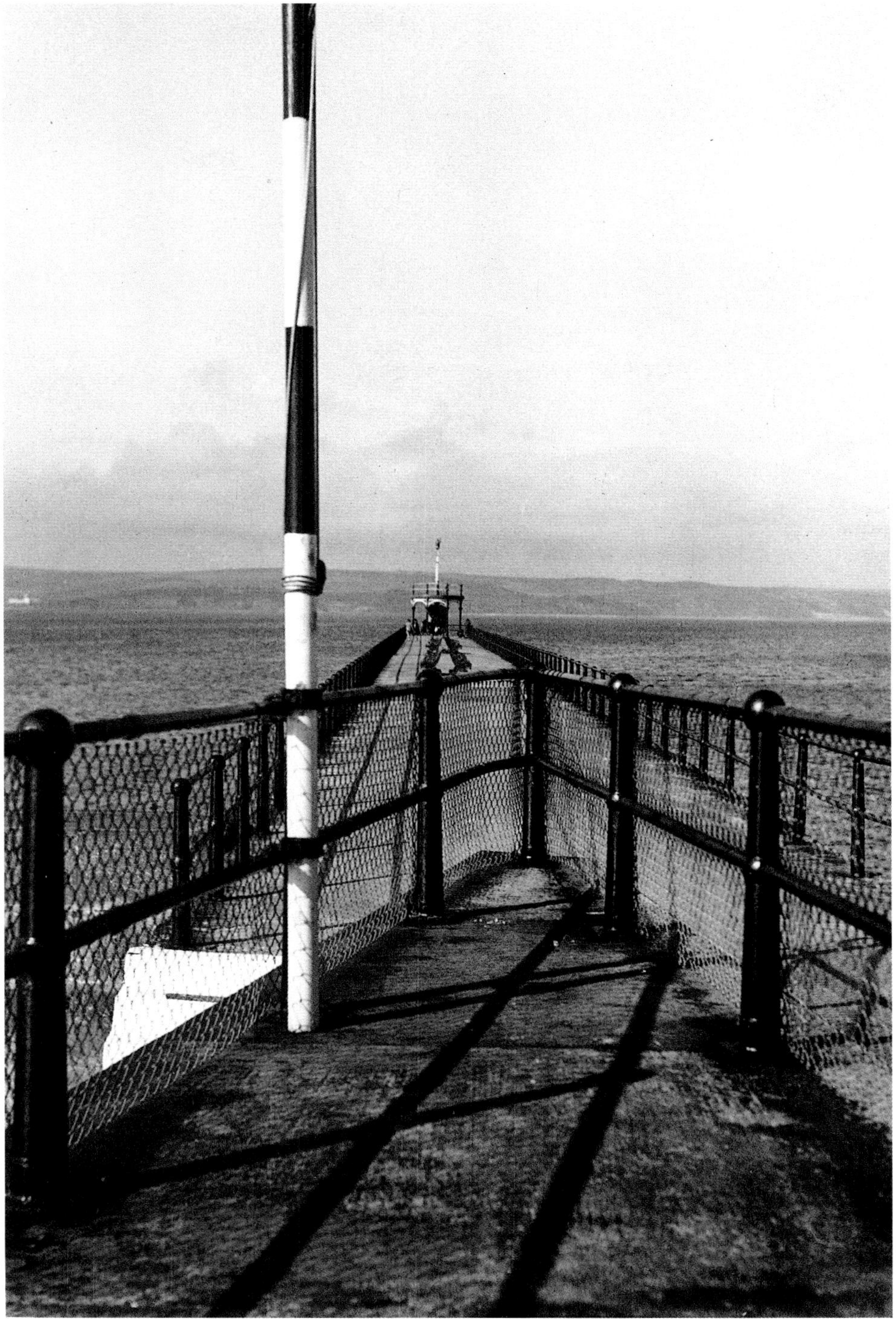

1 Weymouth Pier, Dorset

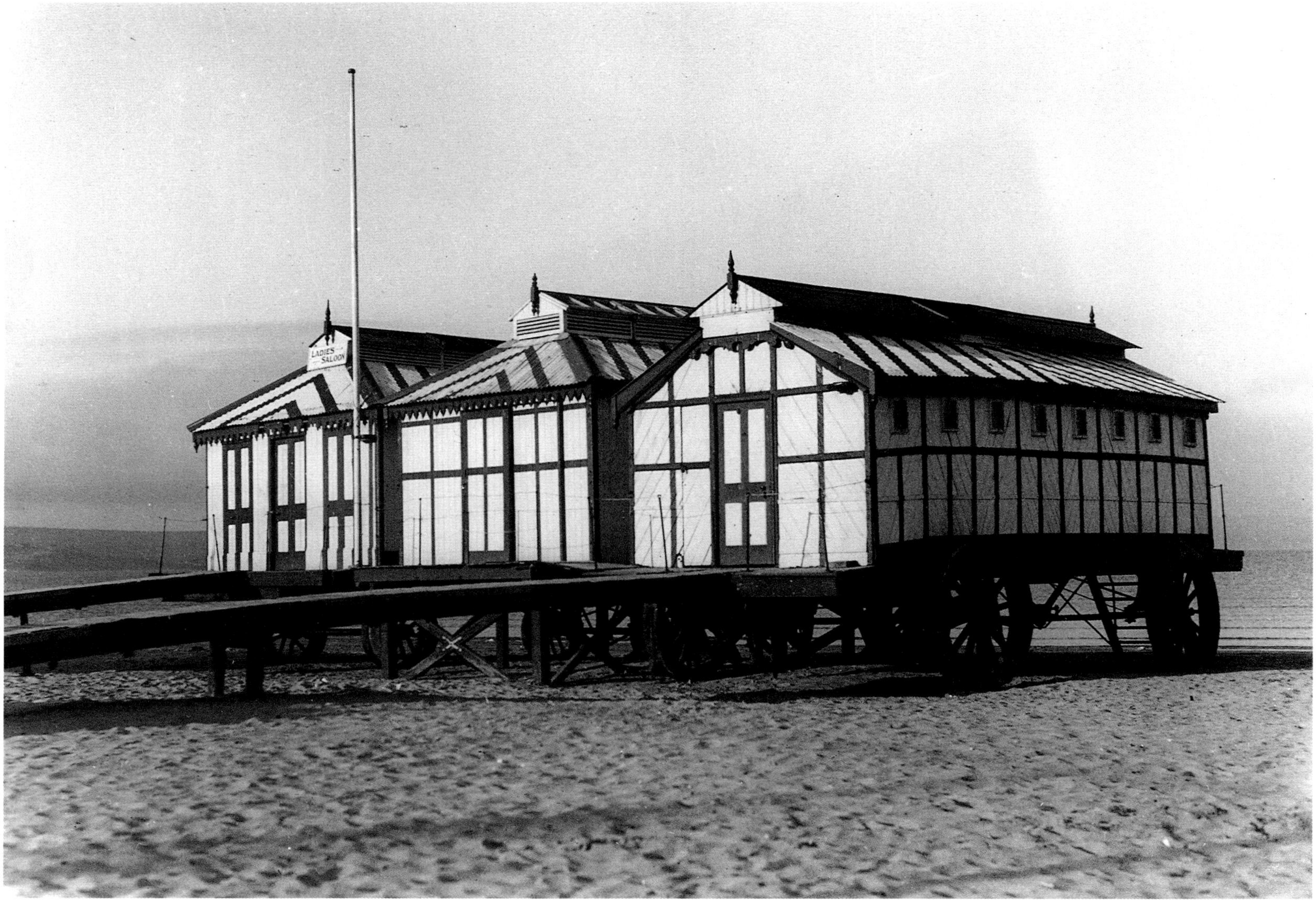

2 Beach huts

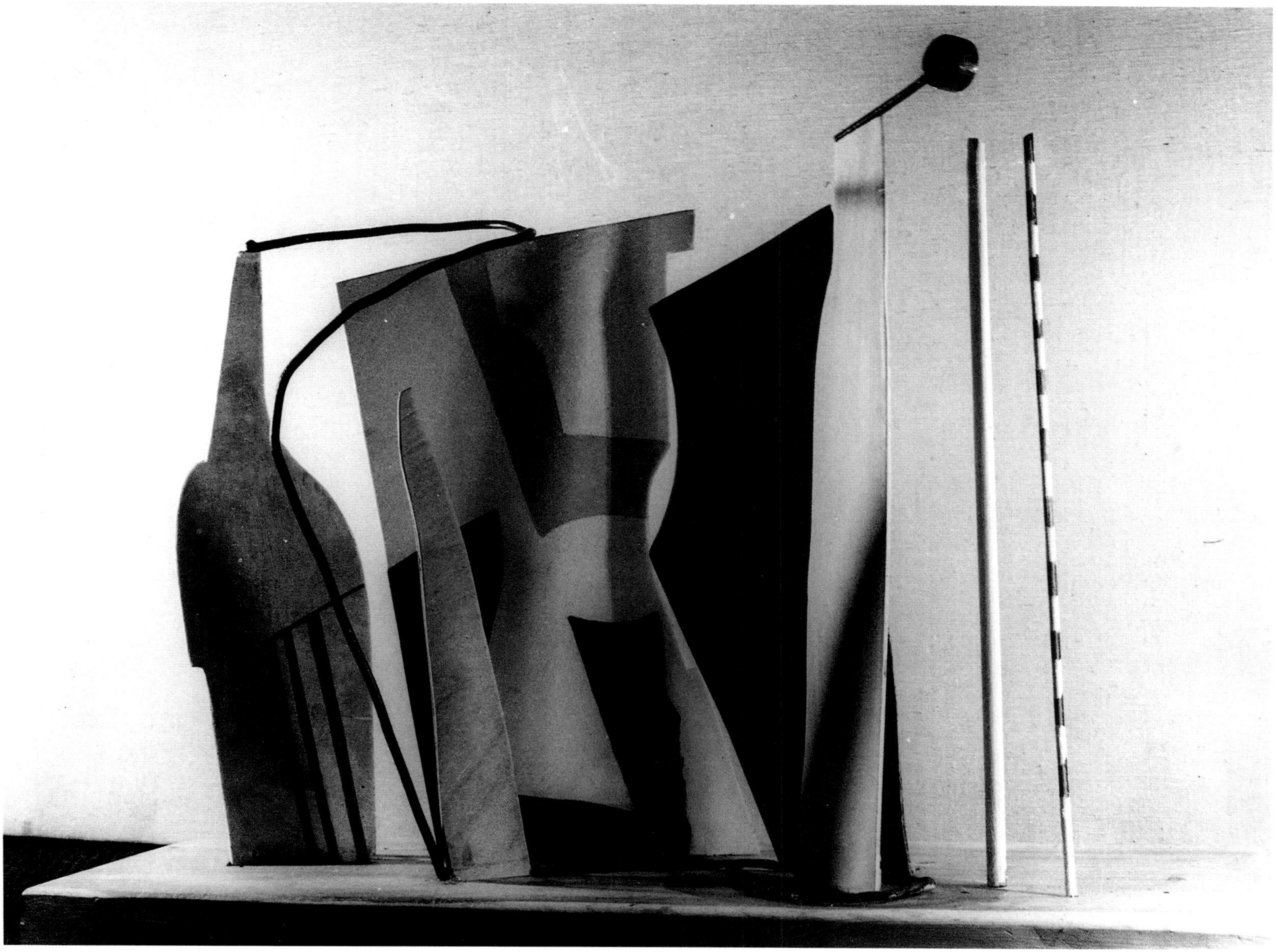

3 Beach Object, Construction by John Piper, 1937

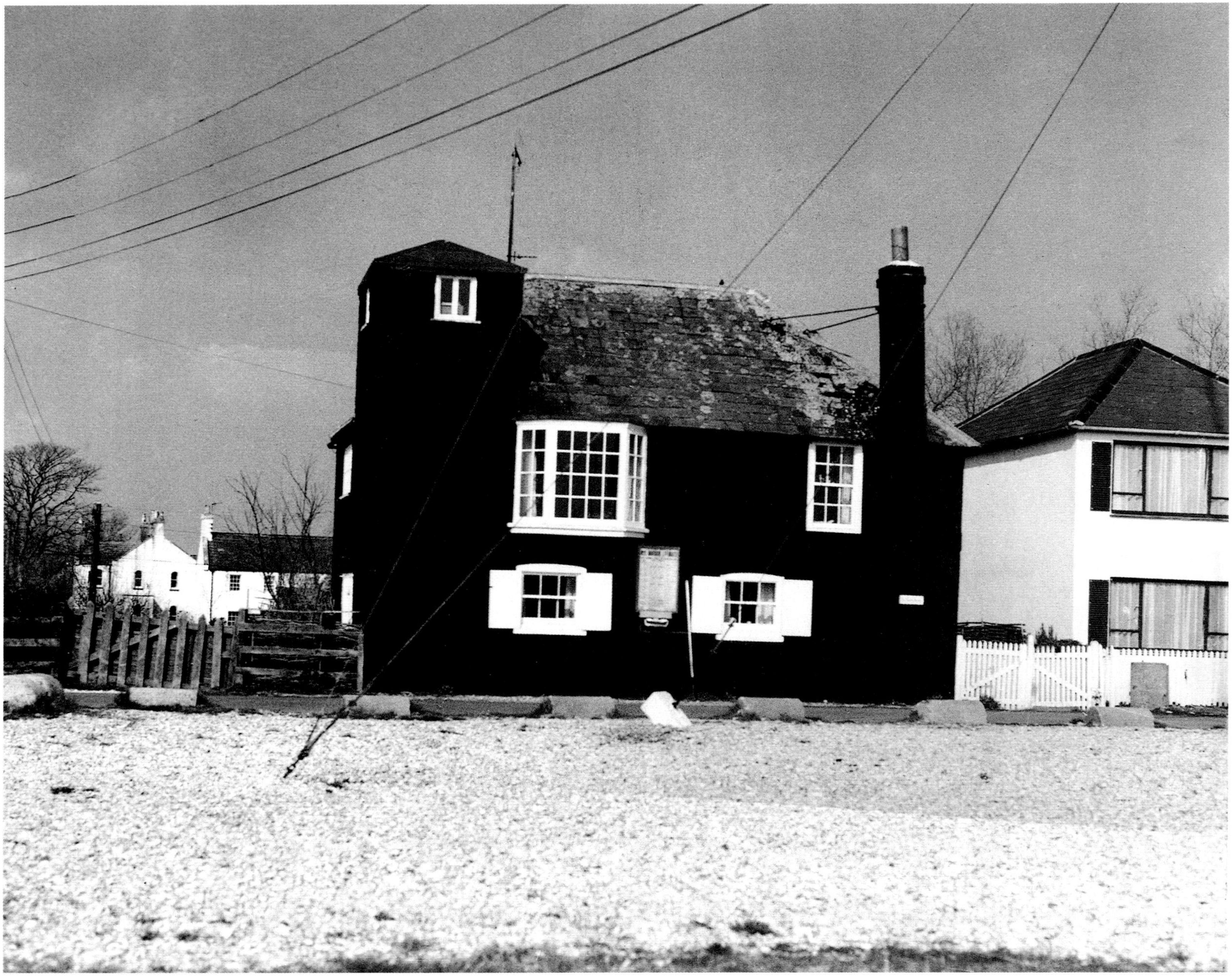

4 Coastguard Station, Rye Harbour,
East Sussex, 1977

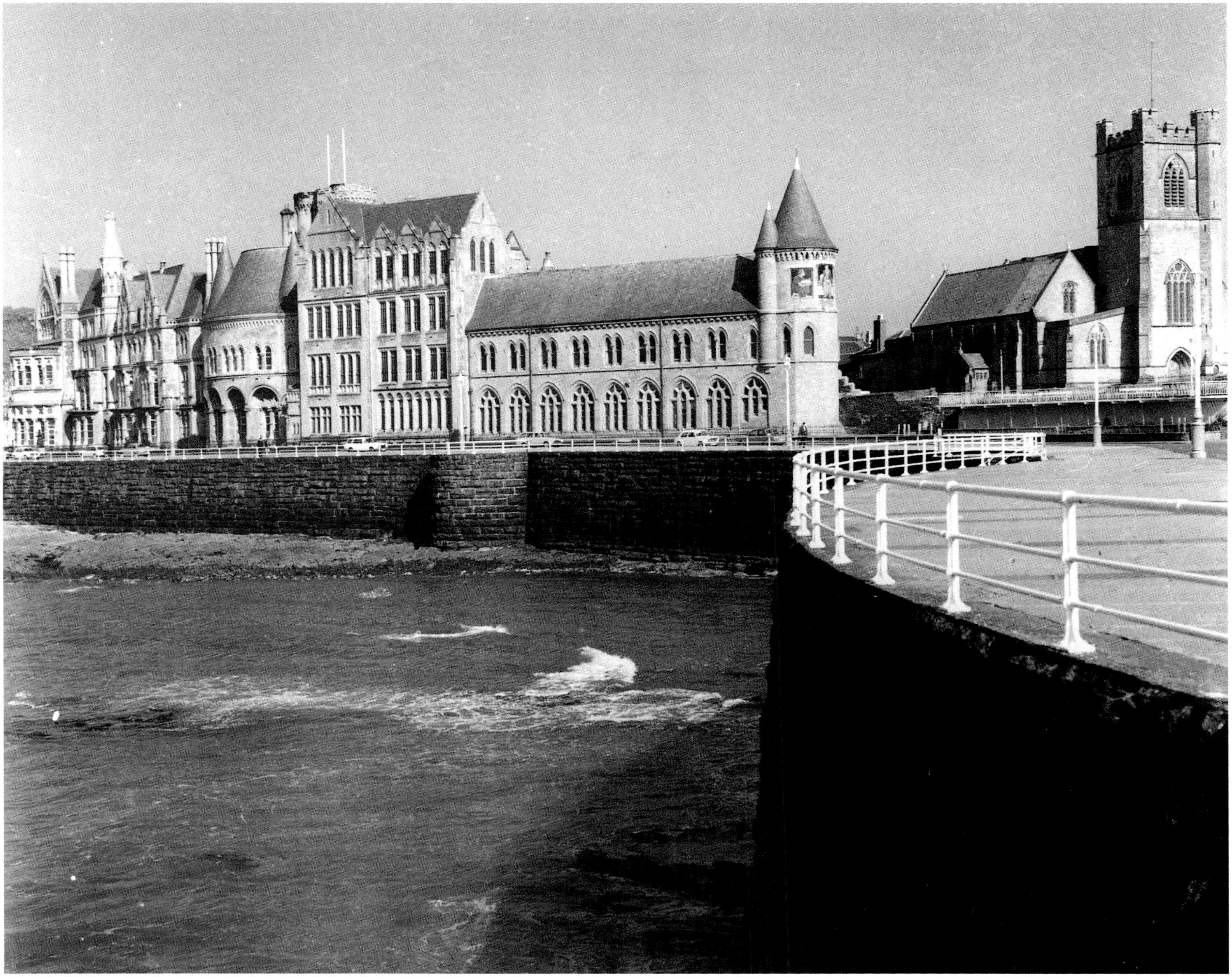

5 J. P. Seddon's University College of Wales, Aberystwyth, Dyfed

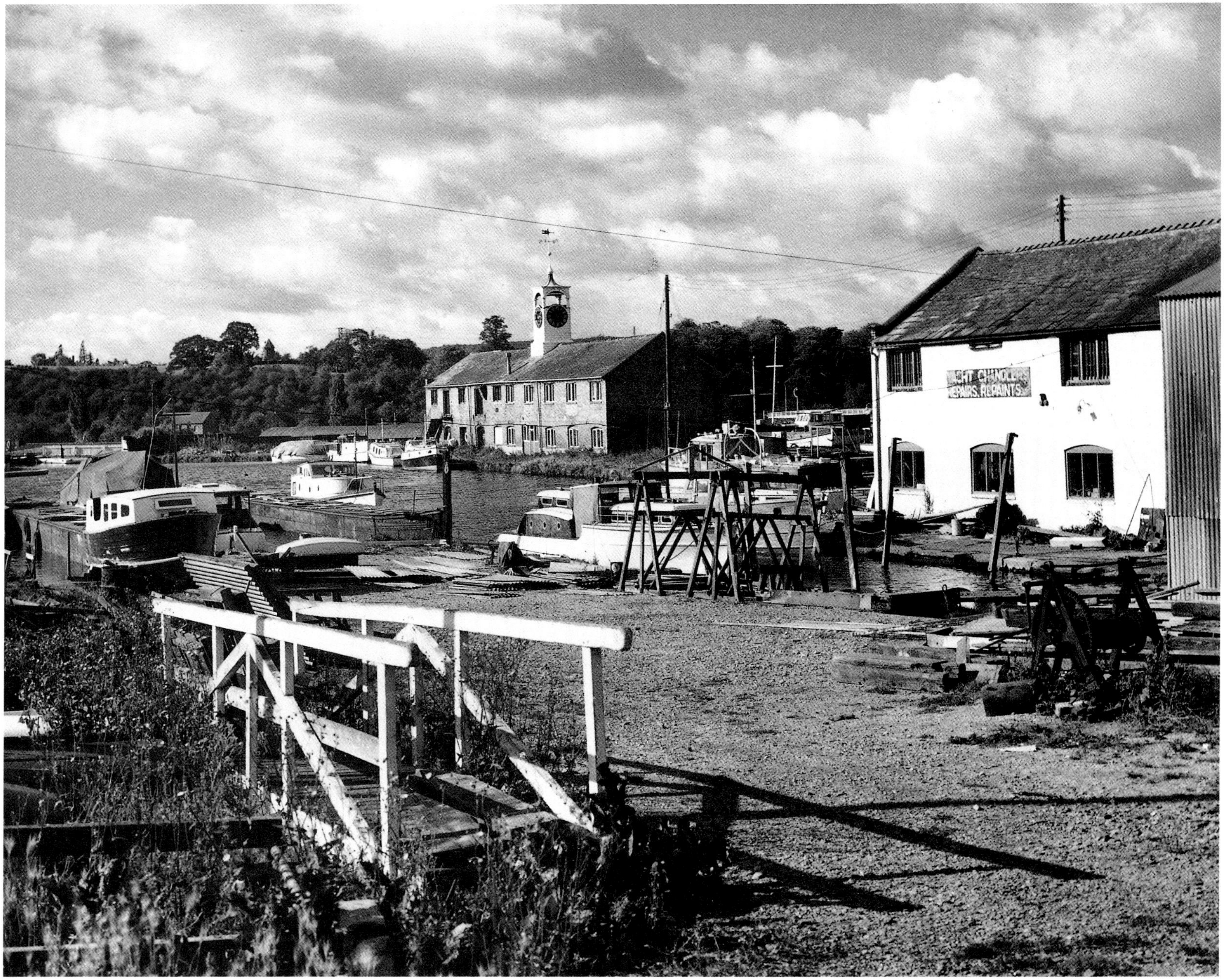

6 Canal Basin, Stourport, Worcestershire

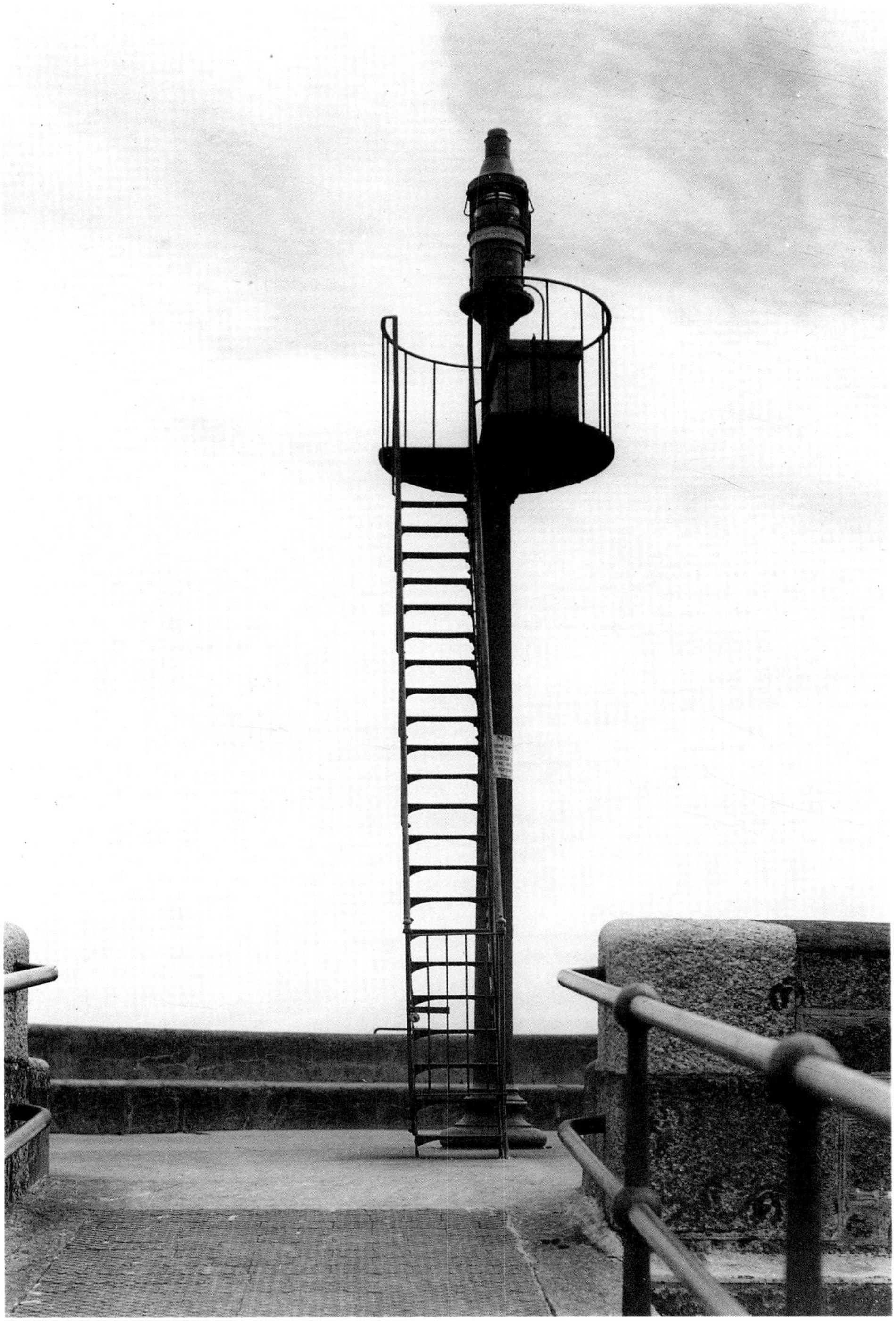

7 A harbour light at Ramsgate, Kent

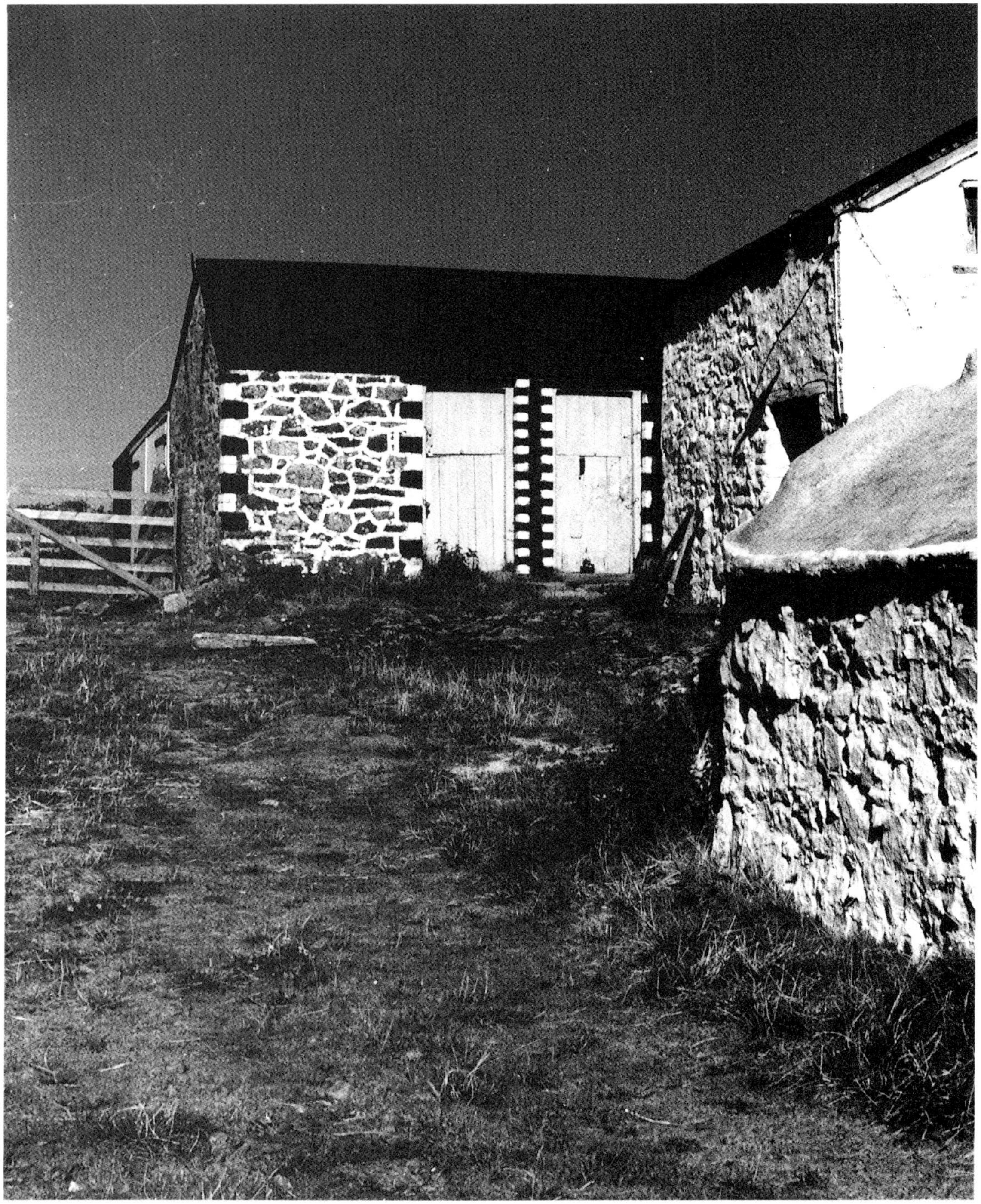

8 Farm buildings, Trefasser, Dyfed

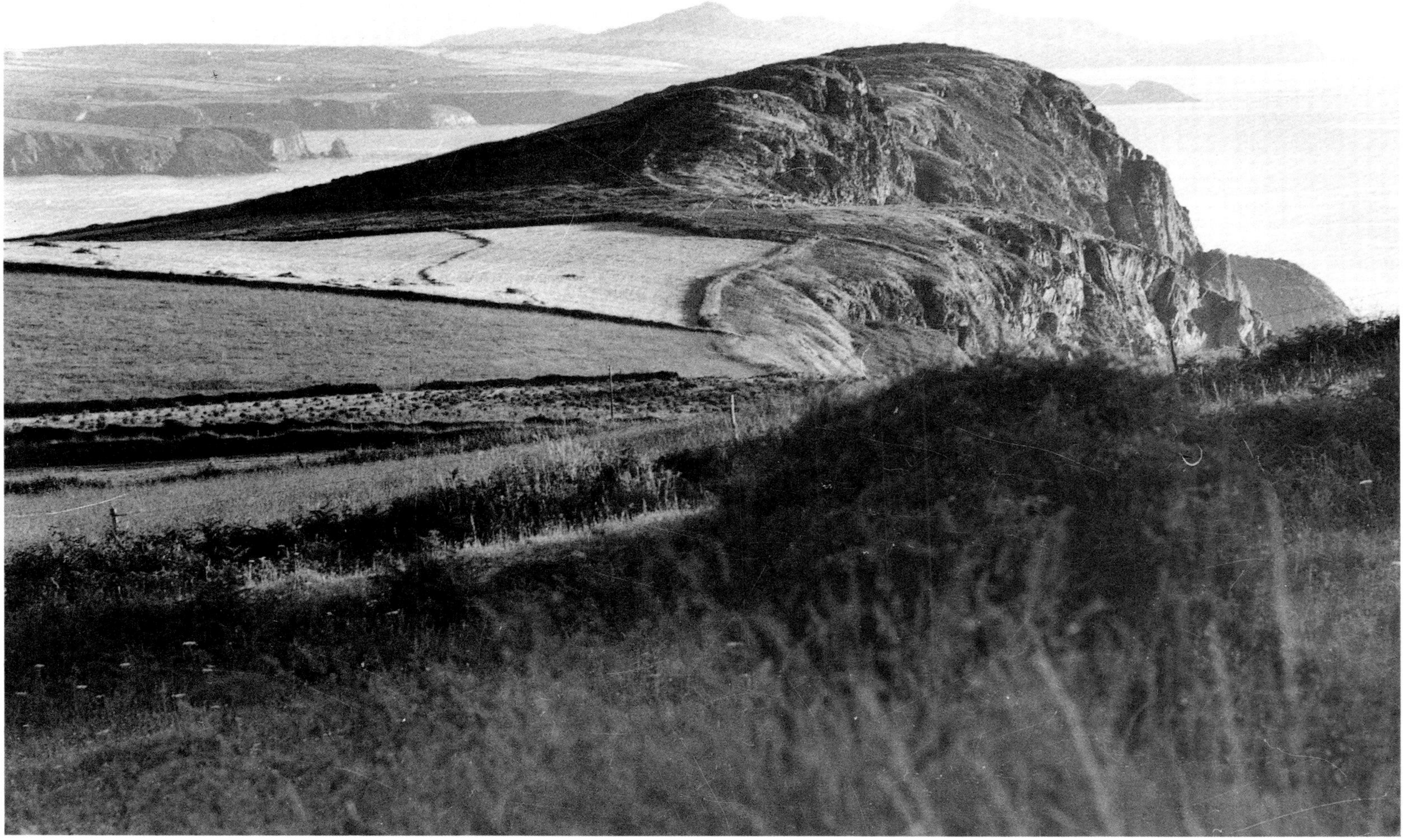

9 From Strumble Head, looking towards
St Davids, Dyfed

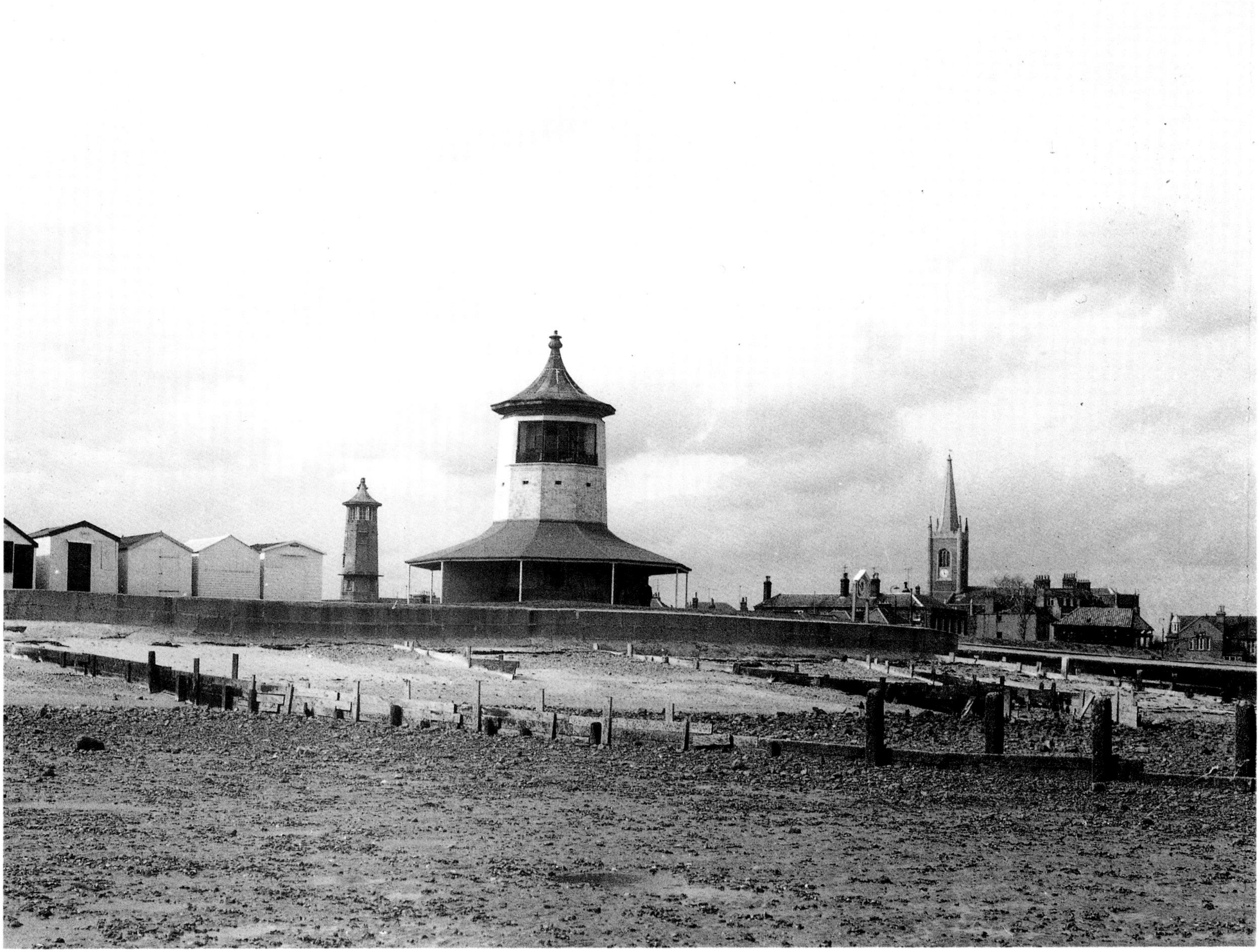

10 Harwich, low light and high light, Essex

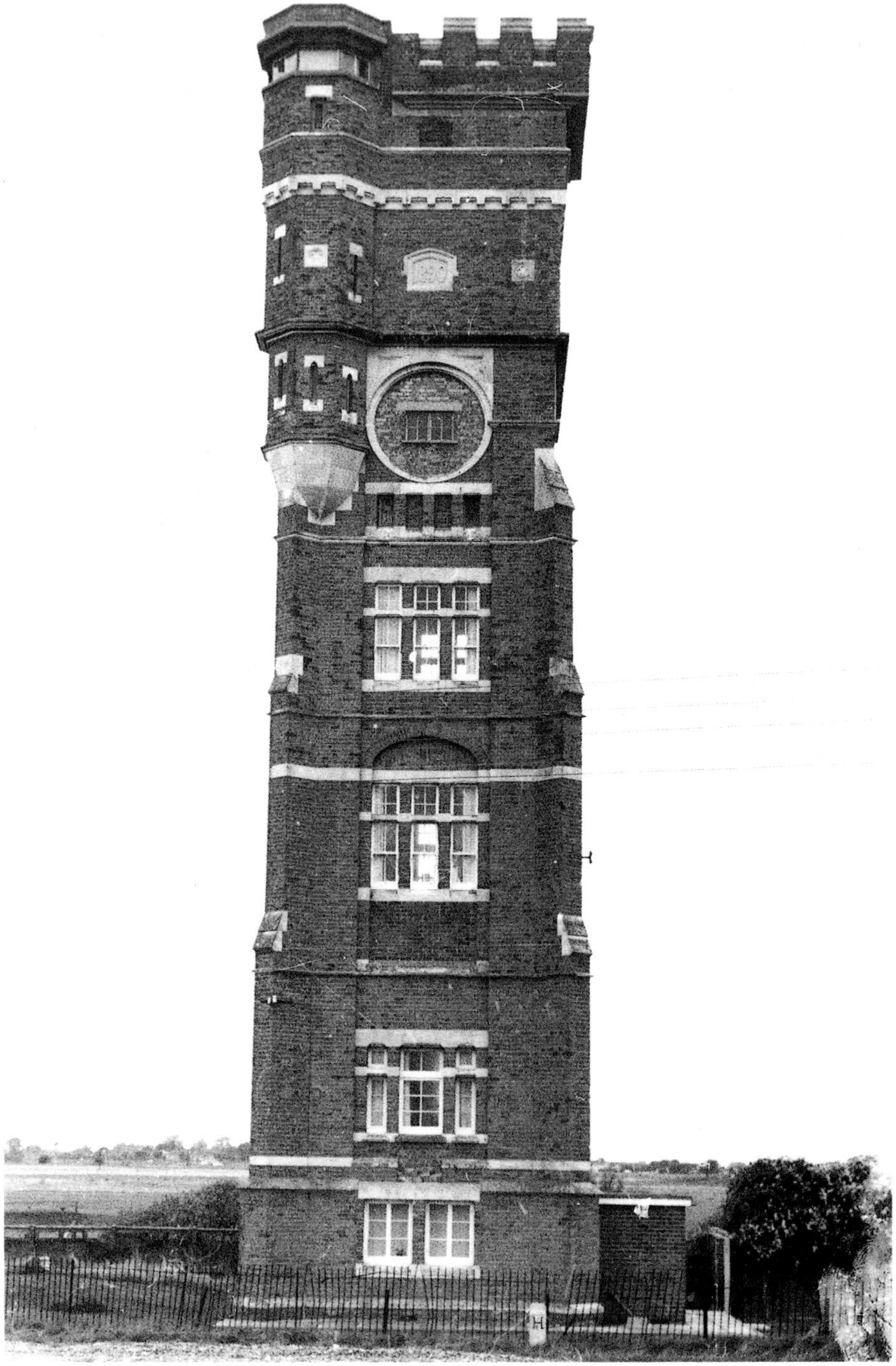

11 Tower house at Littlestone,
Romney Marsh, Kent

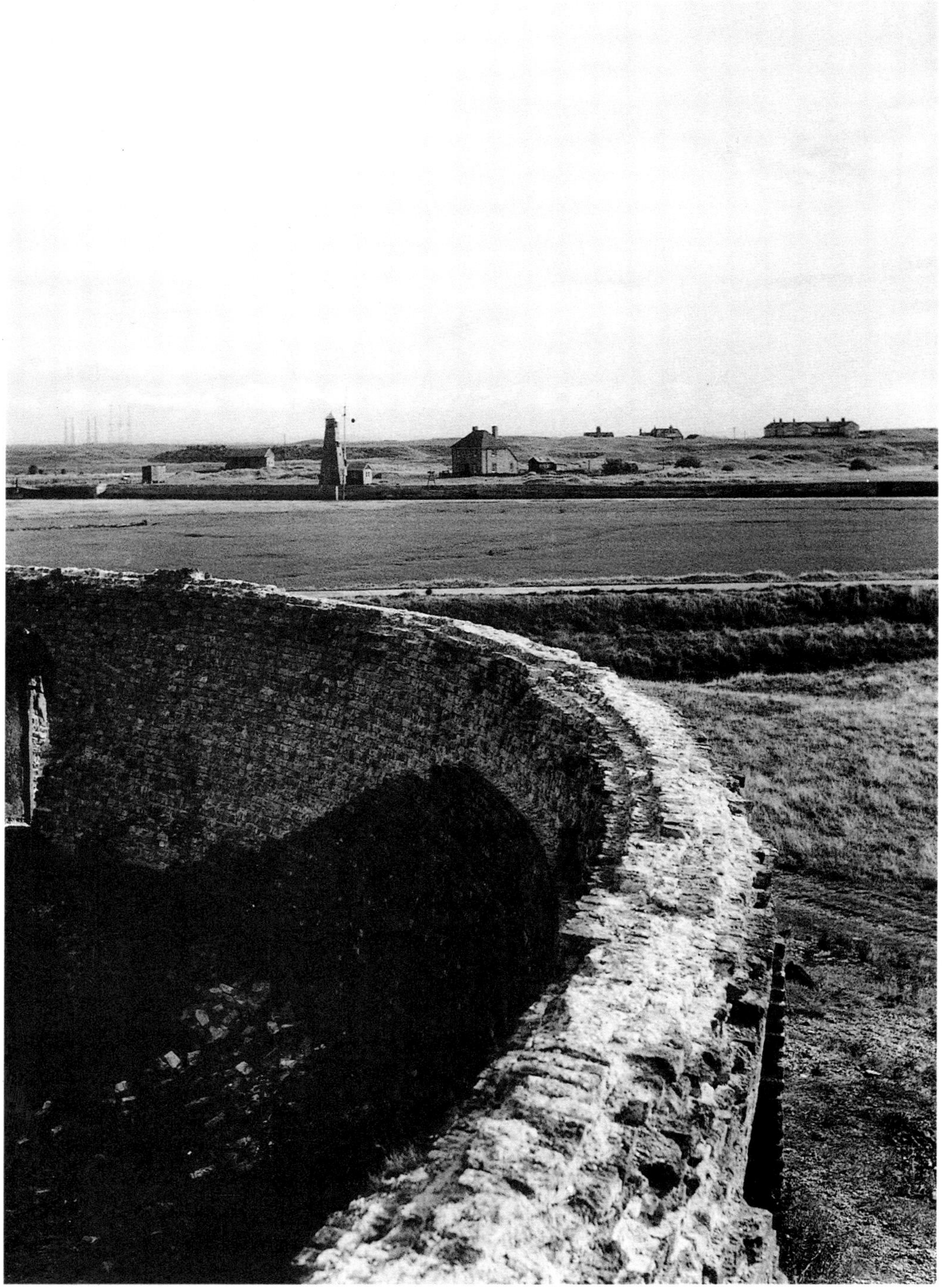

12 Martello tower at Camber

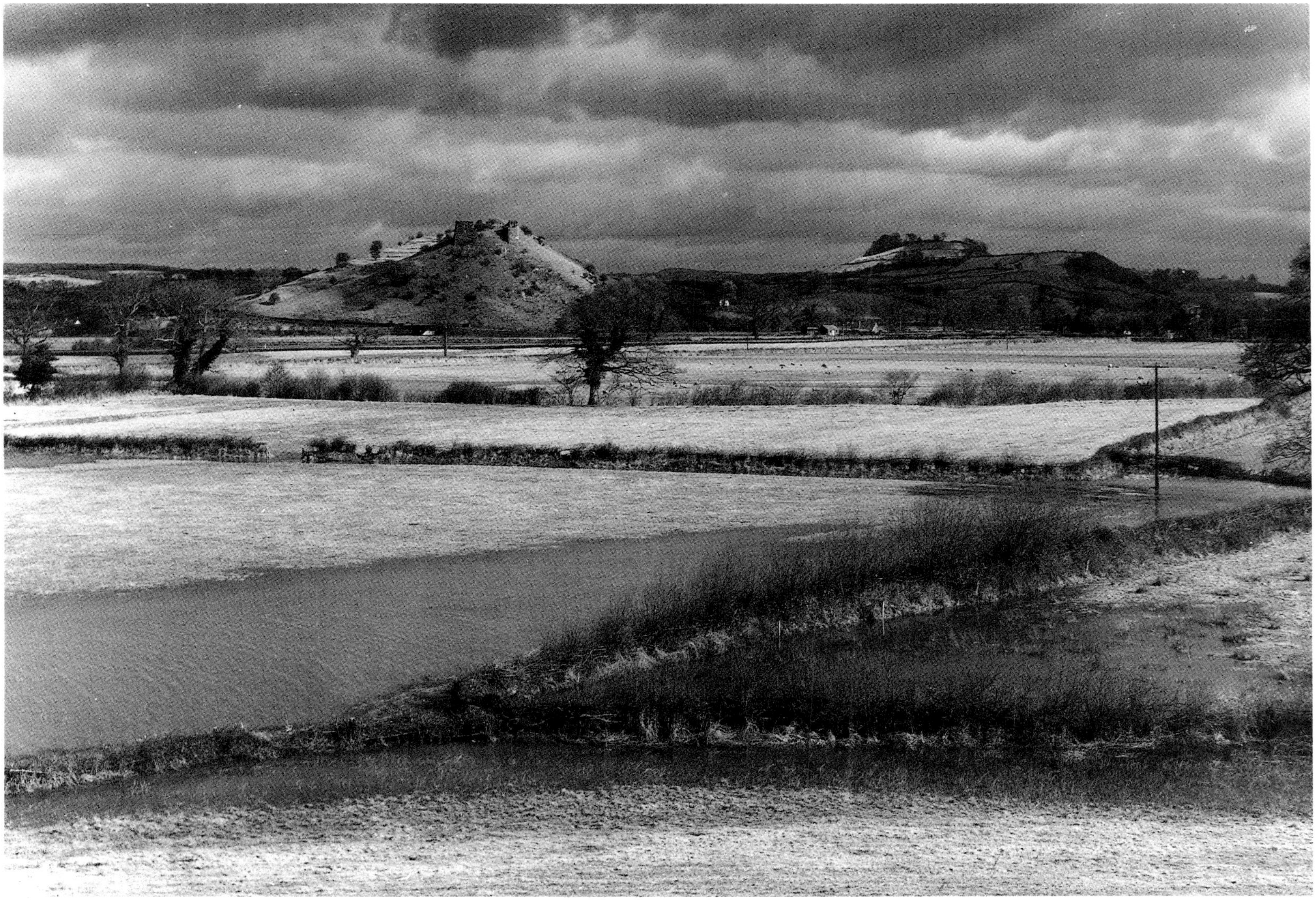

13 Dryslewyn, near Llandeilo, Dyfed

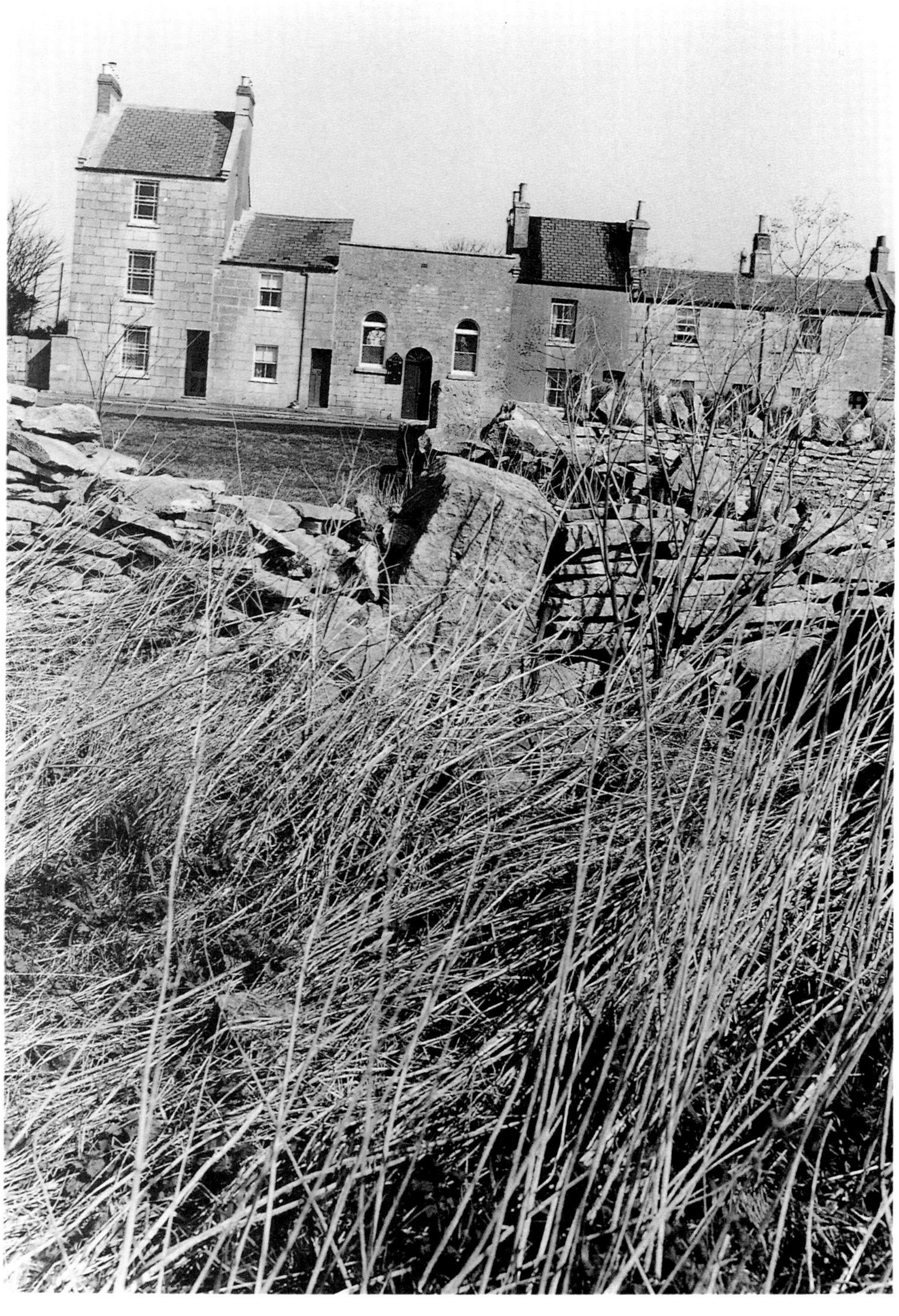

14 Houses at Portland, 1937

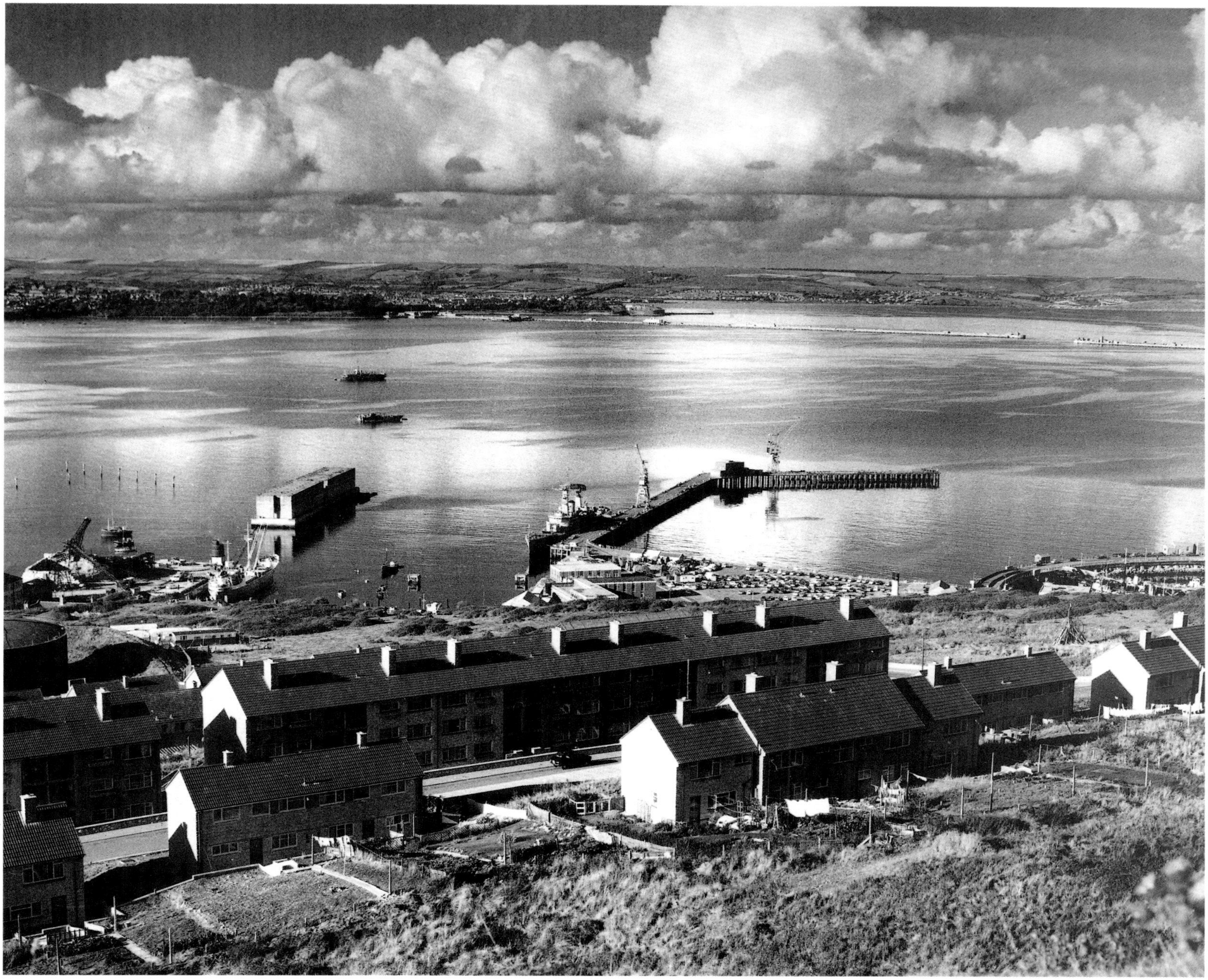

15 Portland Roads looking towards
Weymouth, about 1970

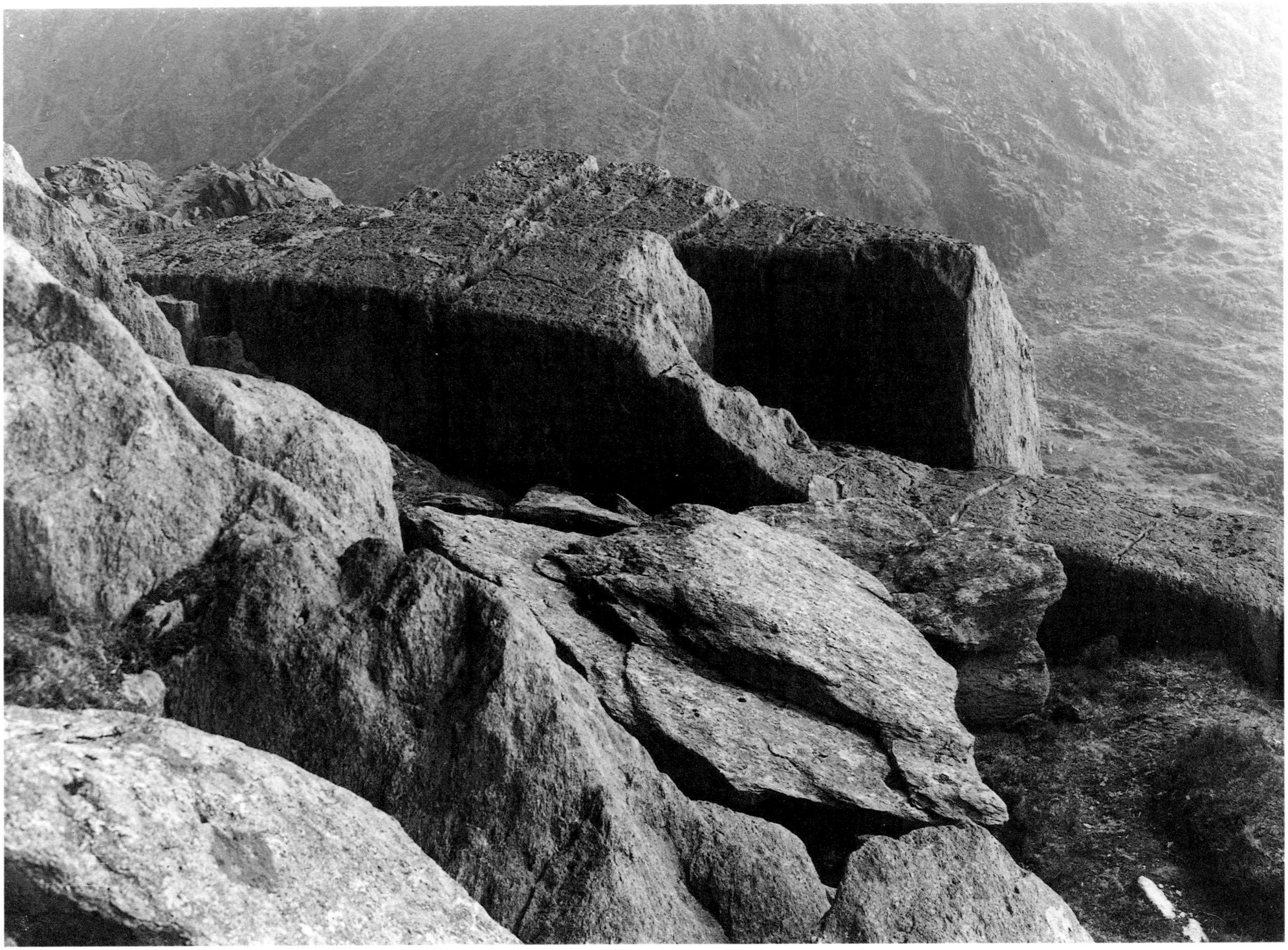

16 Tryfan, Snowdonia, about 1950

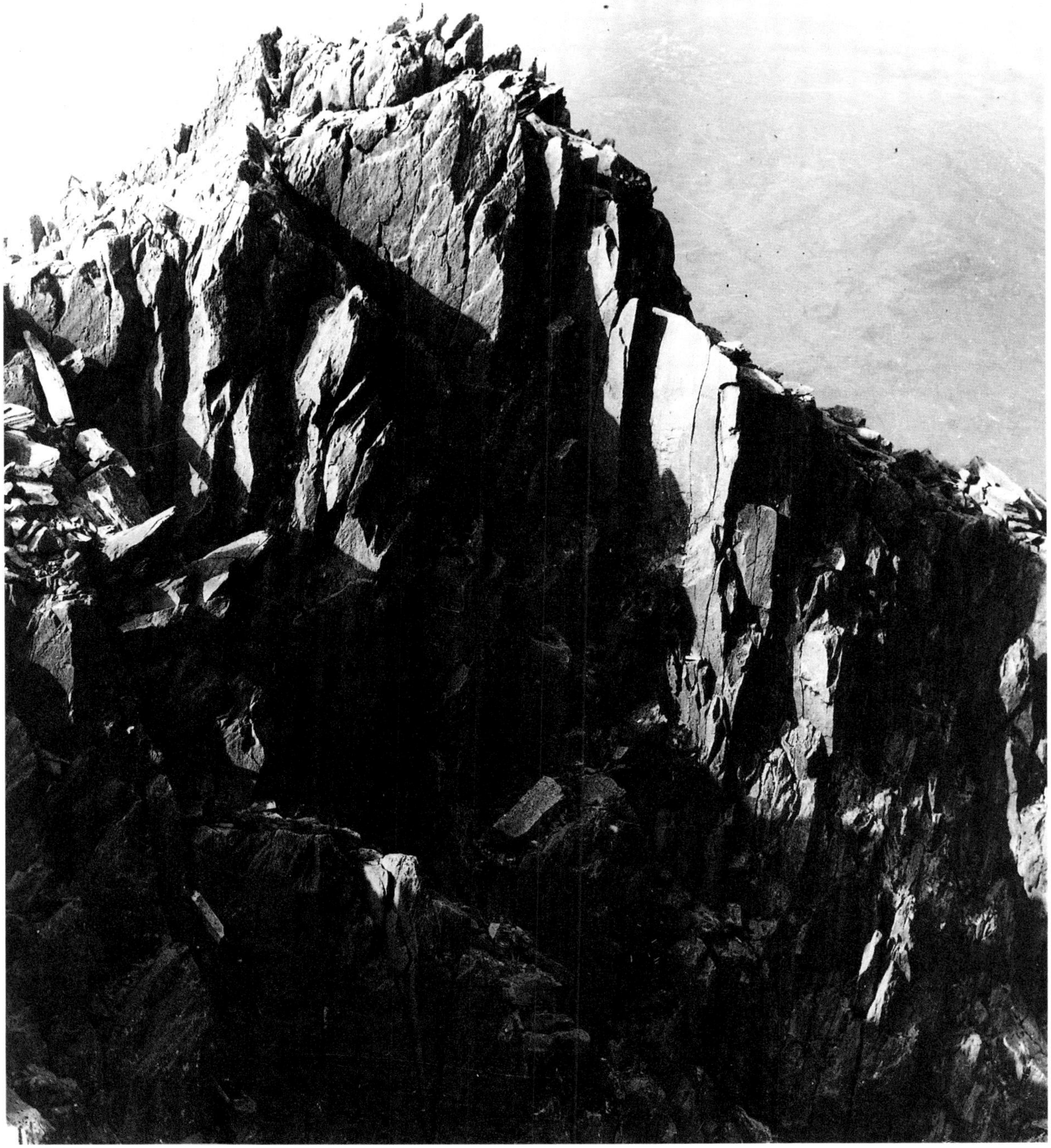

17 The summit of Tryfan, Snowdonia, about 1950

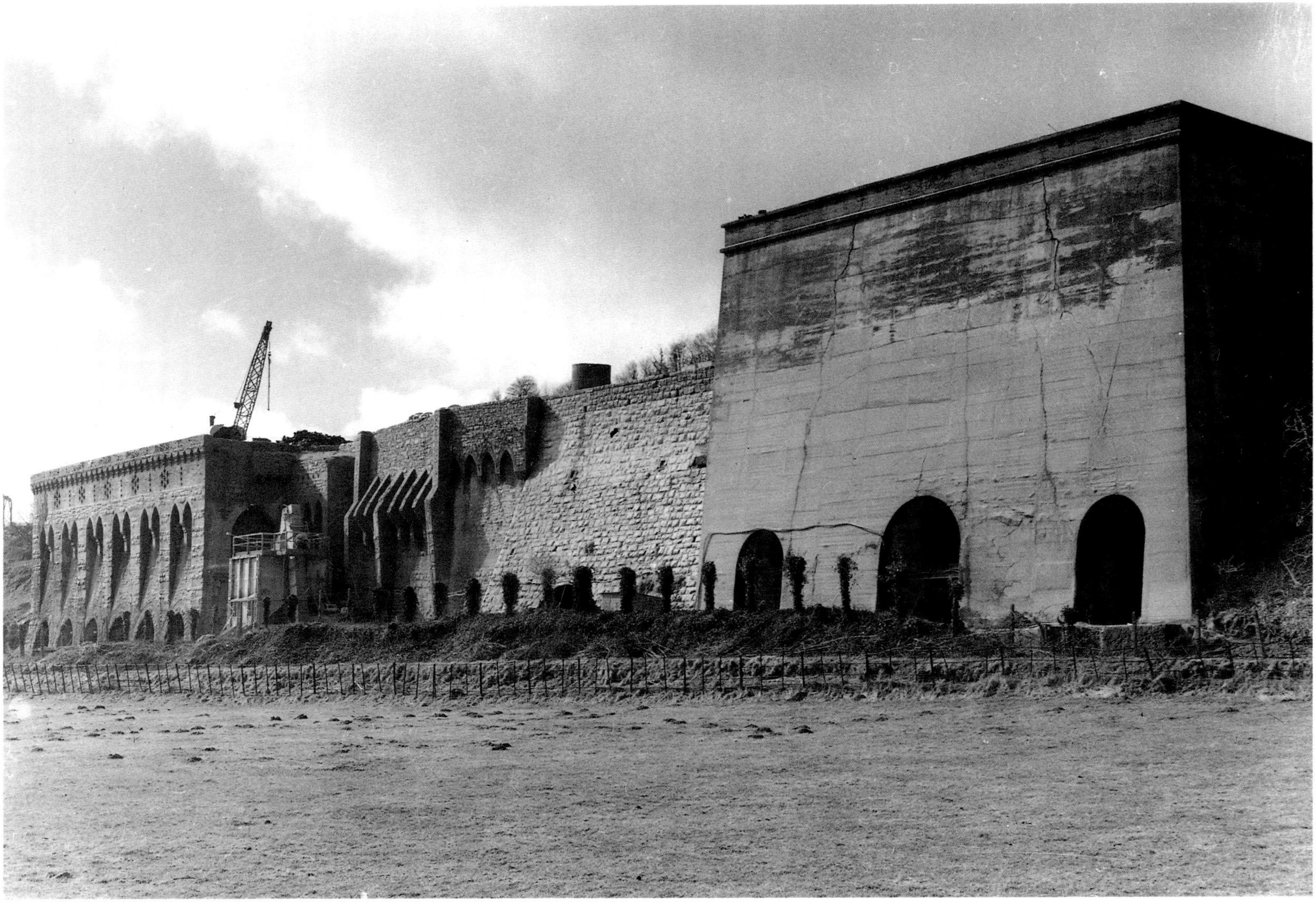

18 Limekilns at Llandybie, Dyfed

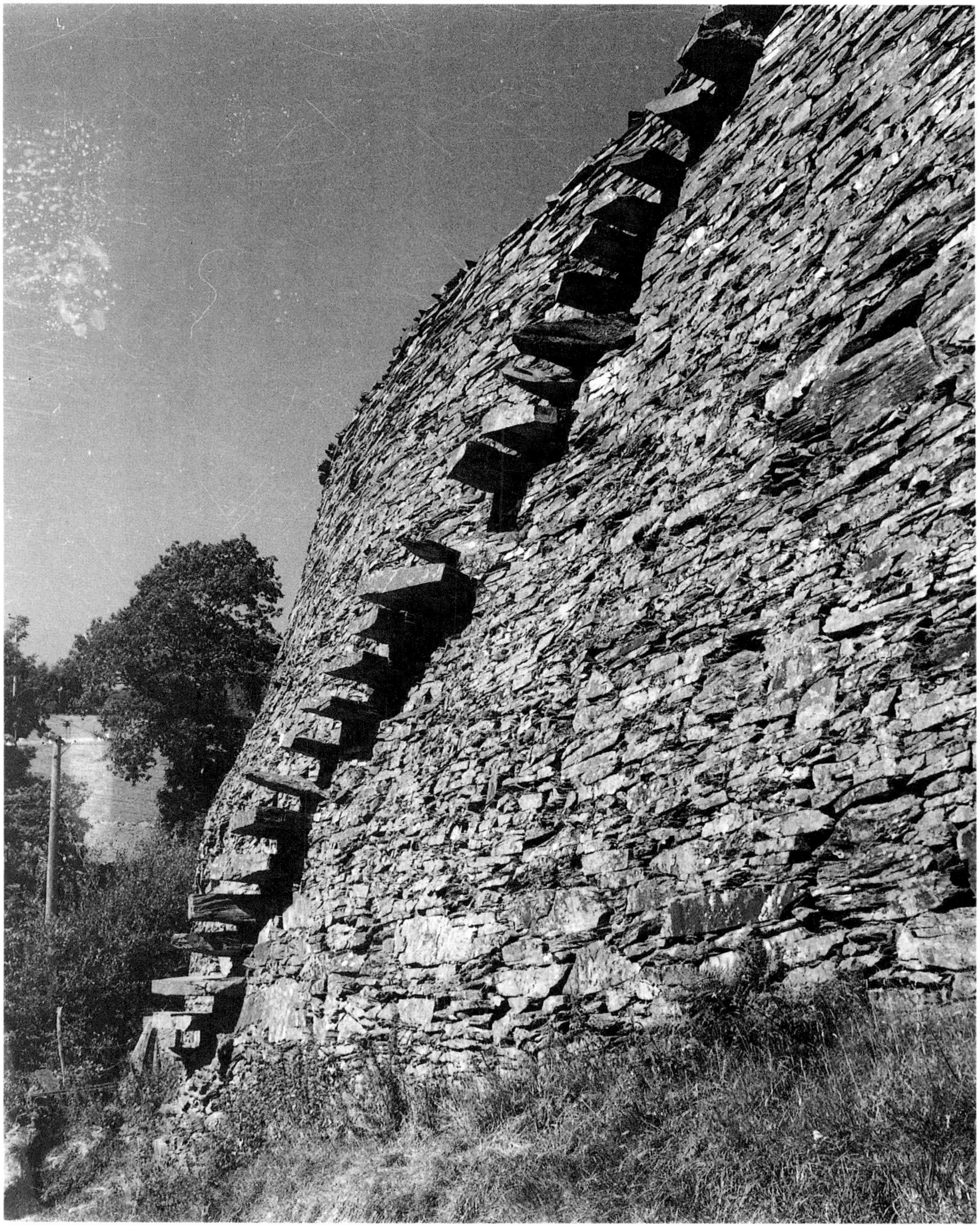

19 Quarryman's staircase, Corris, Gwynedd

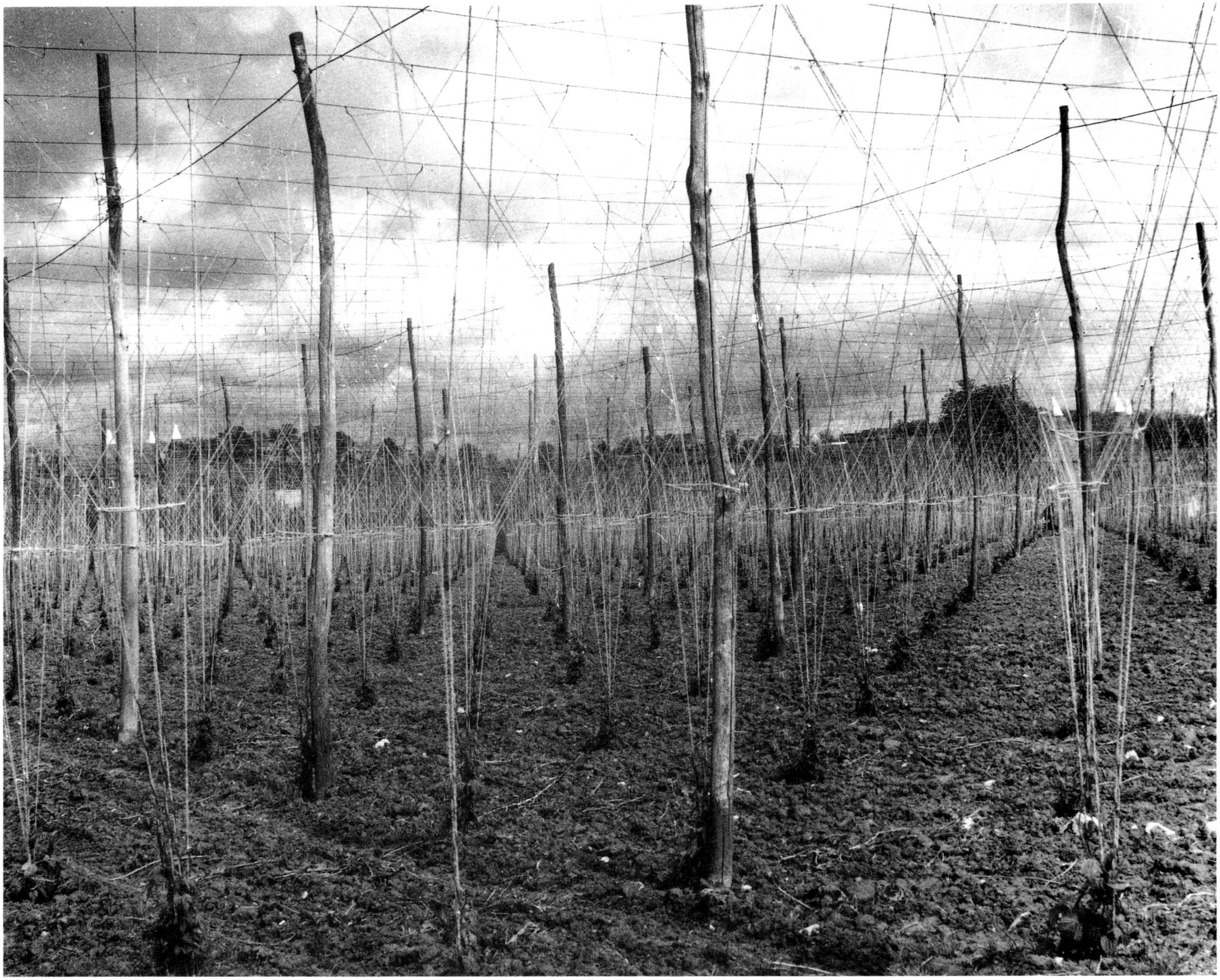

20 Hopfield at Horsmonden, Kent

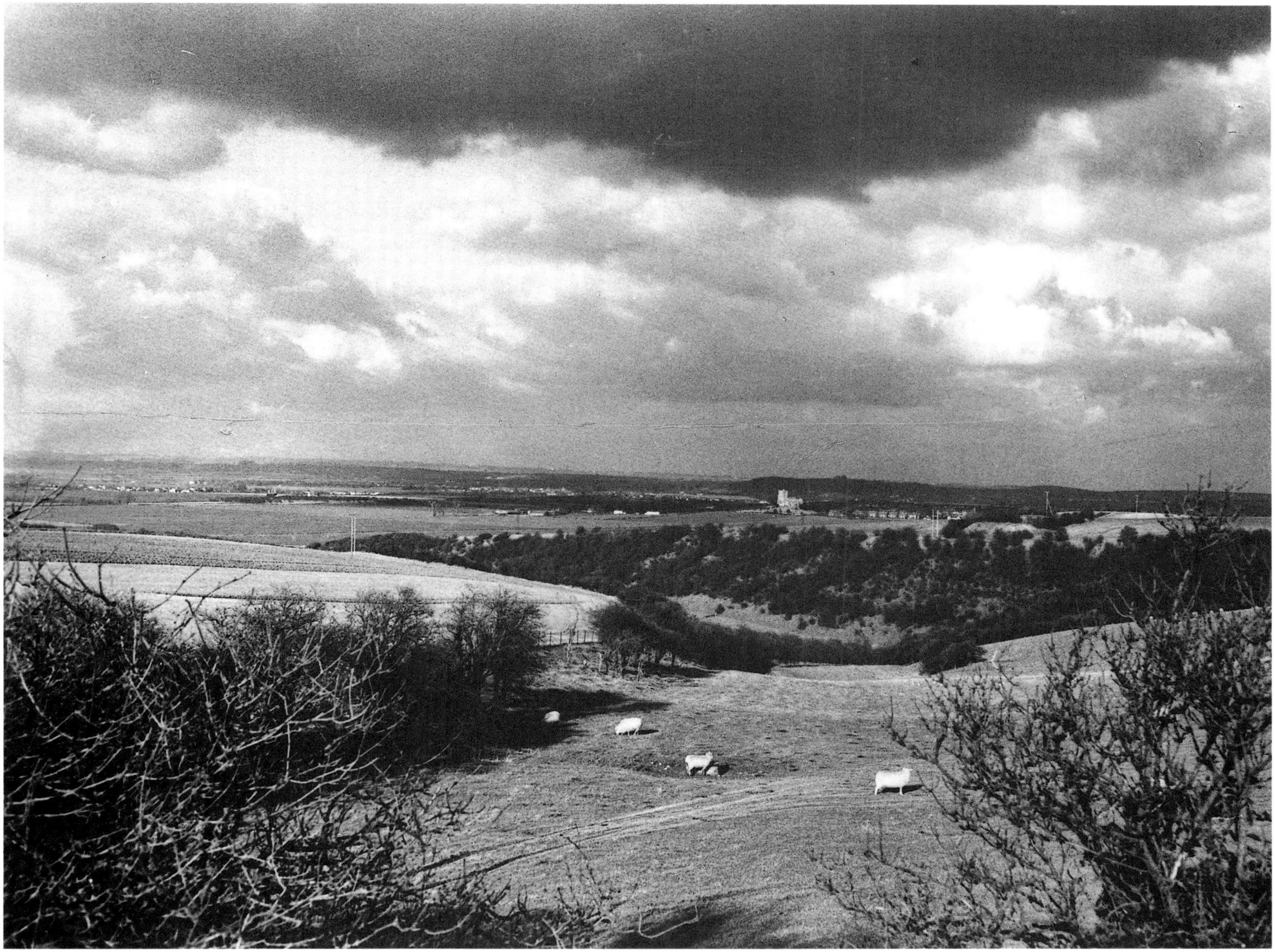

21 Edlesborough, Buckinghamshire

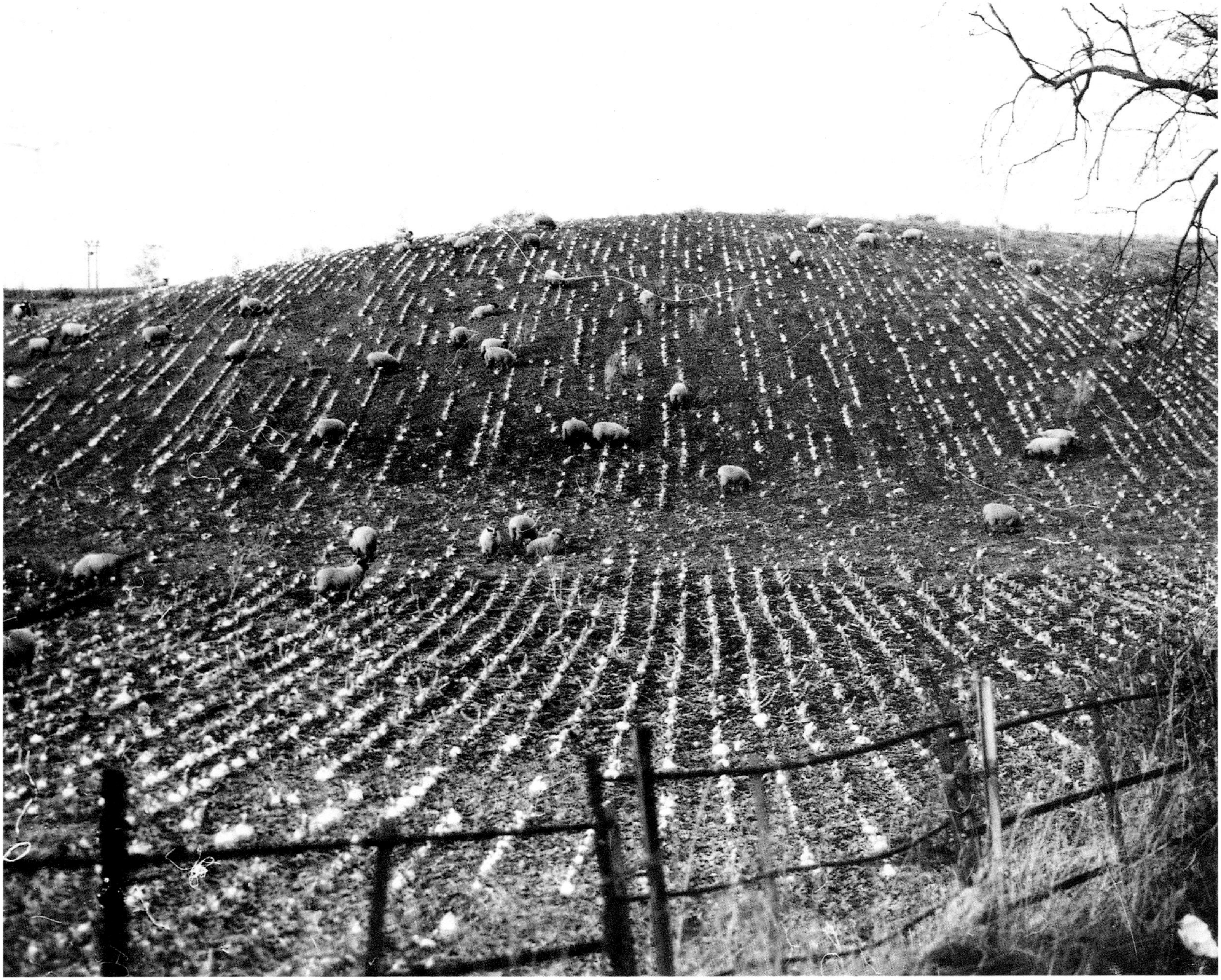

22 Sheep in brussels sprouts, near Claverly, Worcestershire, about 1980

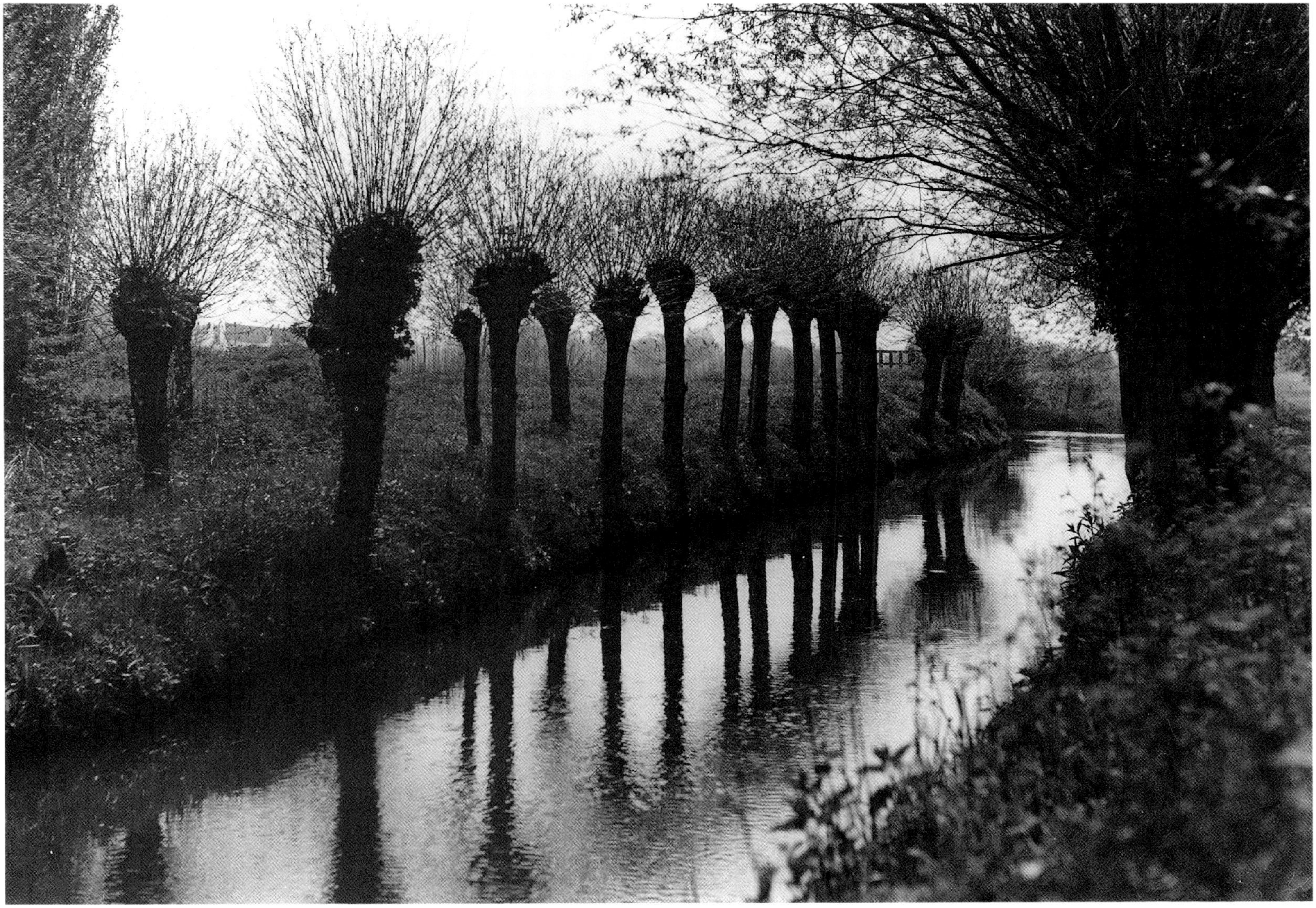

23 Backwater of the Thames, Lechlade,
Gloucestershire, 1936

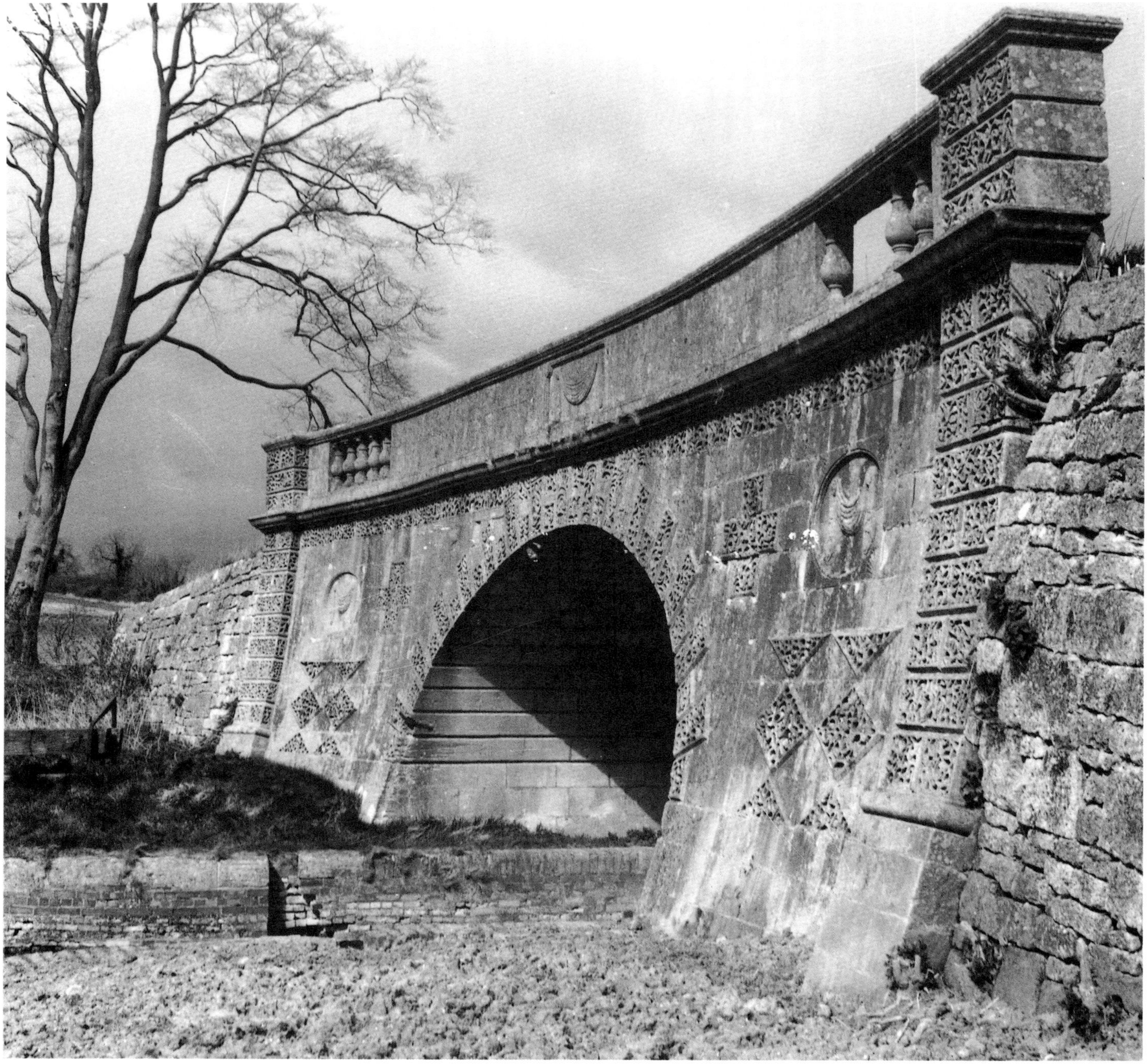

24 Ladie's Bridge on the Kennet and Avon Canal, Wilcot, Wiltshire

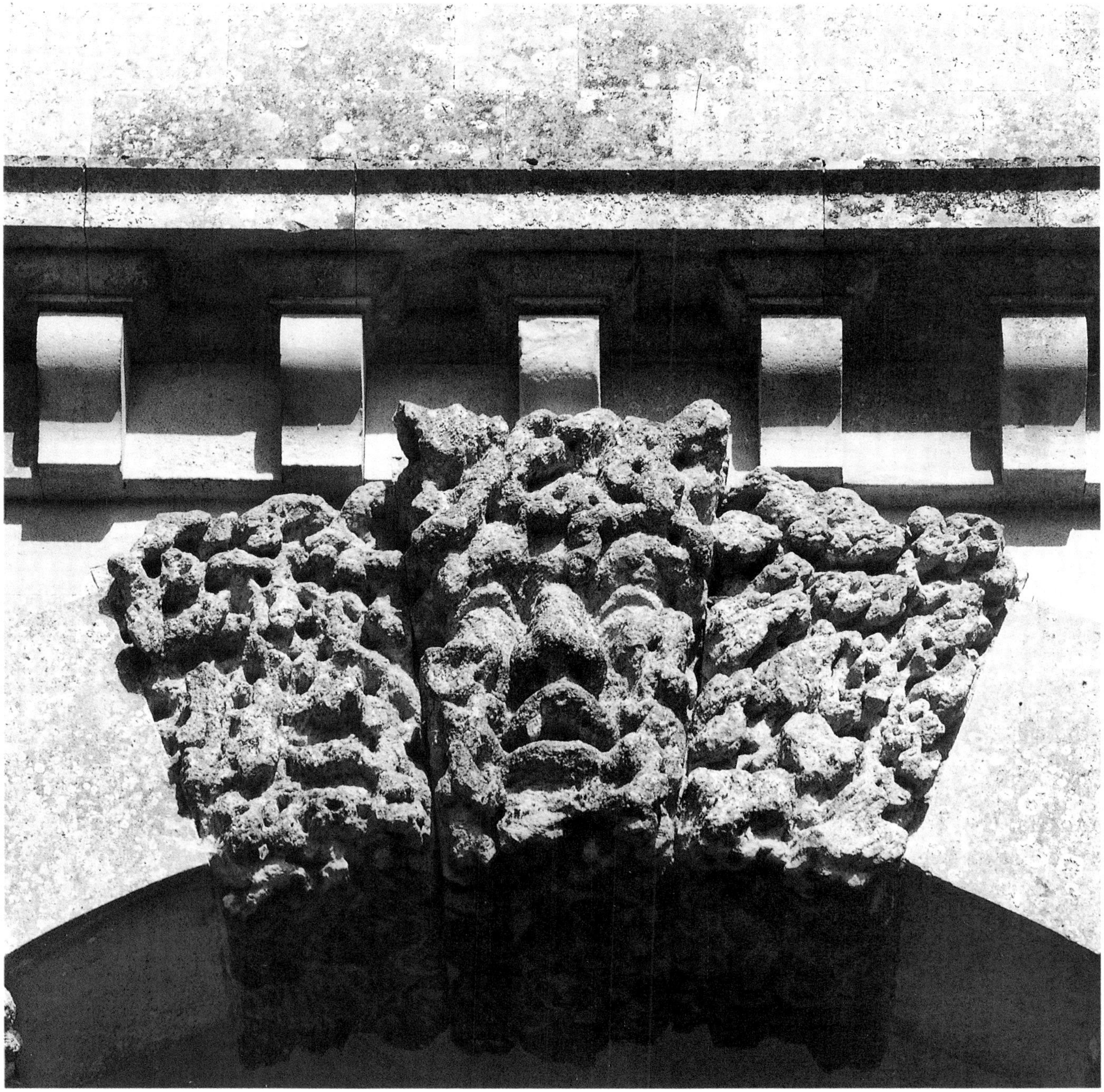

25 Keystone of gateway to Fonthill Abbey, Wiltshire

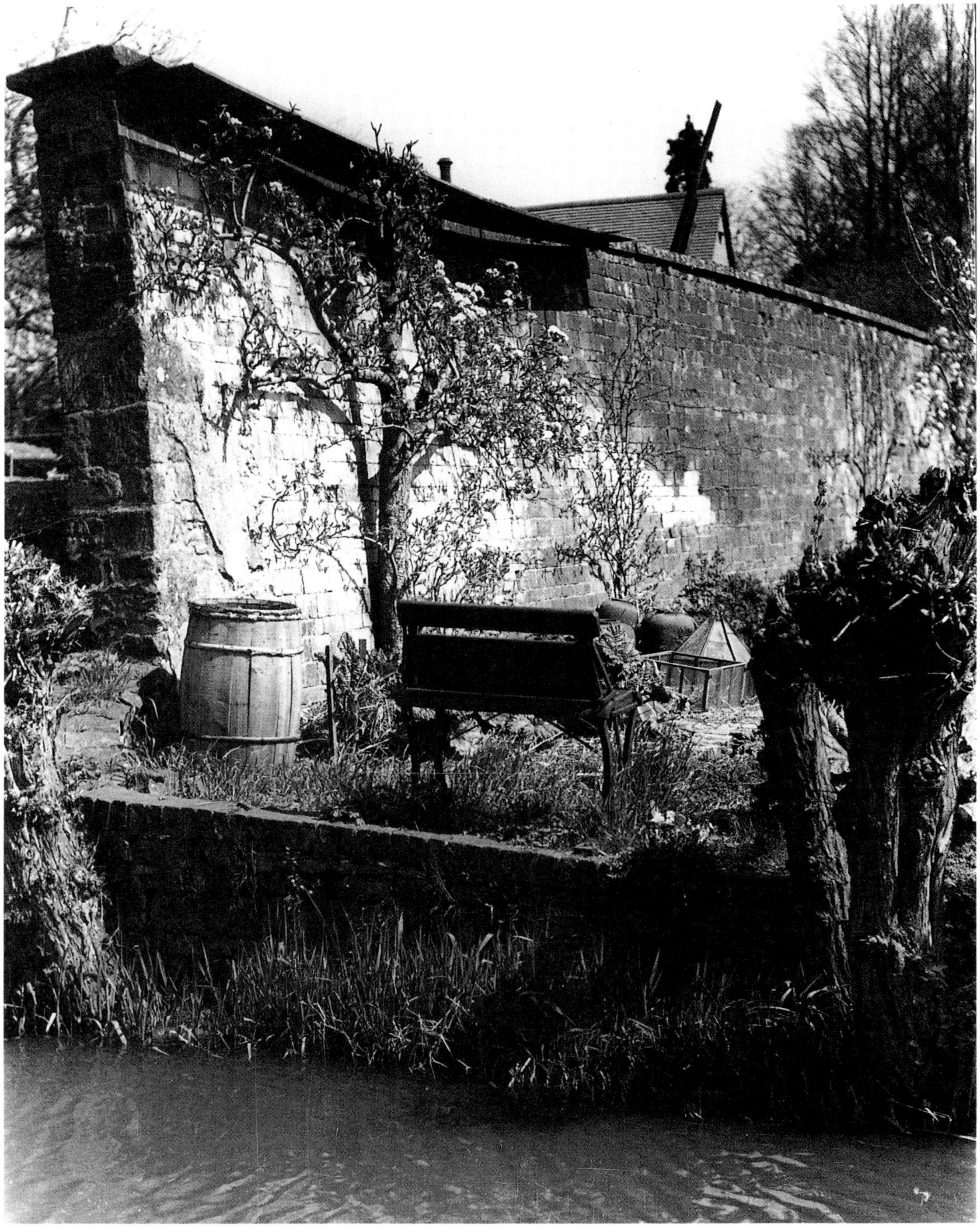

26 A back garden at Adderbury, Oxfordshire, 1937

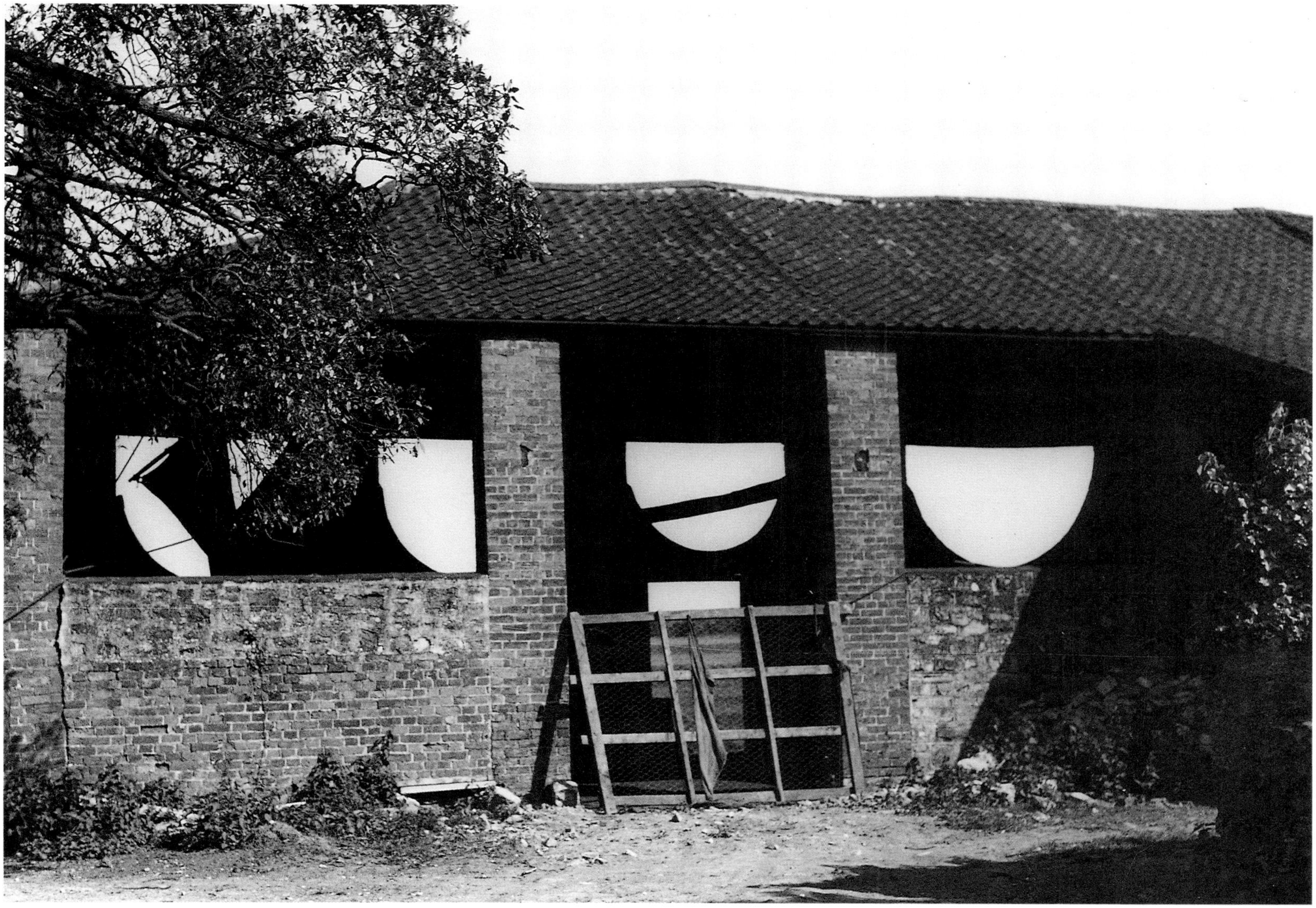

27 Barn at Combwich, on the Parrett near Bridgwater, Somerset about 1938

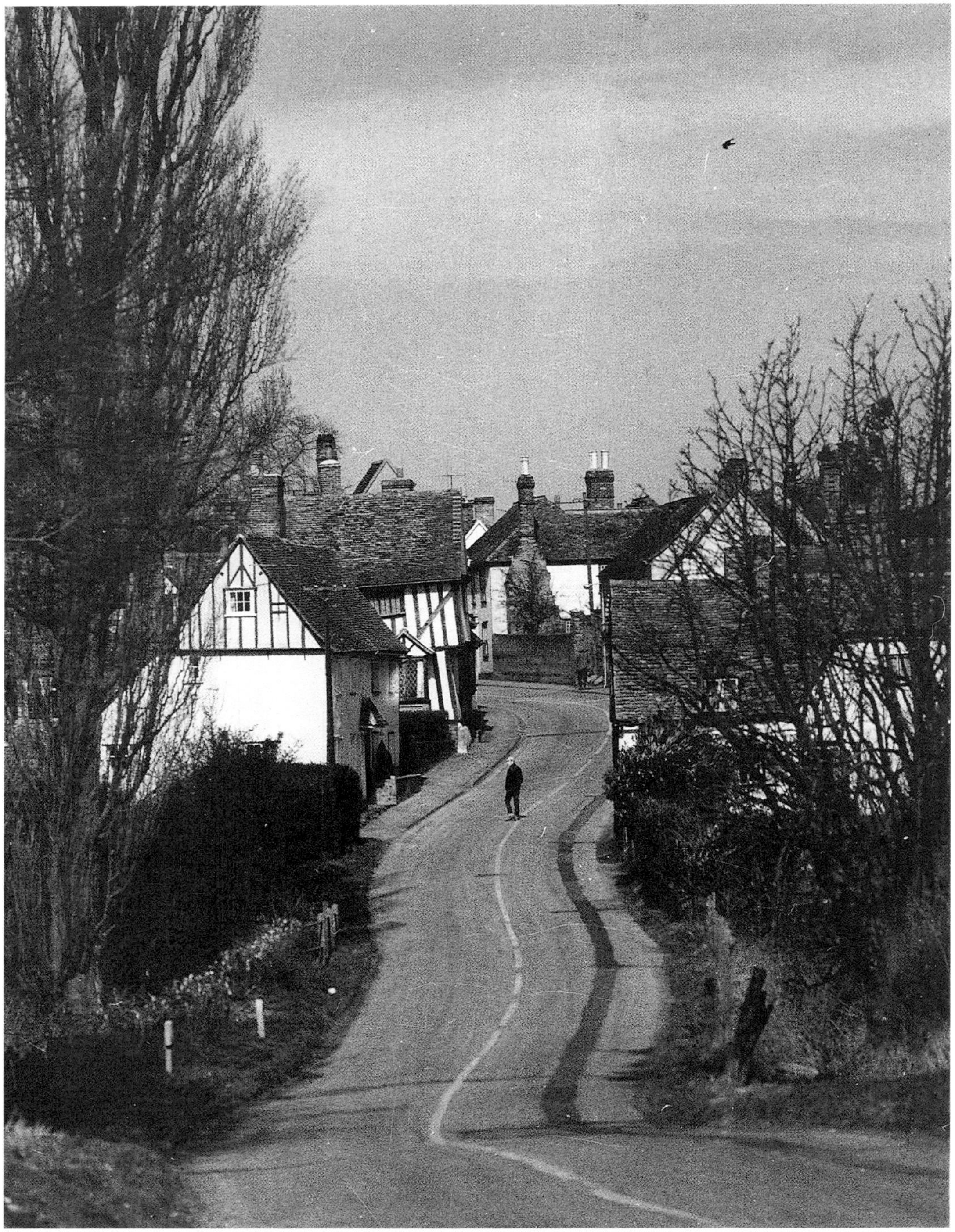

28 Stebbing, Essex

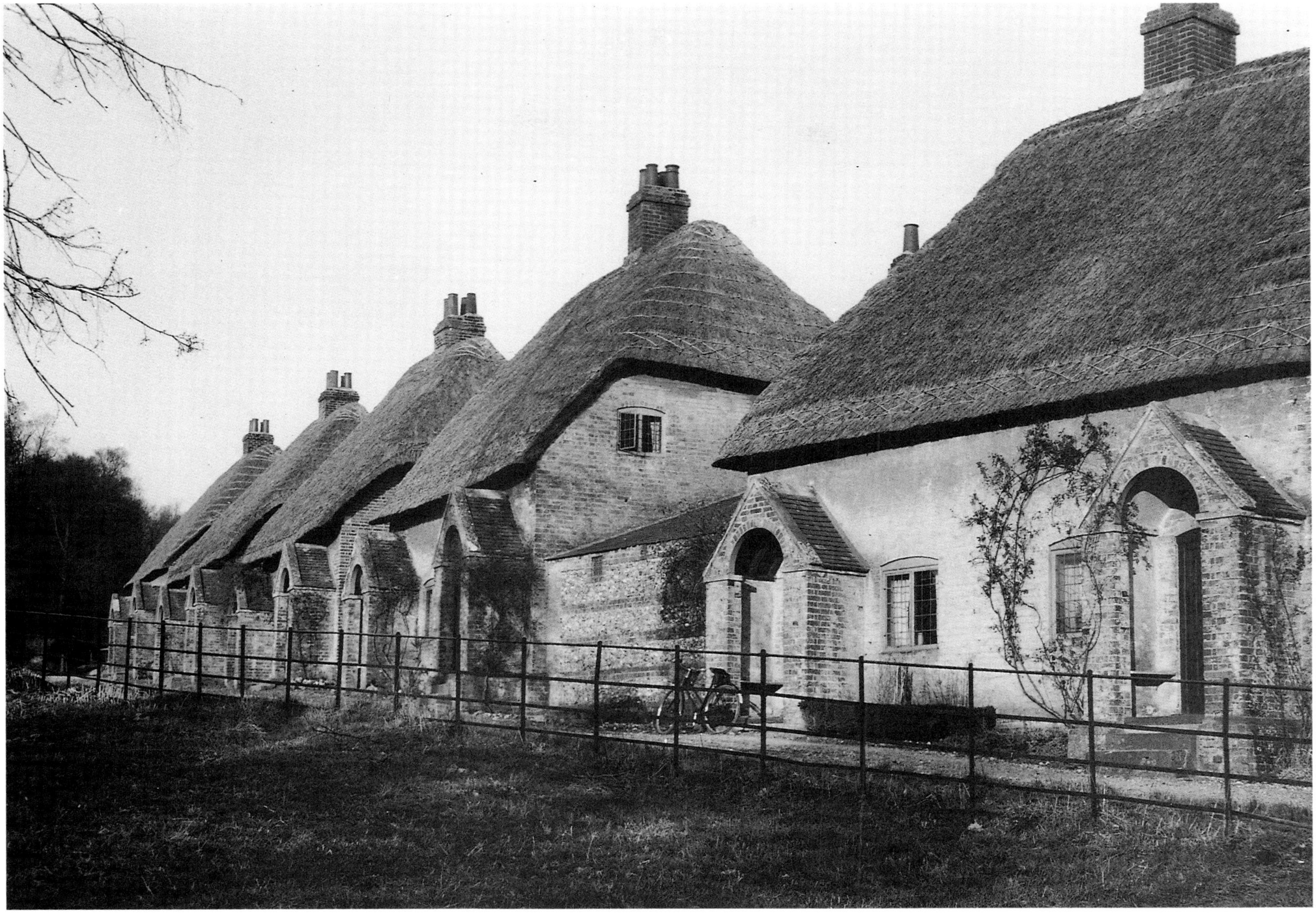

29 Model Village, Milton Abbas, Dorset

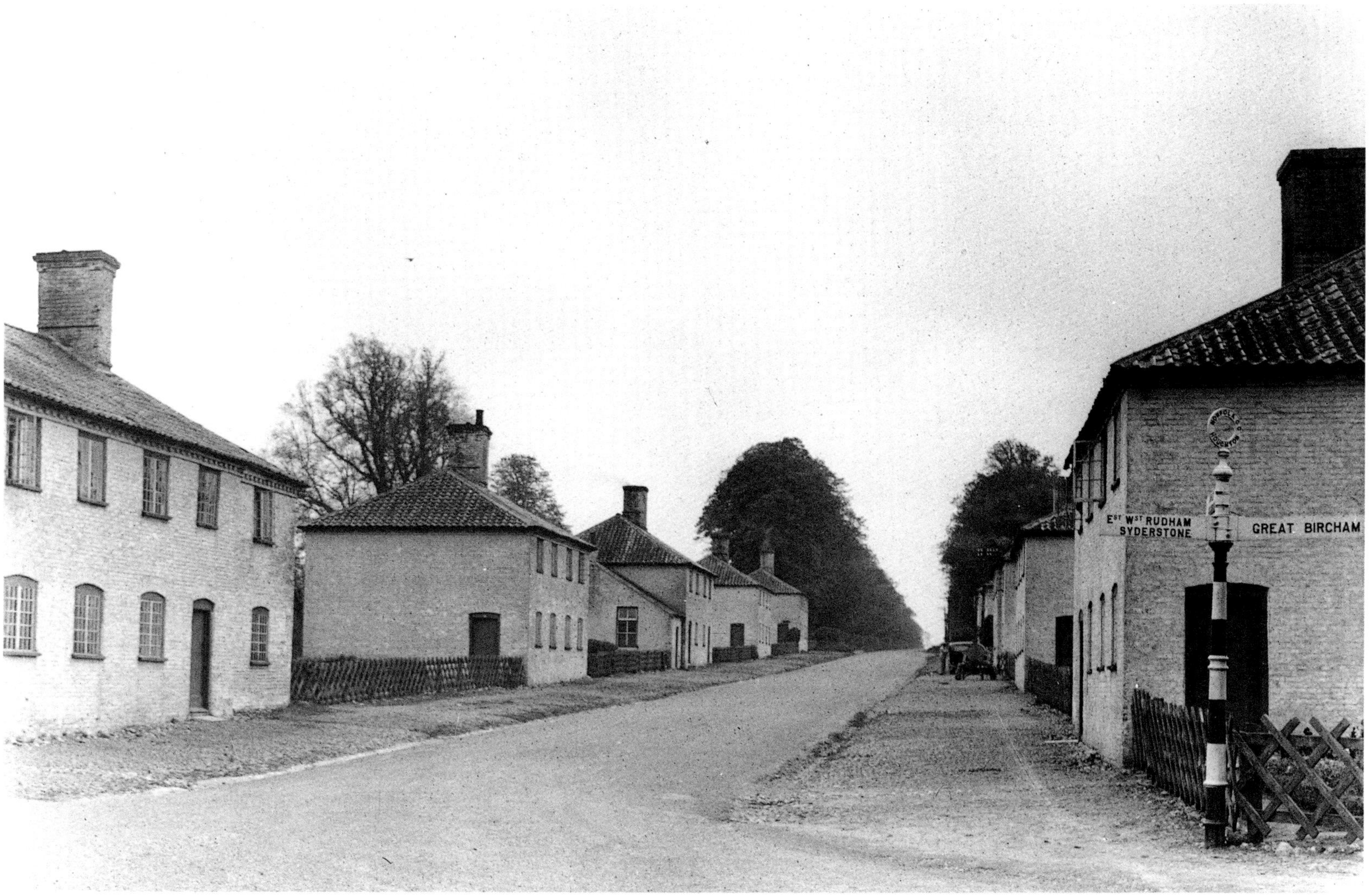

30 South Creake, Norfolk

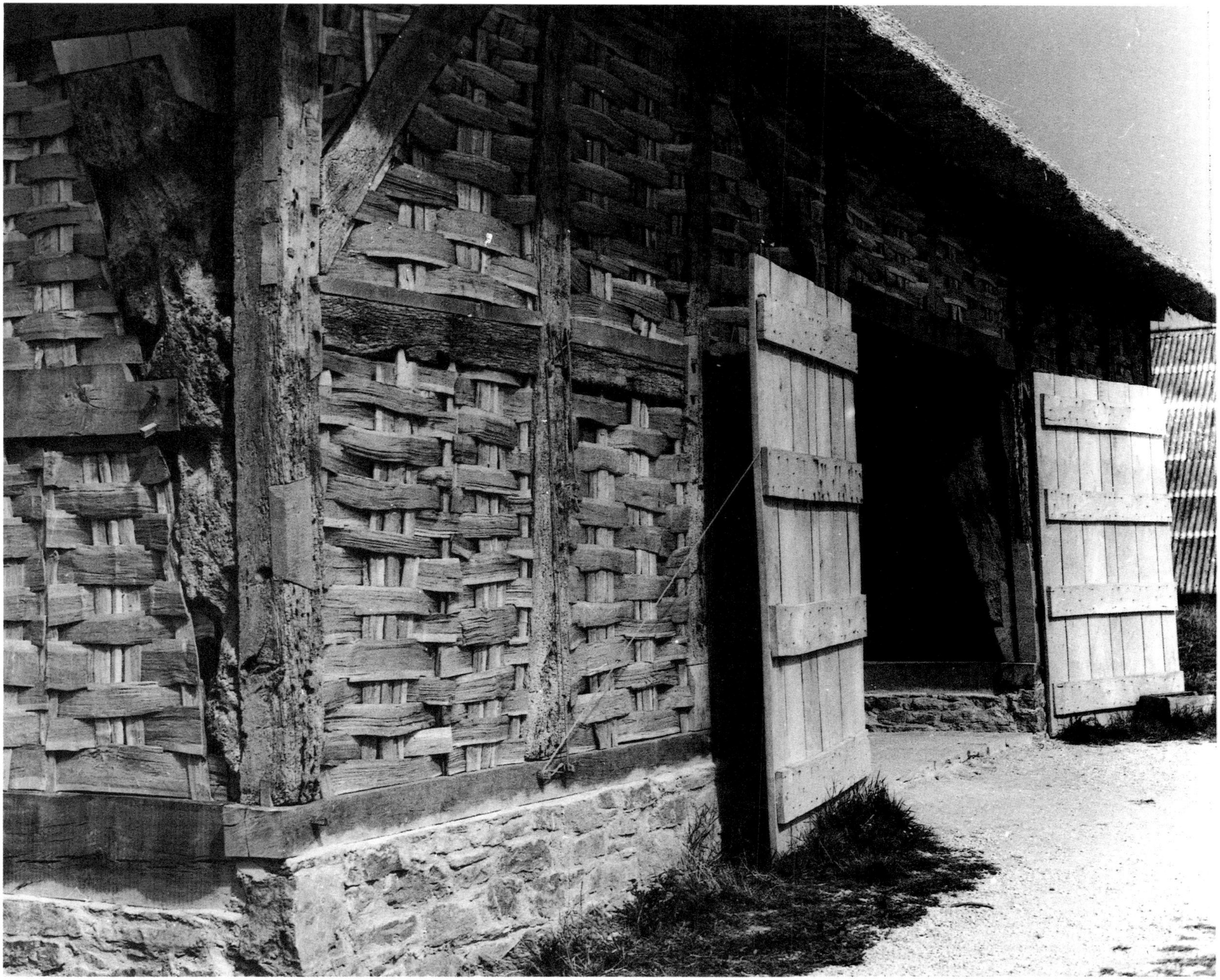

31 Avoncroft Museum of Buildings,
Bromsgrove, Warwickshire

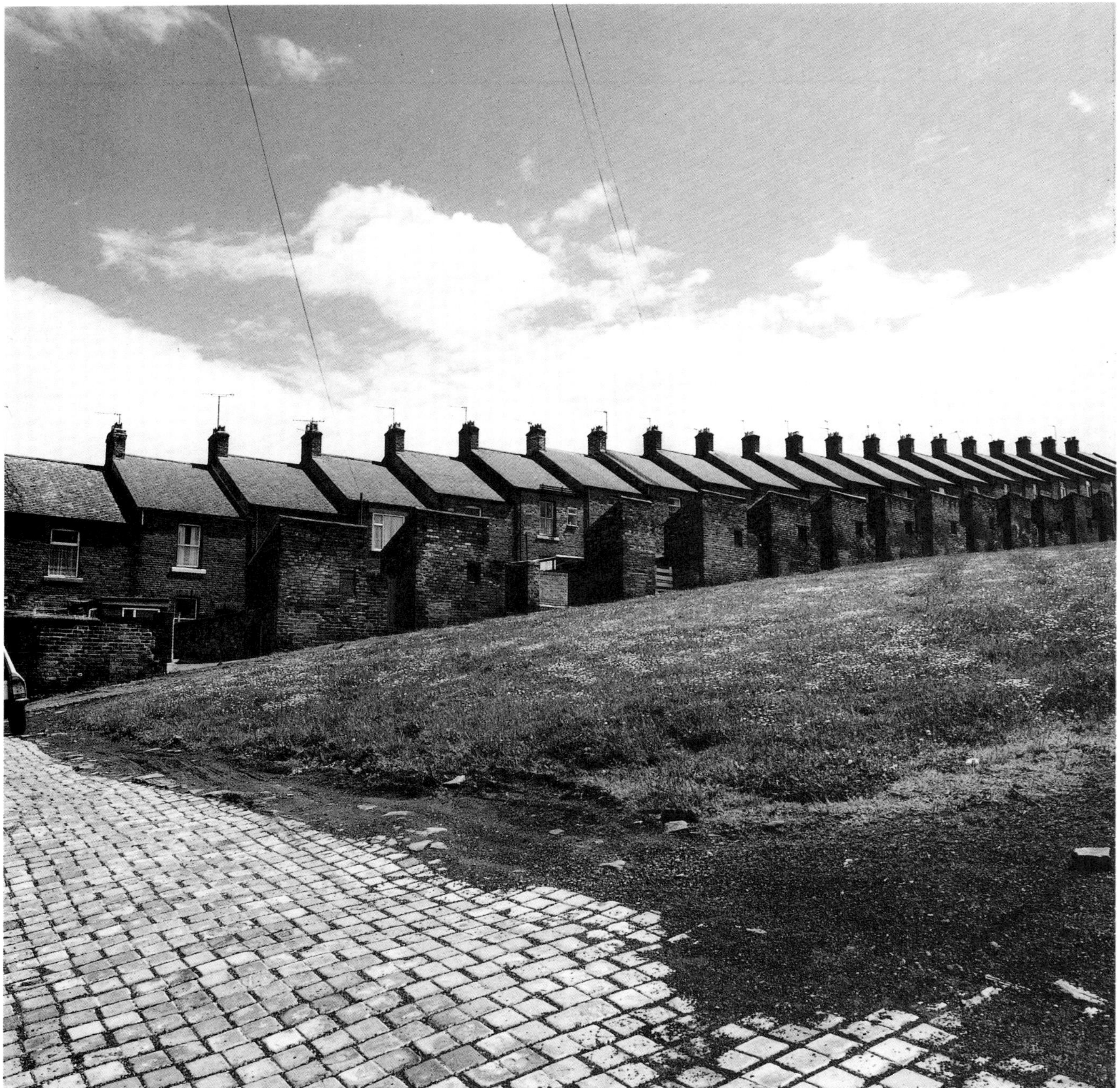

32 Bishop Auckland, Durham

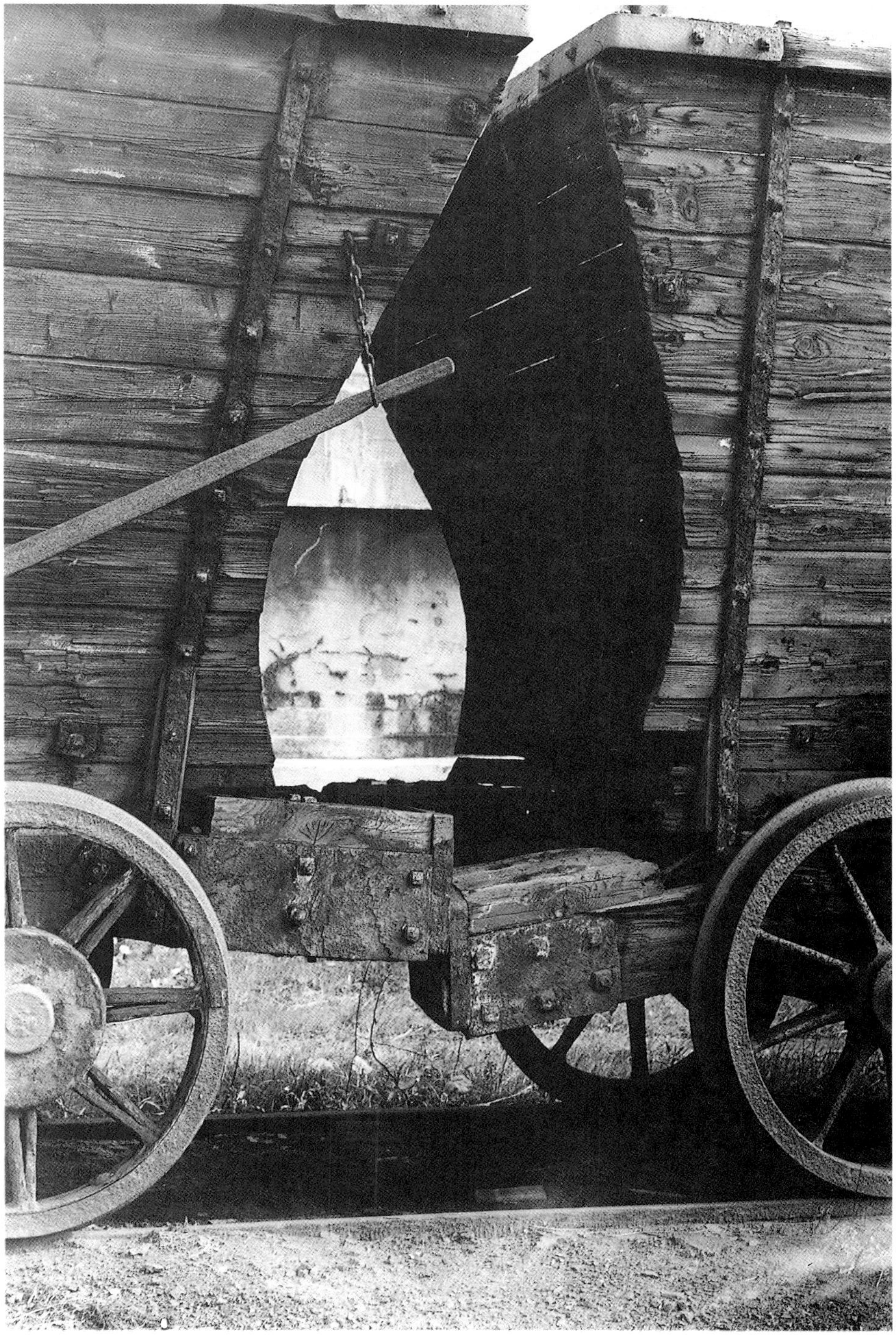

33 Coal wagons at Middlesbrough, about 1938

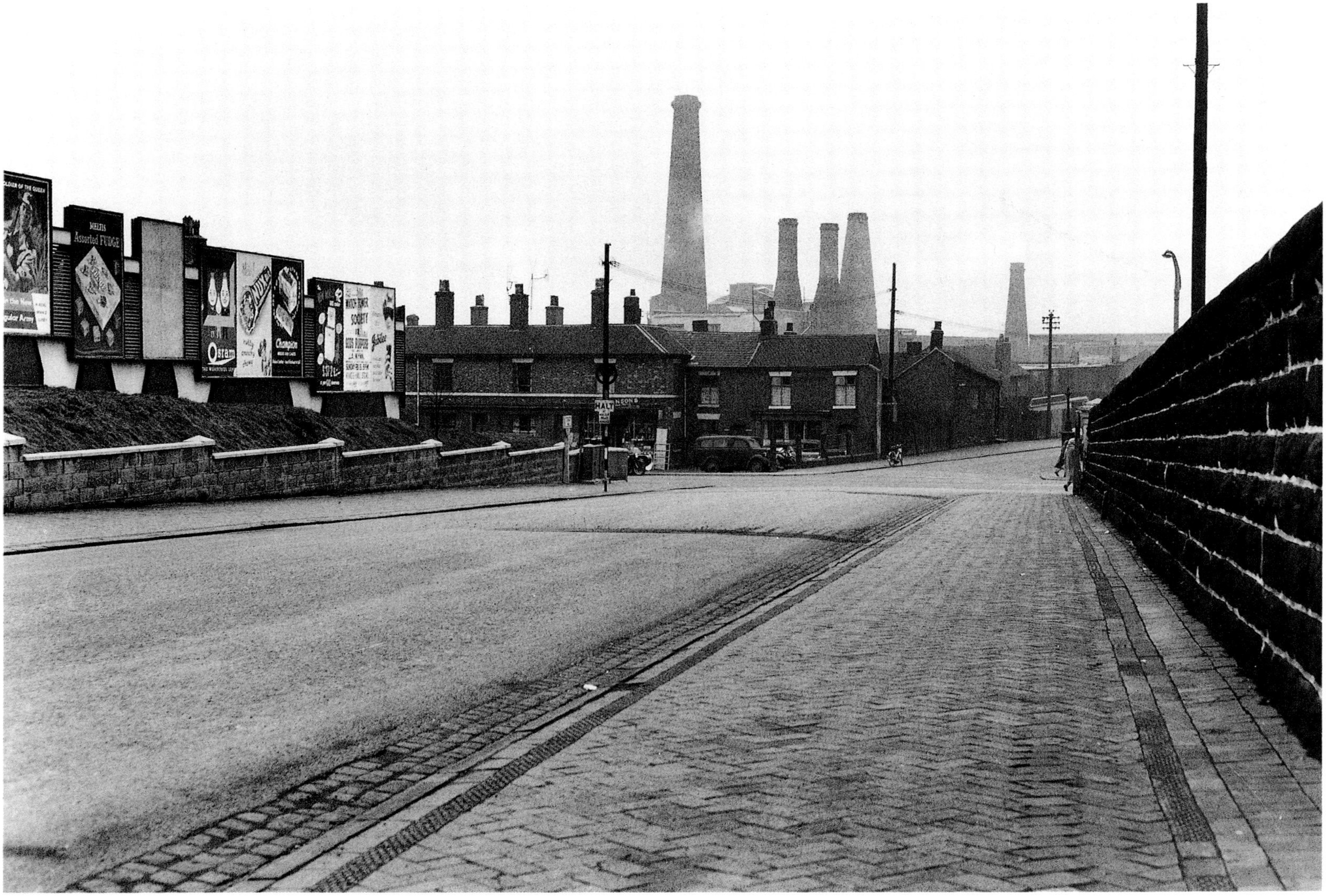

34 Stoke on Trent, 1953

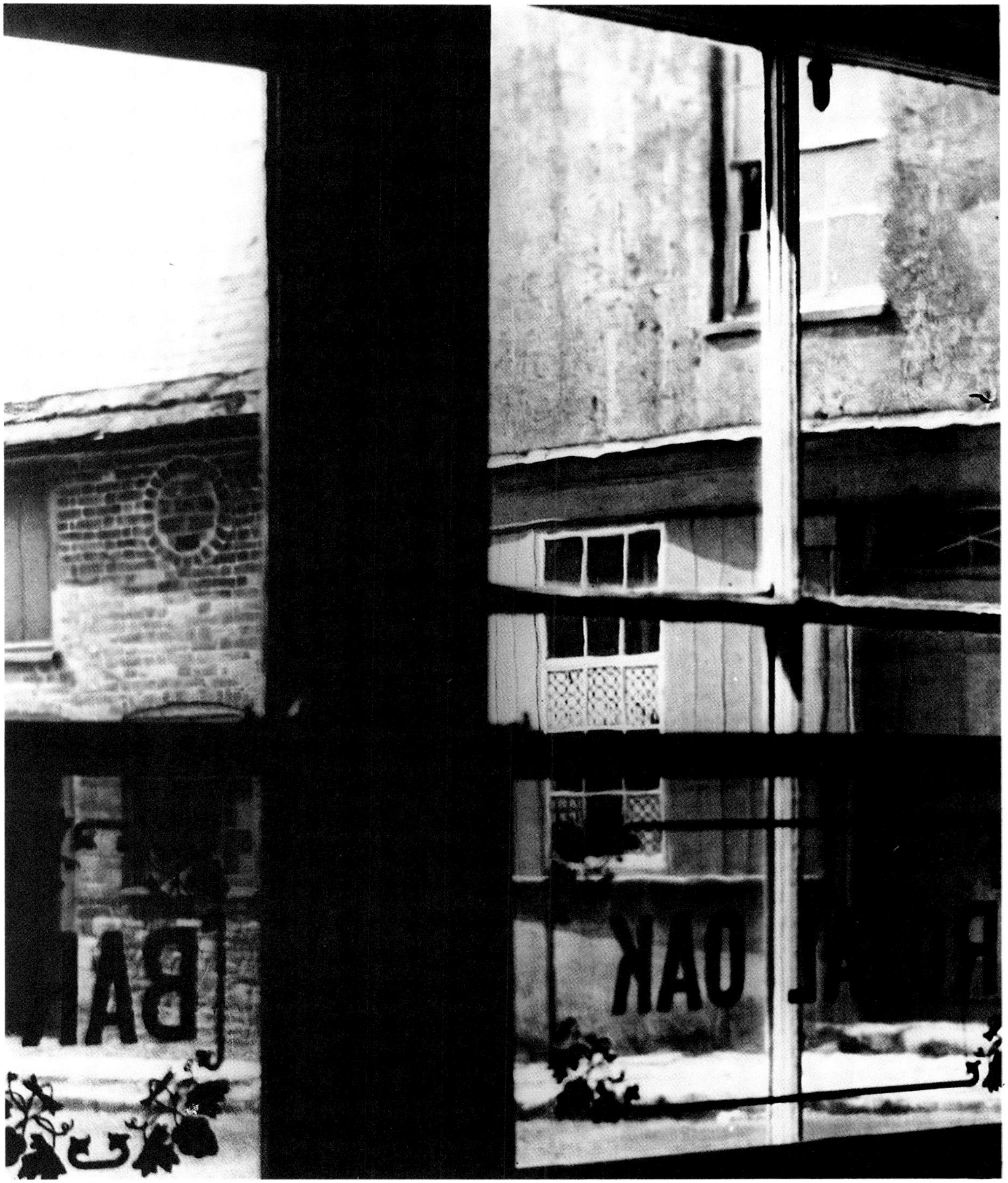

35 Bar in the Royal Oak,
Cerne Abbas, 1936

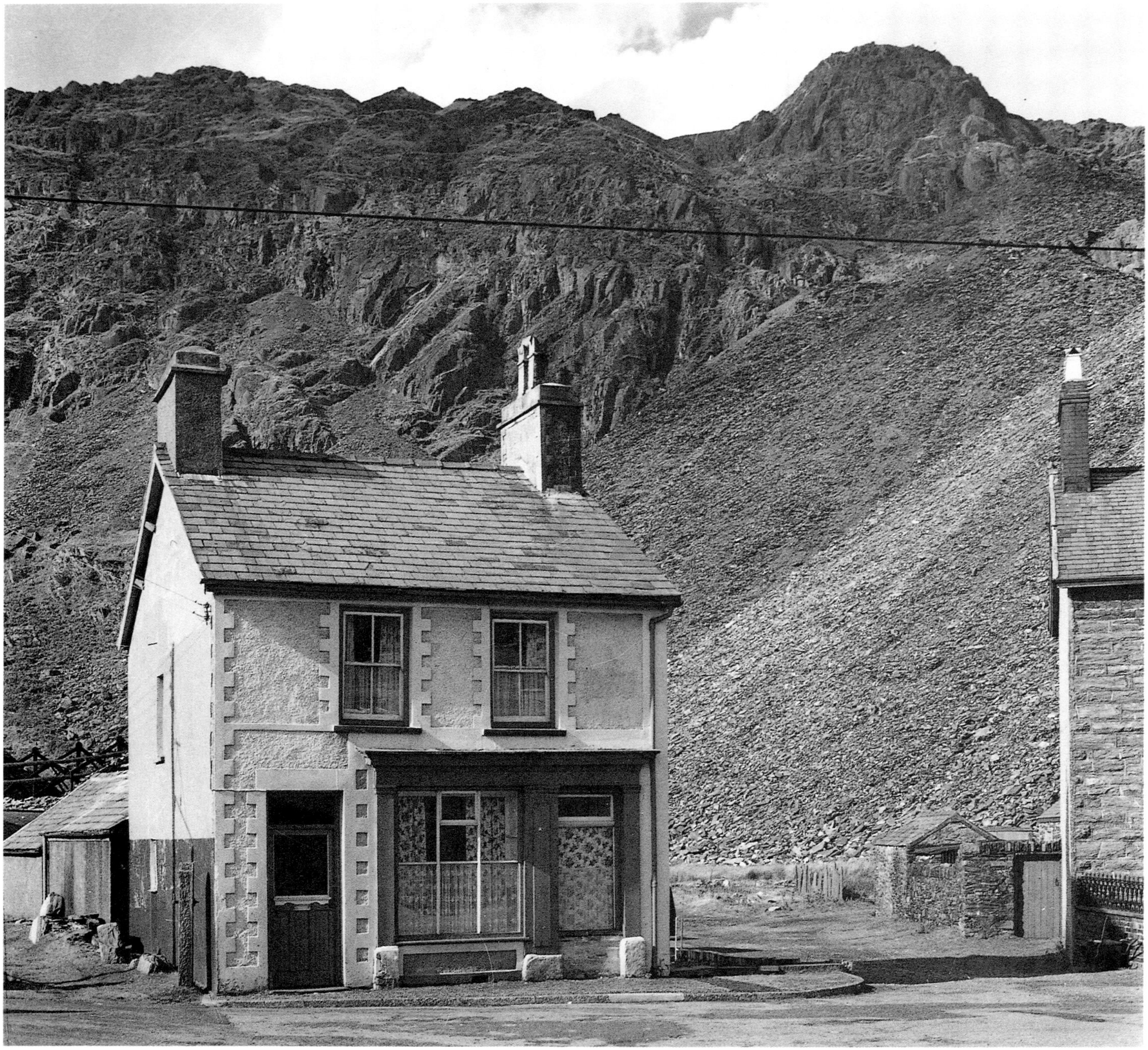

36 Slate quarry, Blaenau Ffestiniog, Gwynedd

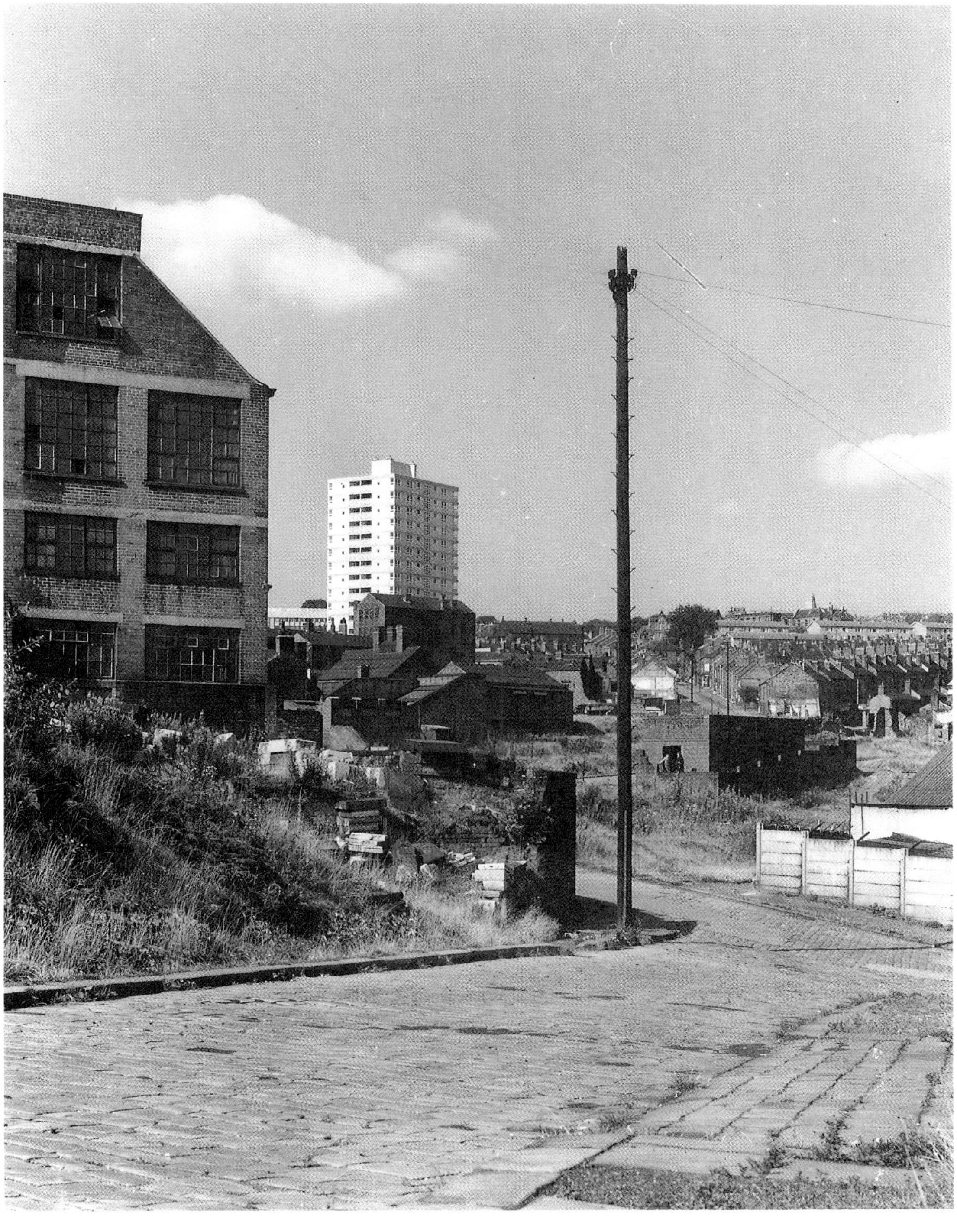

37 Sheffield

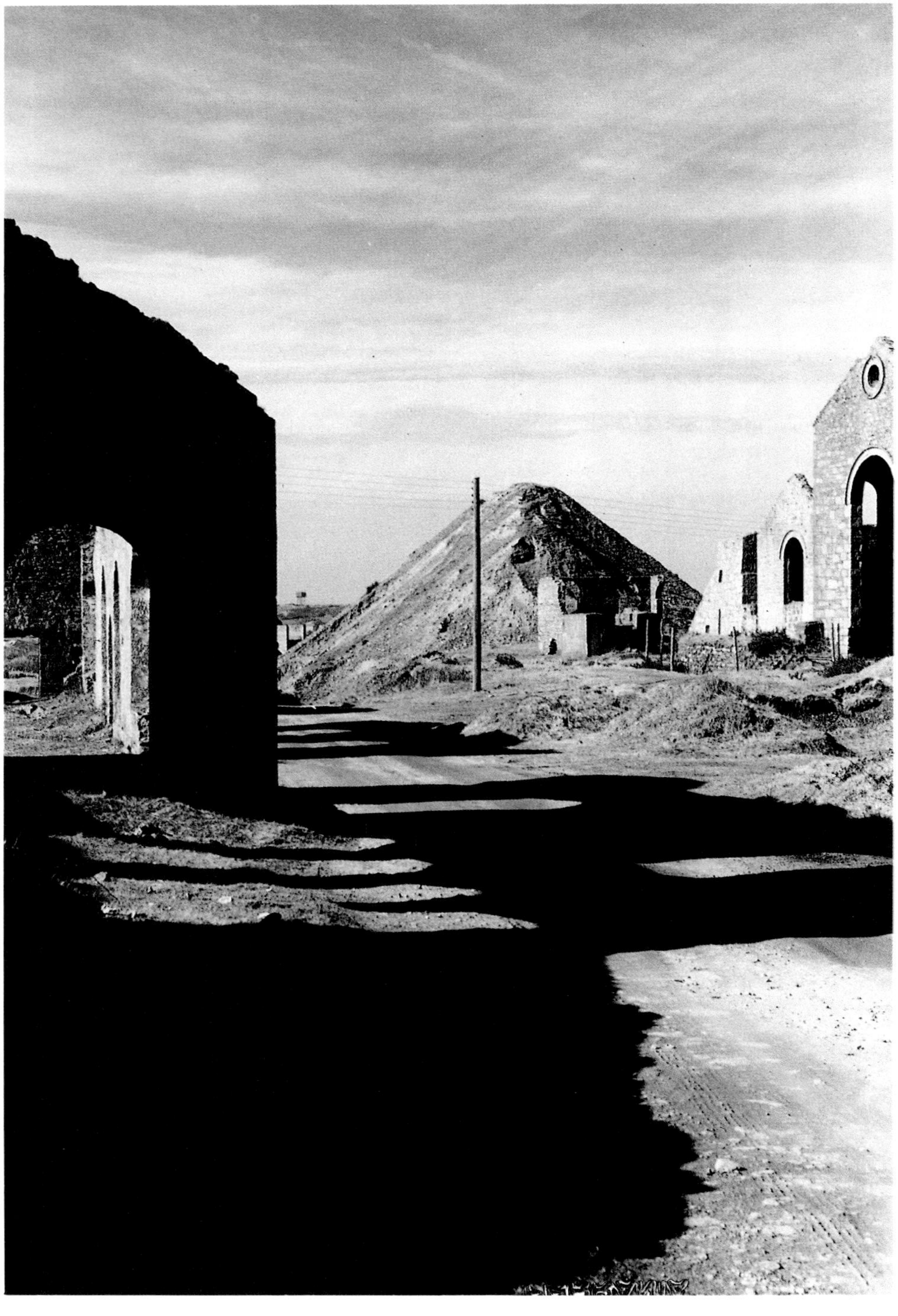

38 Mine buildings at Redruth, Cornwall

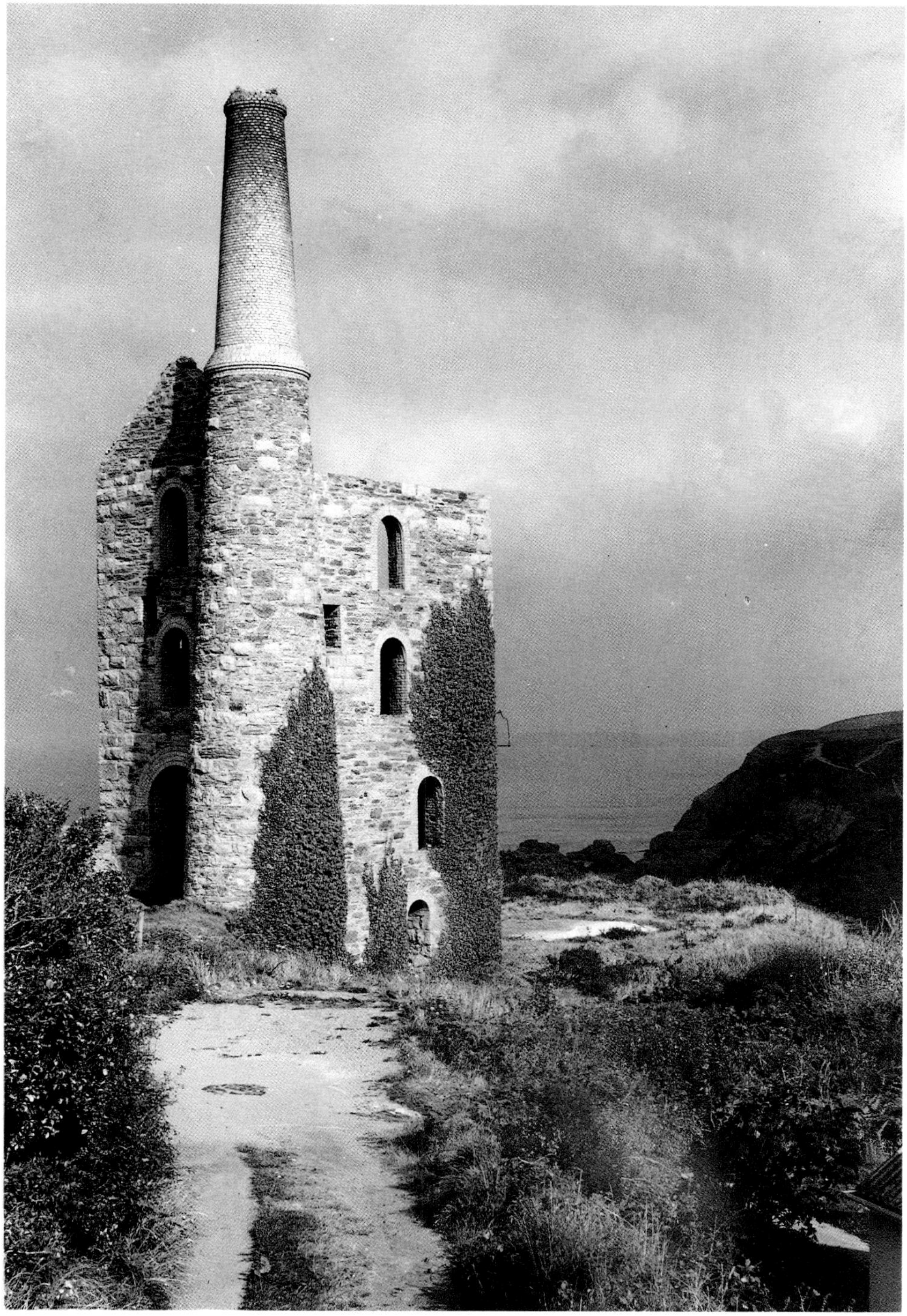

39 Deserted tin mine near St Austell, Cornwall

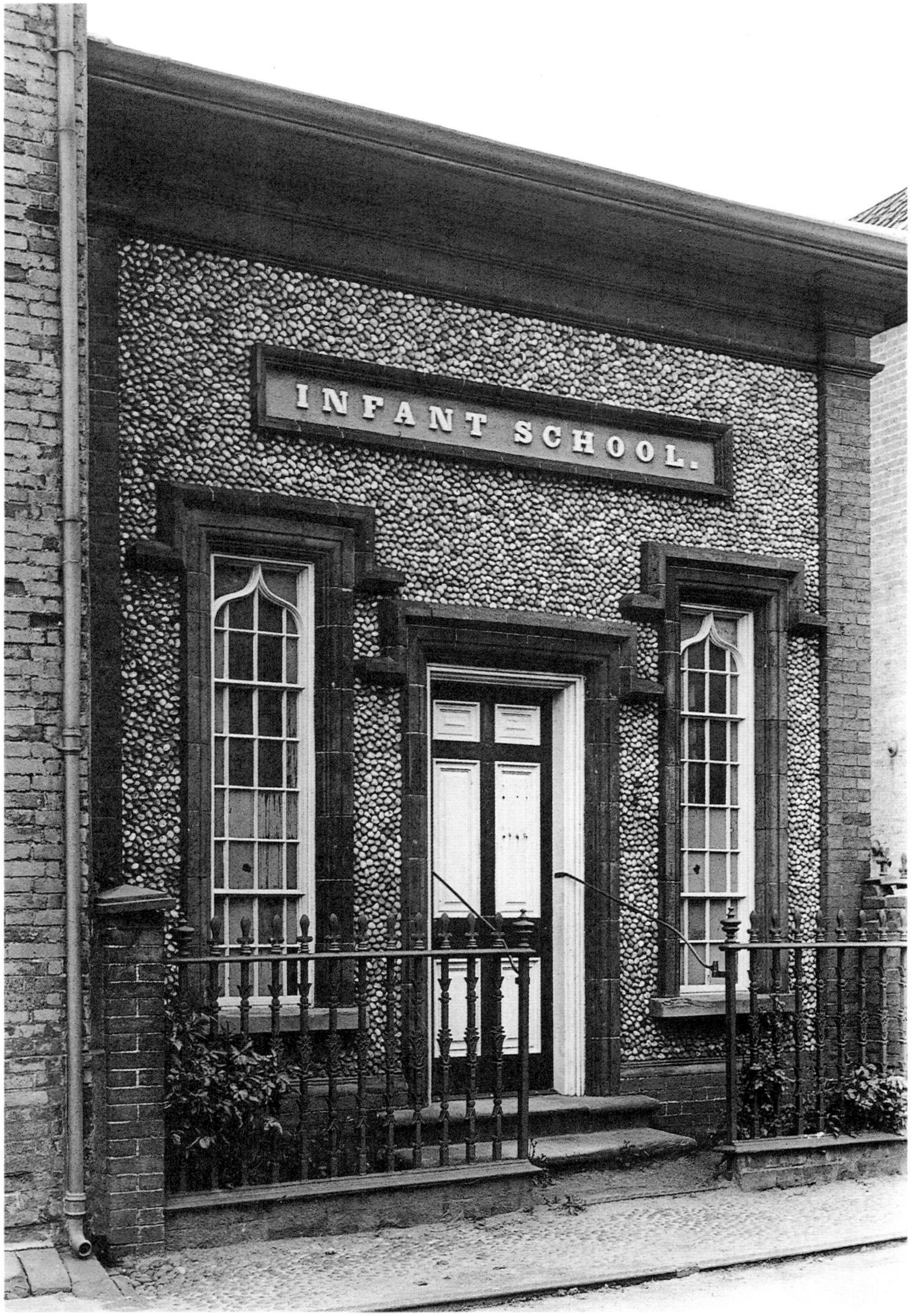

40 Infant School

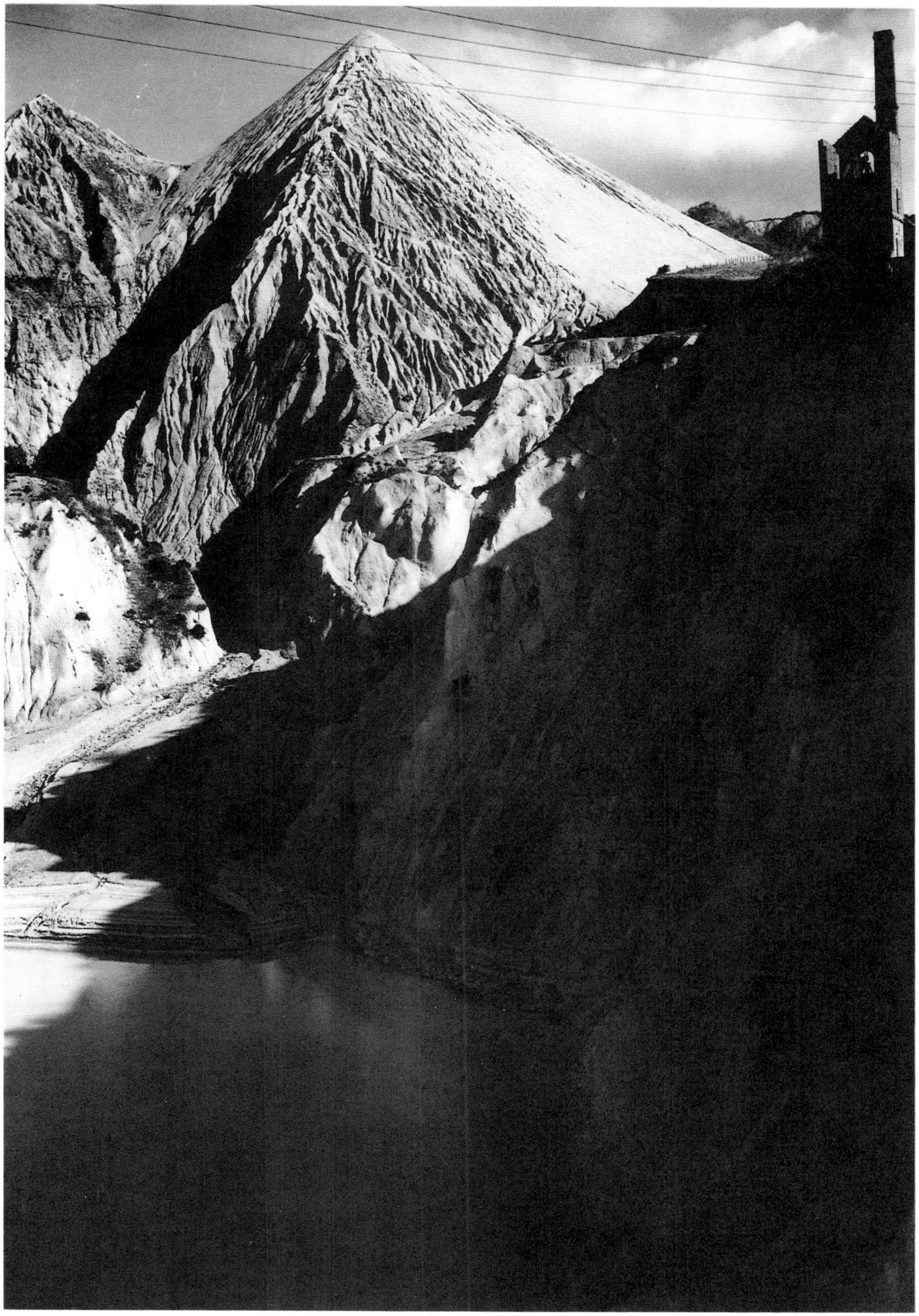

41 China clay tip, Nanpean, Cornwall

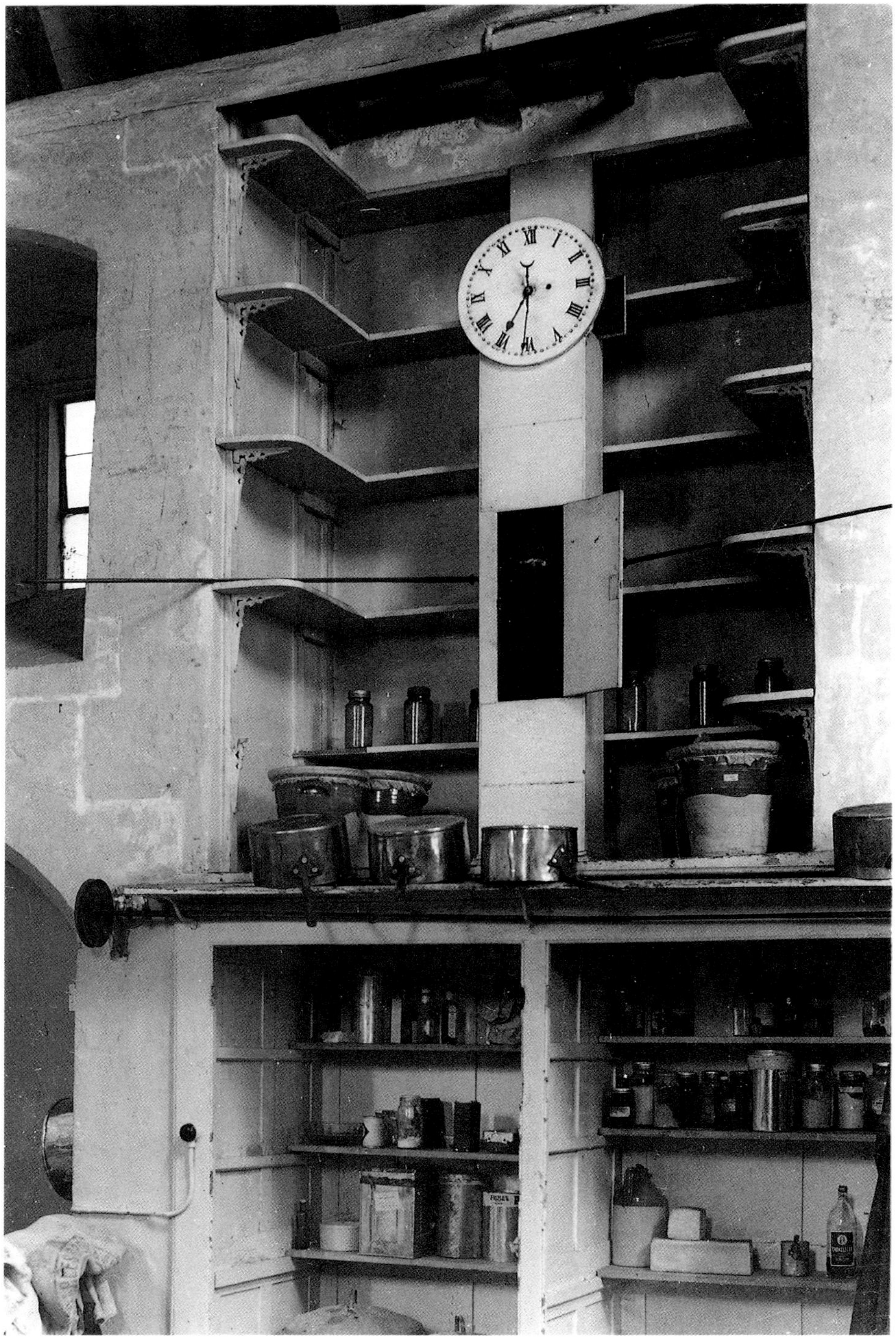

42 The kitchen of an Oxford College, about 1936

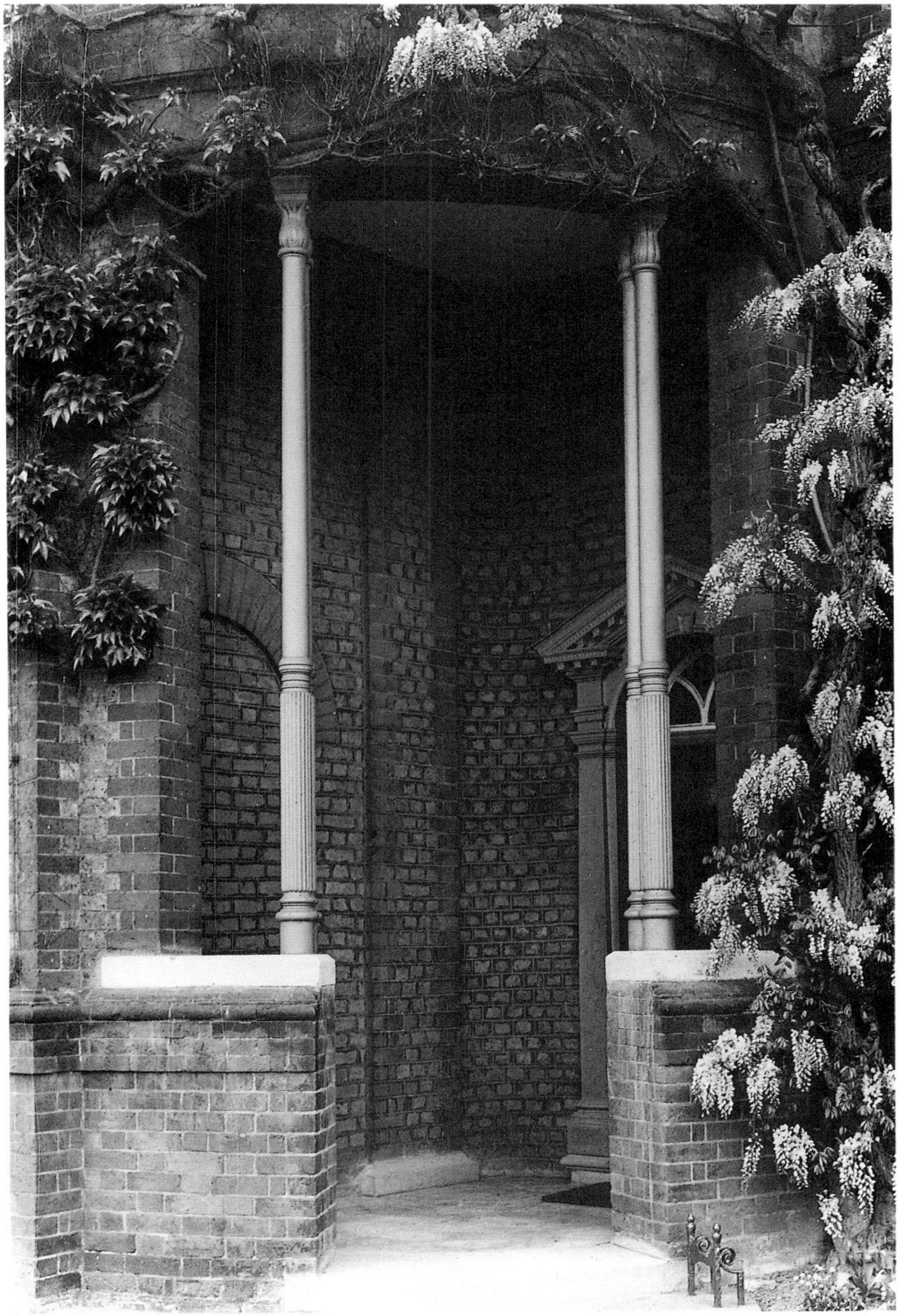

43 Wisteria at Bretforton, Worcestershire

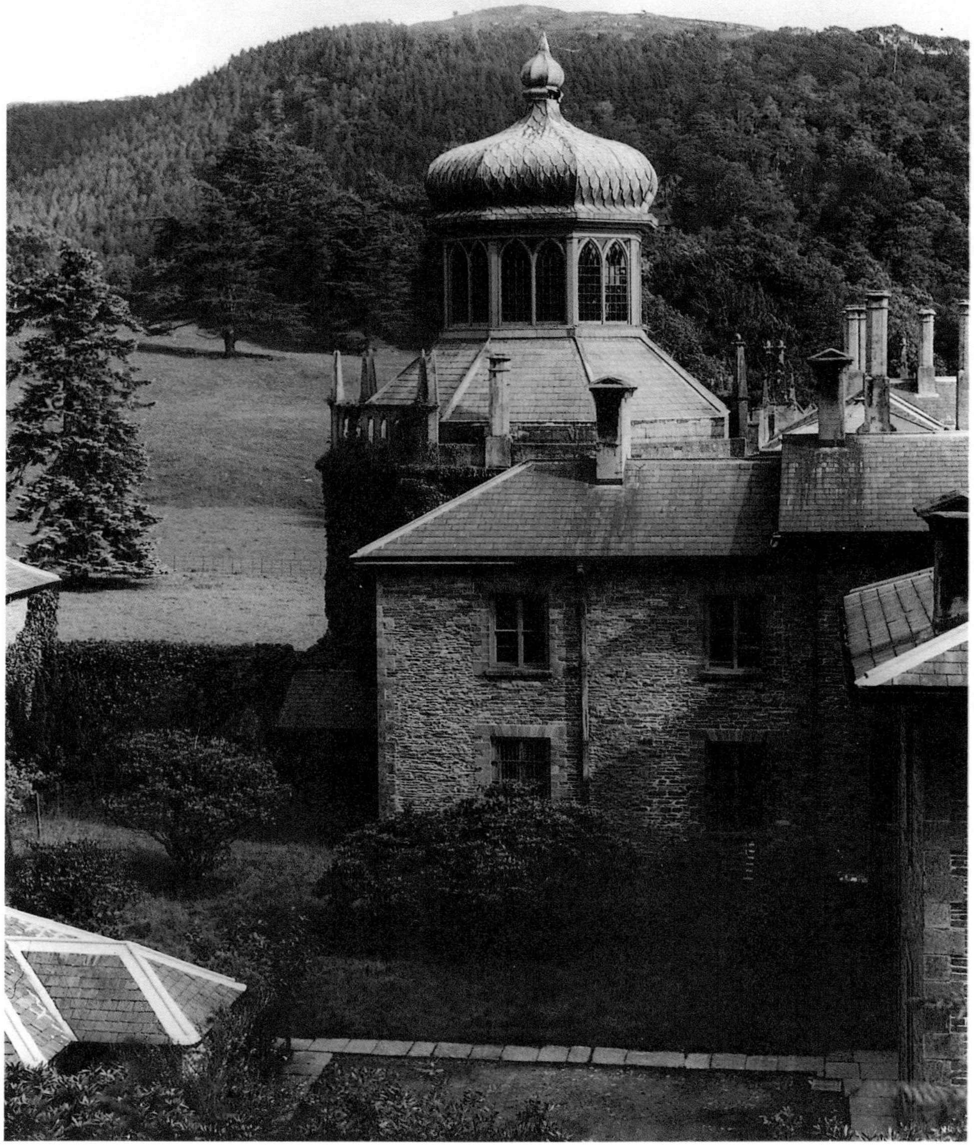

44 The Library, Hafod House, Dyfed, 1939

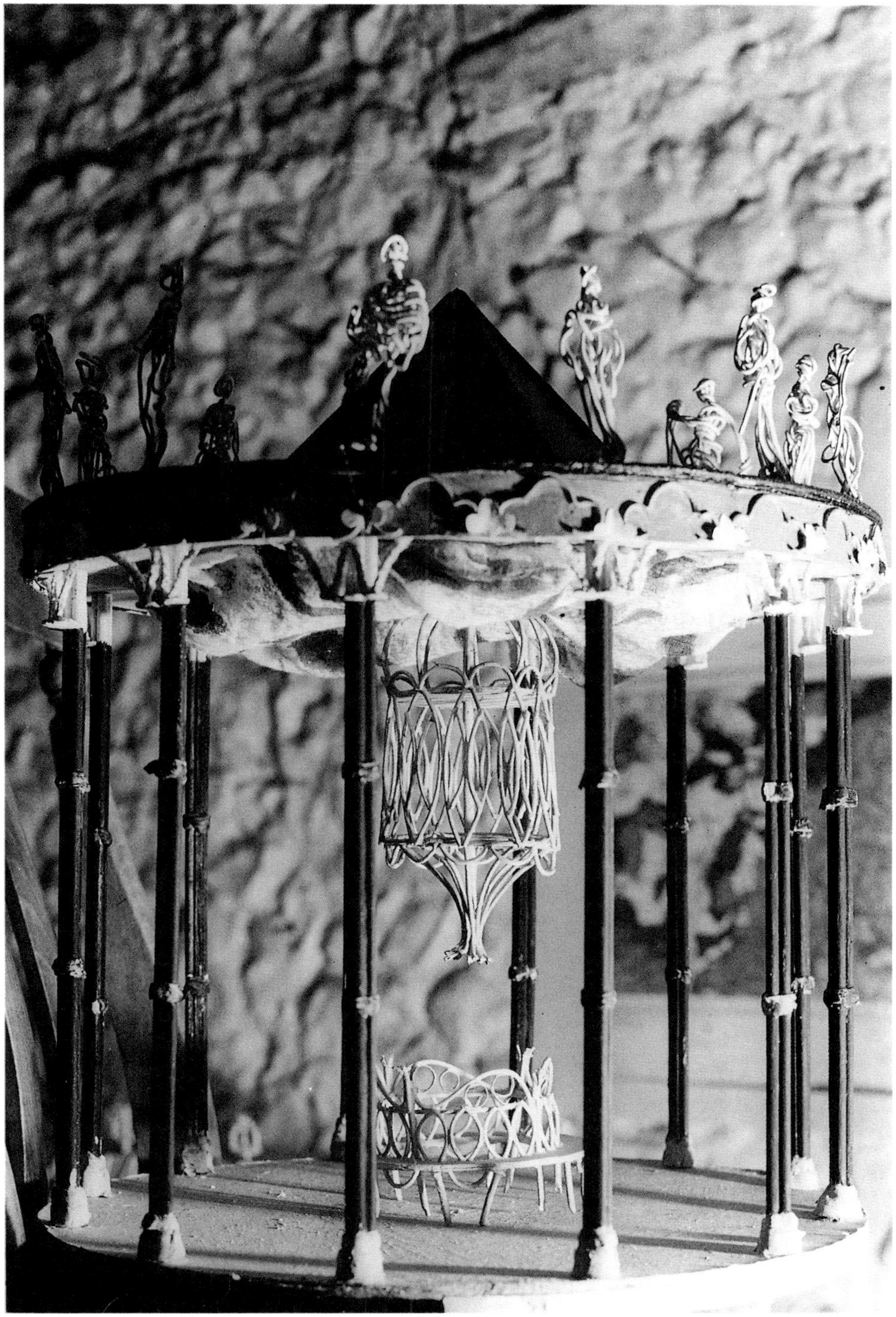

45 Model made by Joy Mills of John Piper's design for the Festival Gardens, Battersea Park, 1951

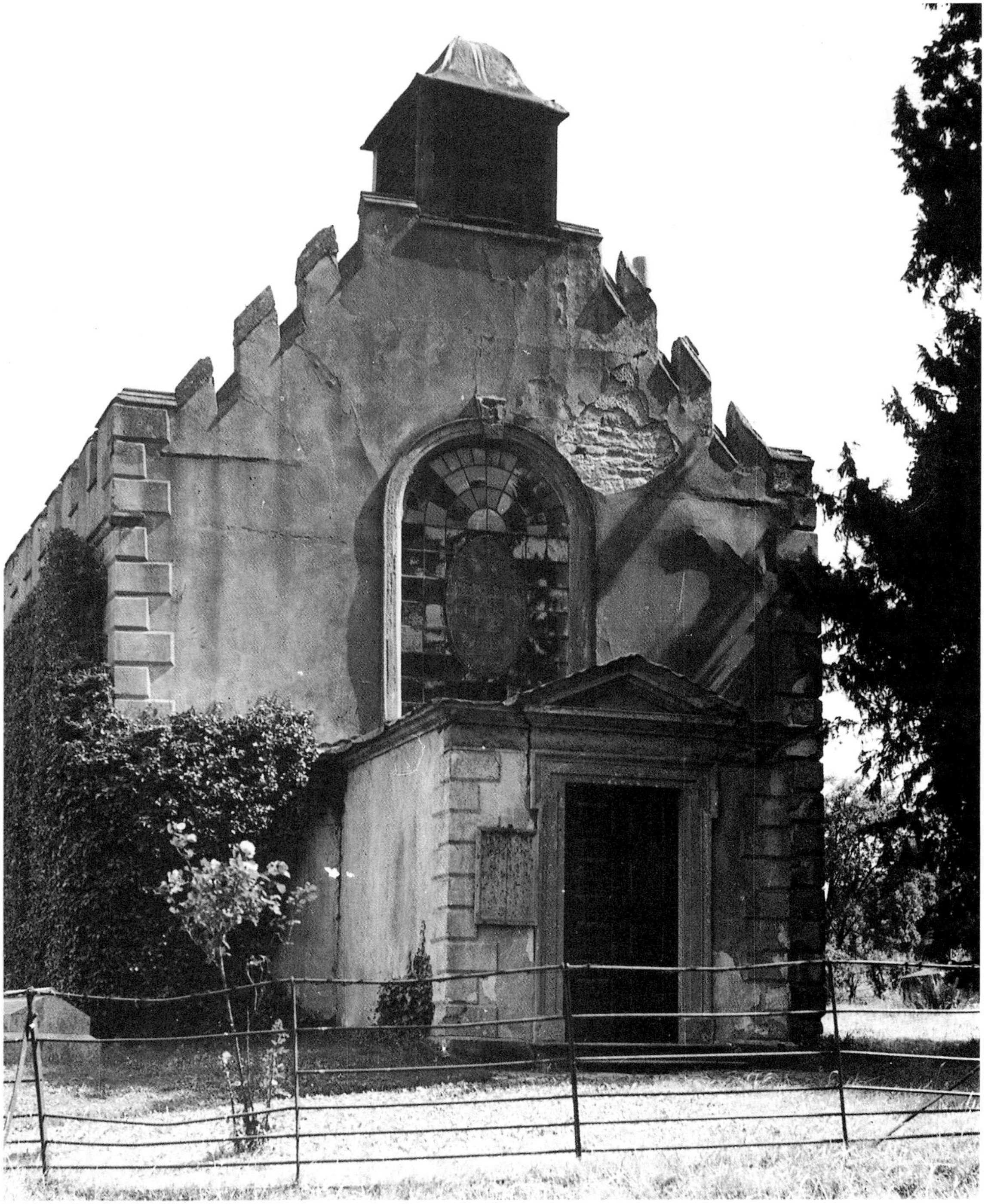

46 Wheatfield, Oxfordshire

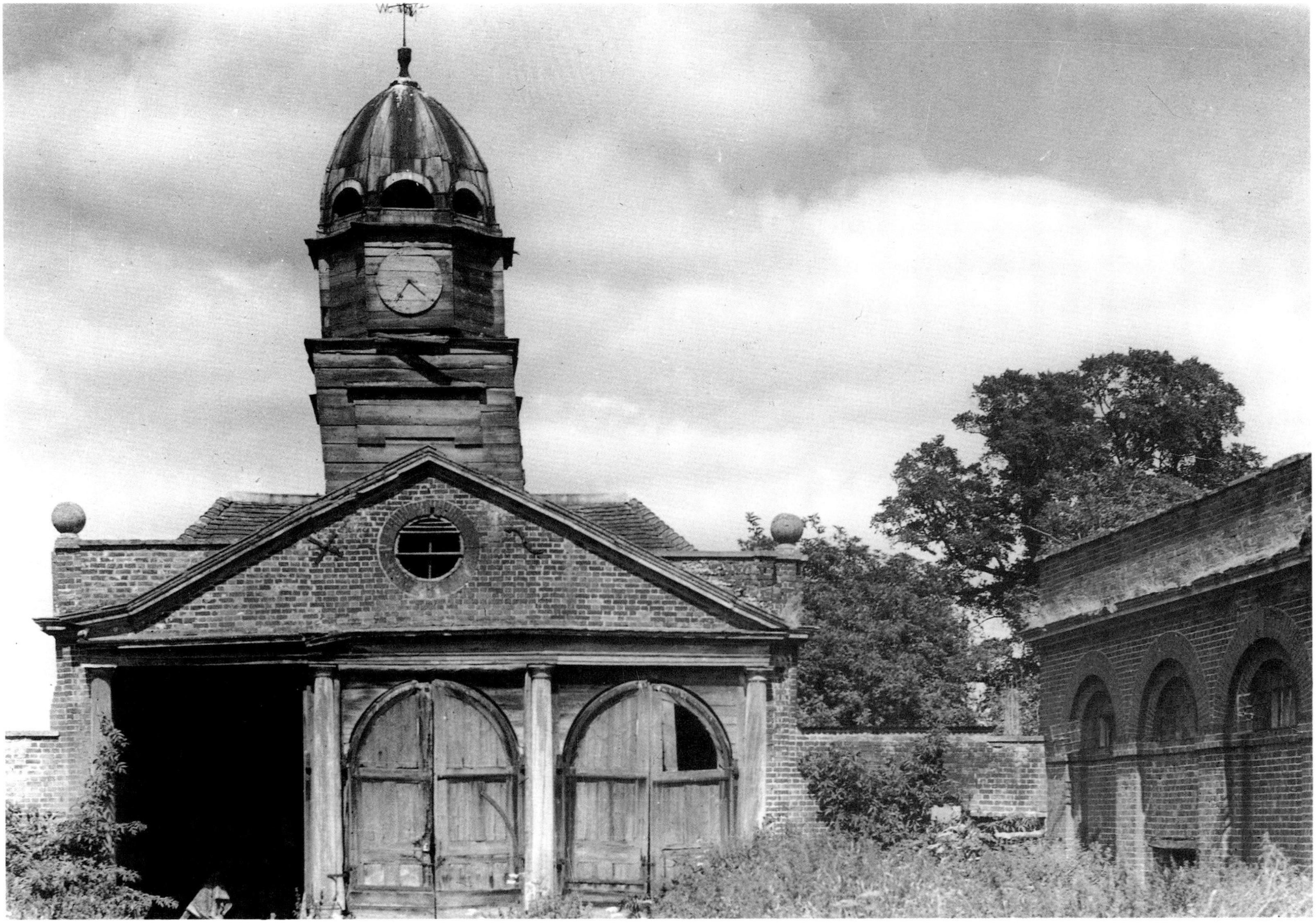

47 Stables of destroyed manor house,
Wheatfield, Oxfordshire

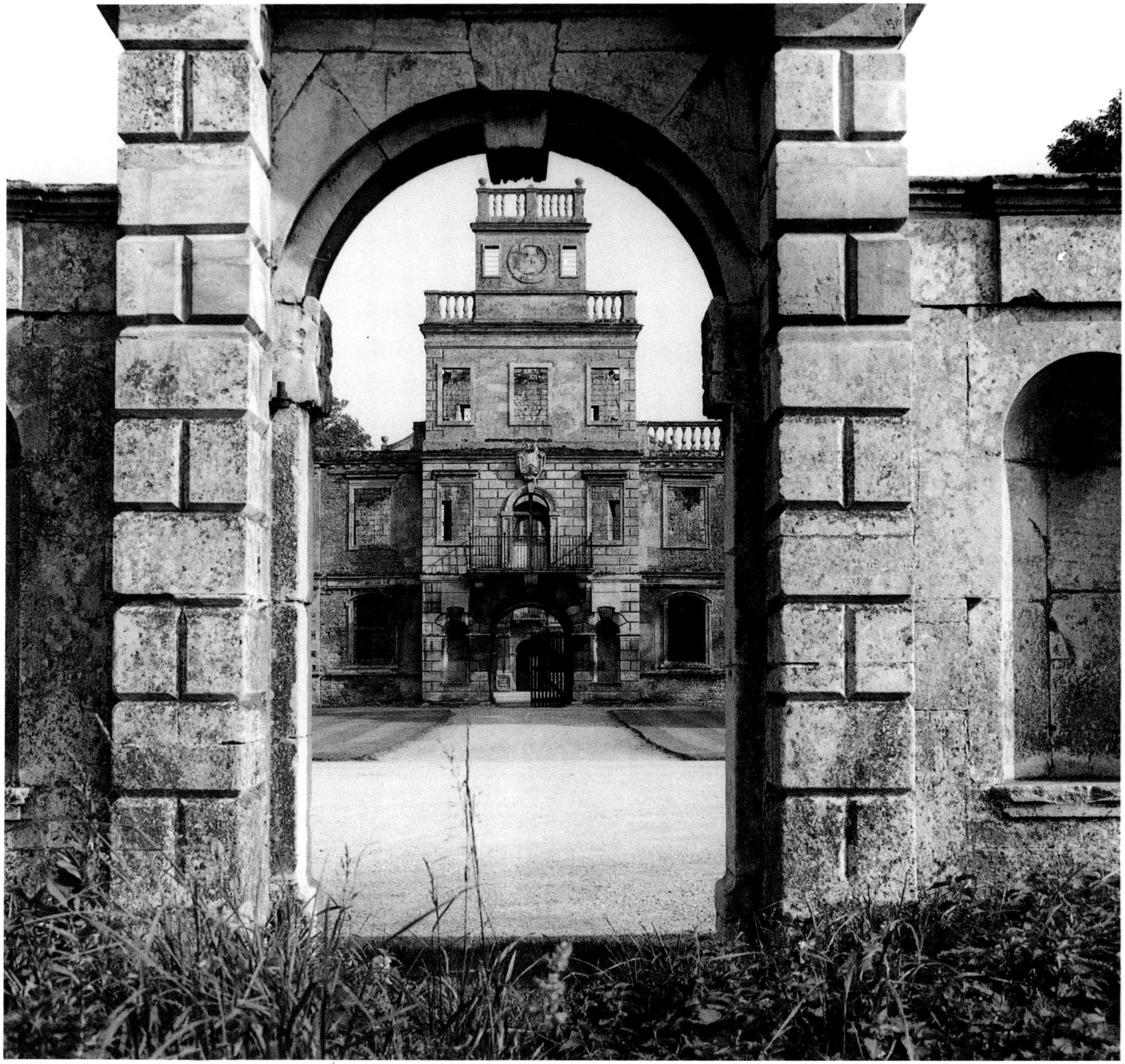

48 Kirby Hall, Northamptonshire

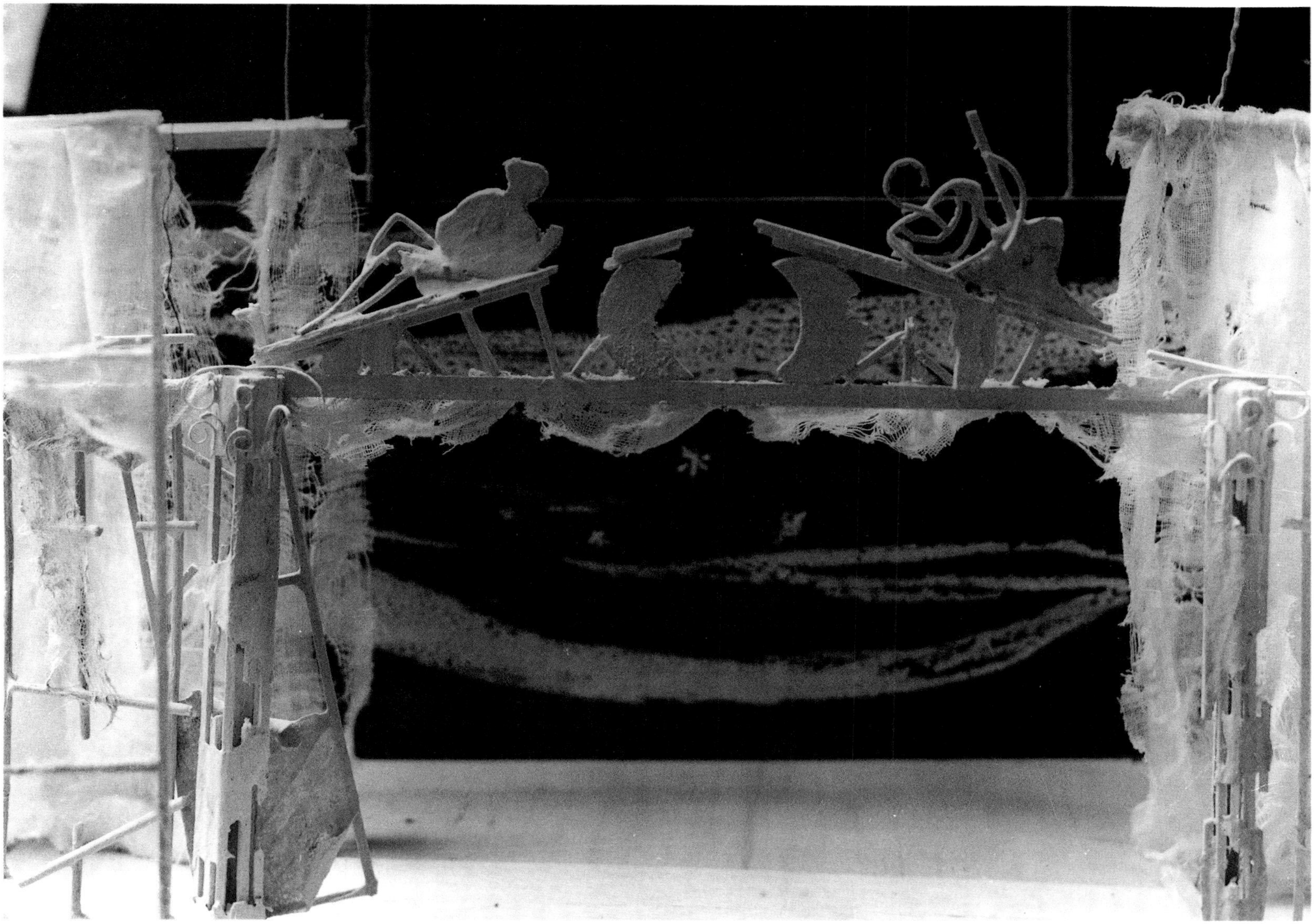

49 Model by John Piper of set for John Cranko's ballet 'Harlequin in April', 1954

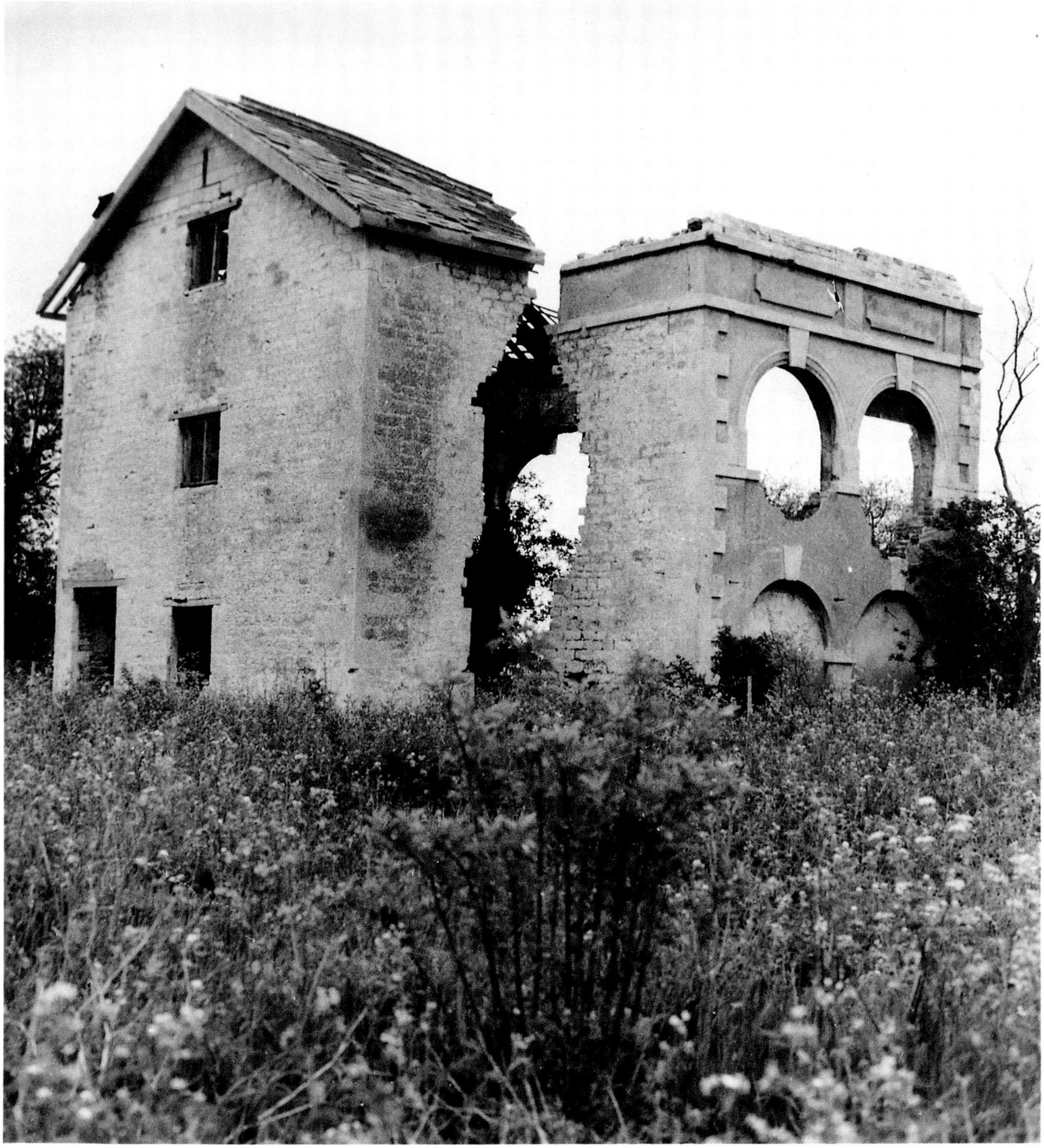

50 Ruined house near Stamford, Northamptonshire

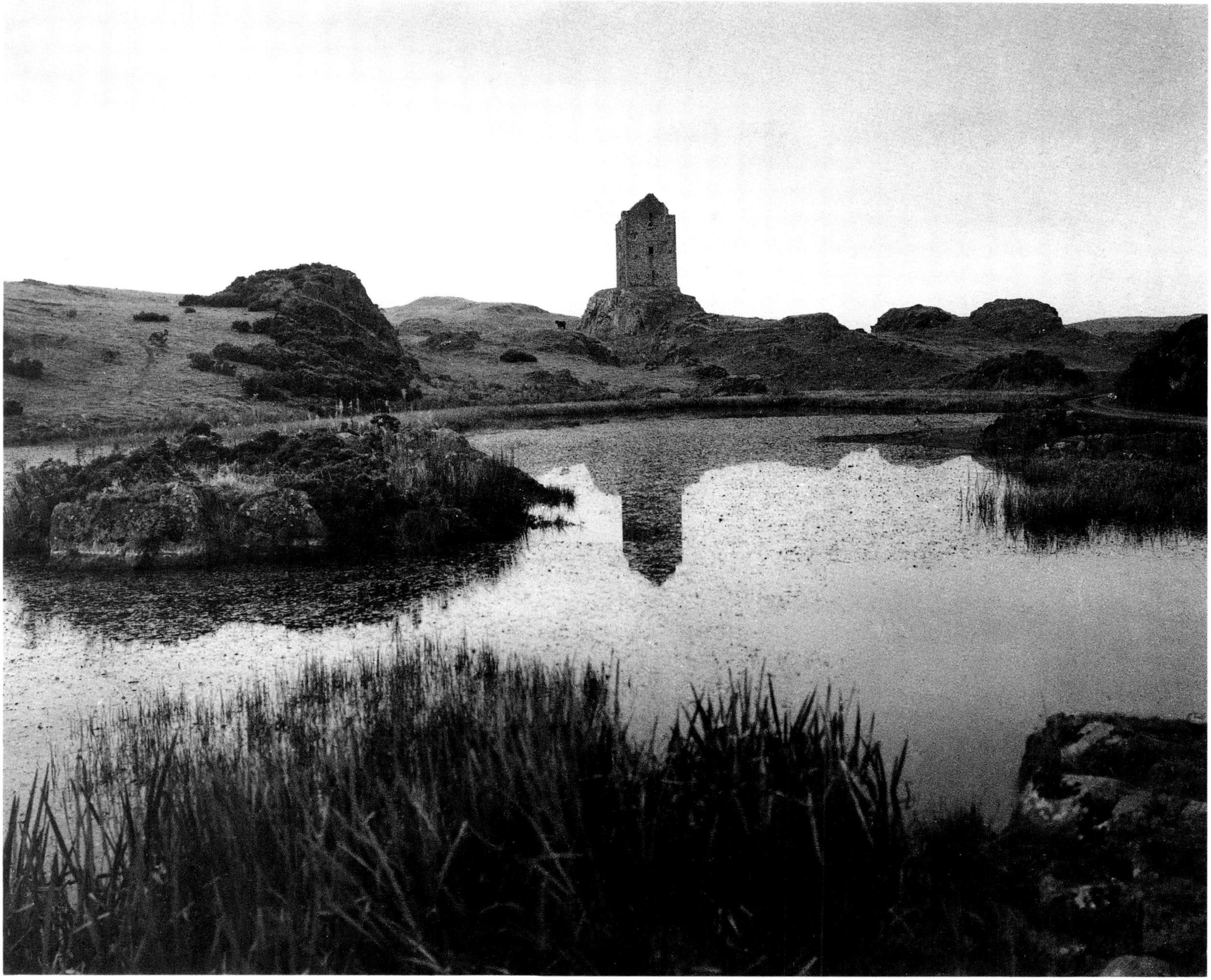

51 Smallholme Tower, near Kelso, 1975

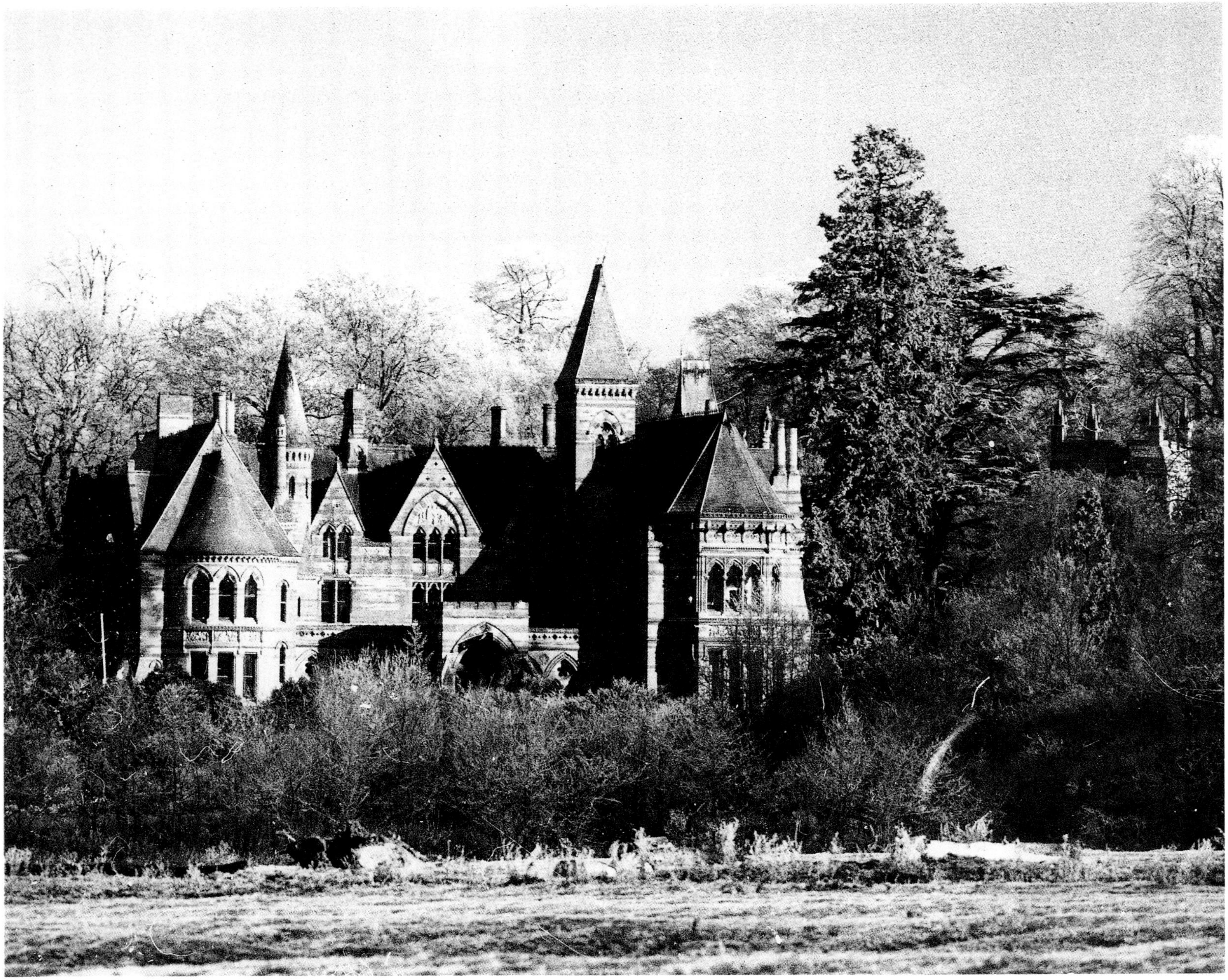

52 Ettington Park, Warwickshire

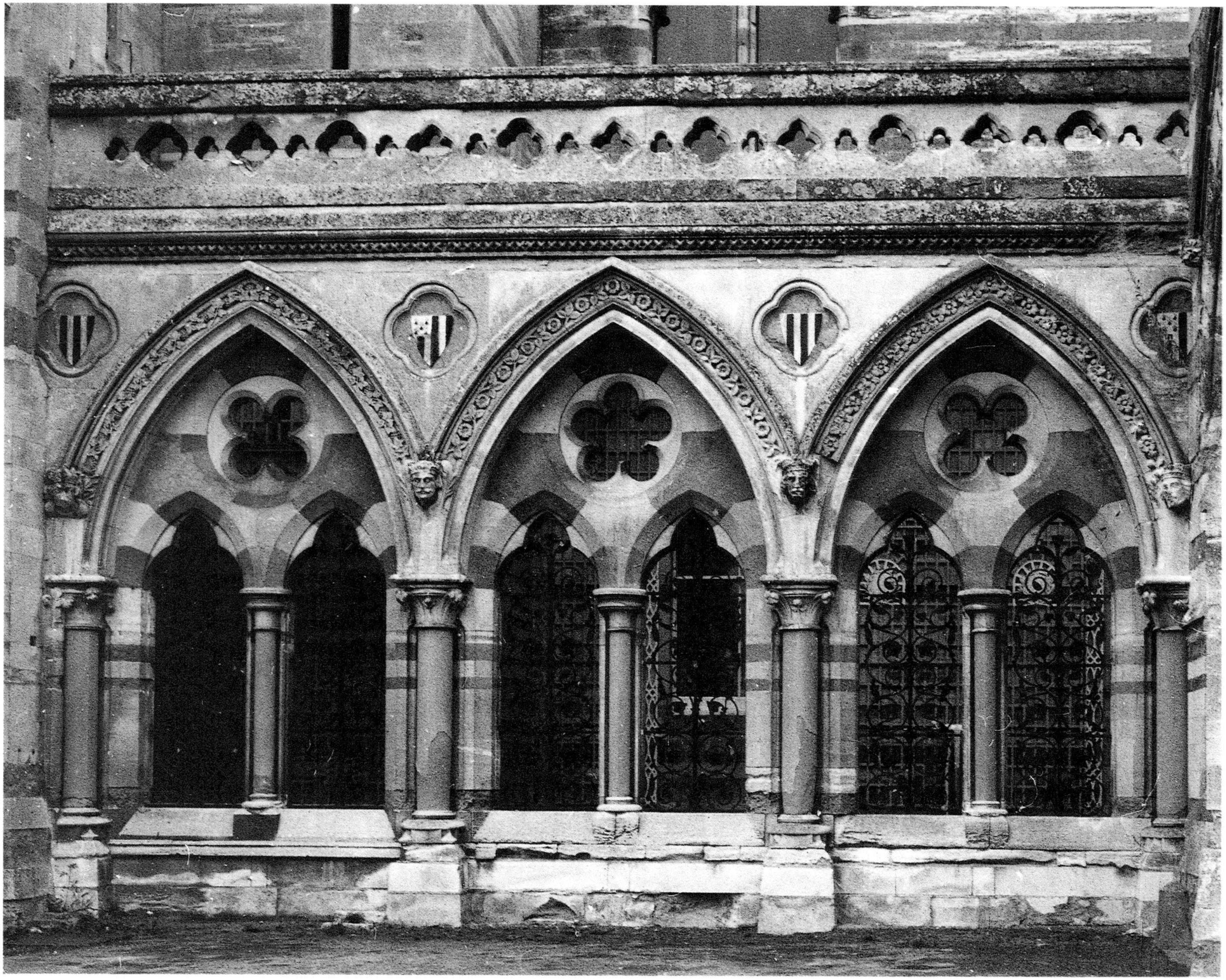

53 Screen at Ettington Park, Warwickshire

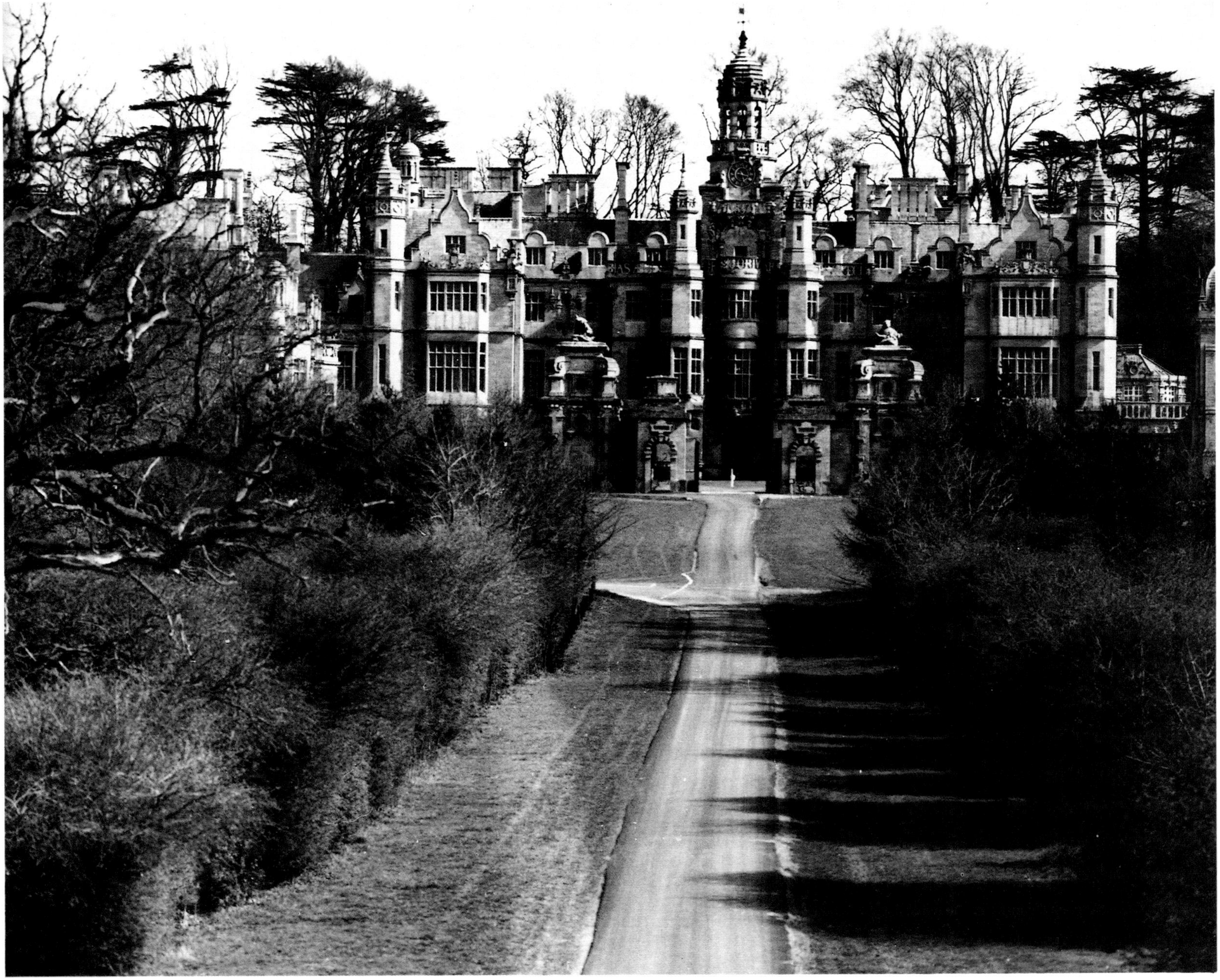

54 Harlaxton Manor, Lincolnshire, 1978

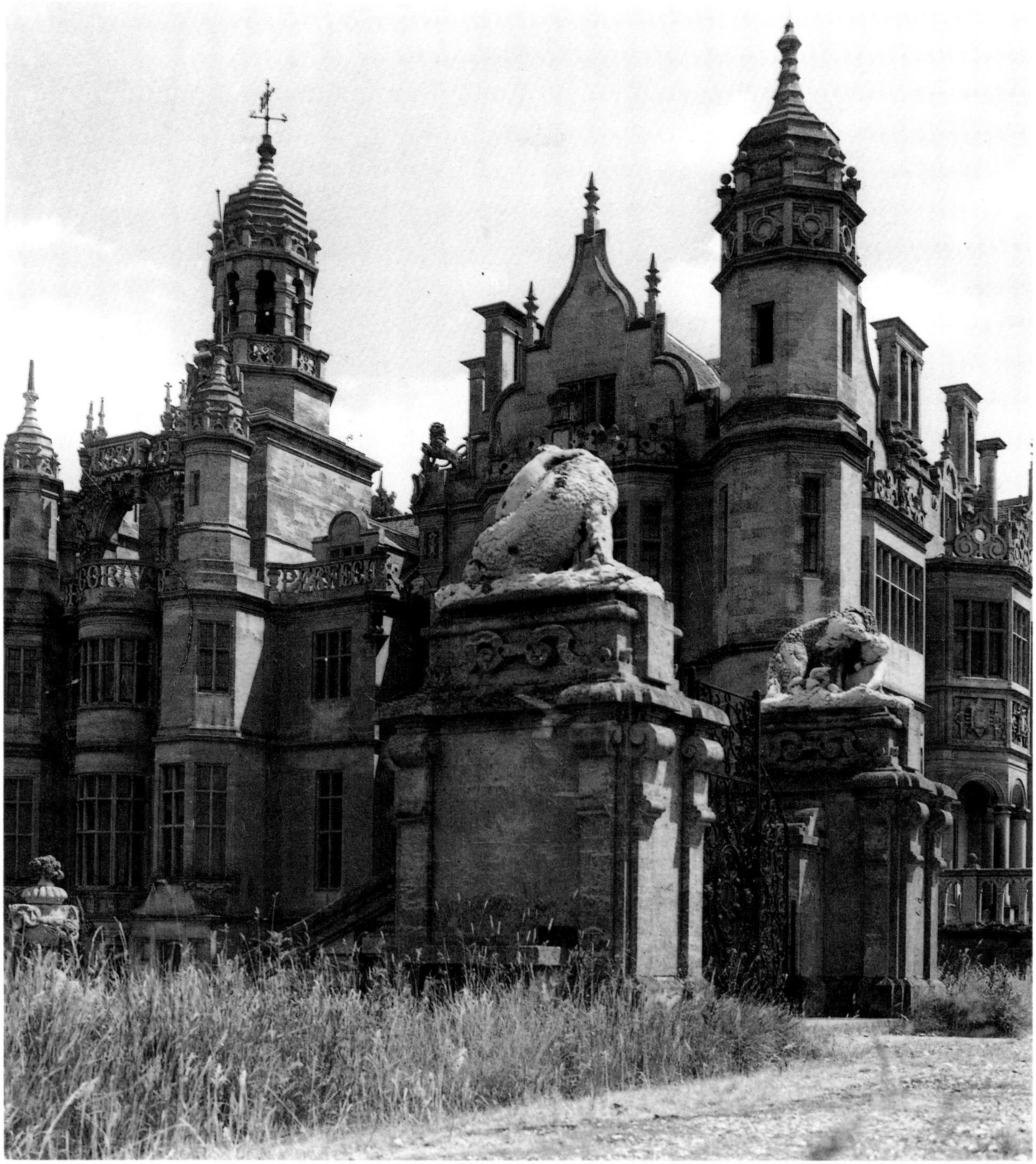

55 Harlaxton Manor,
Lincolnshire, 1965

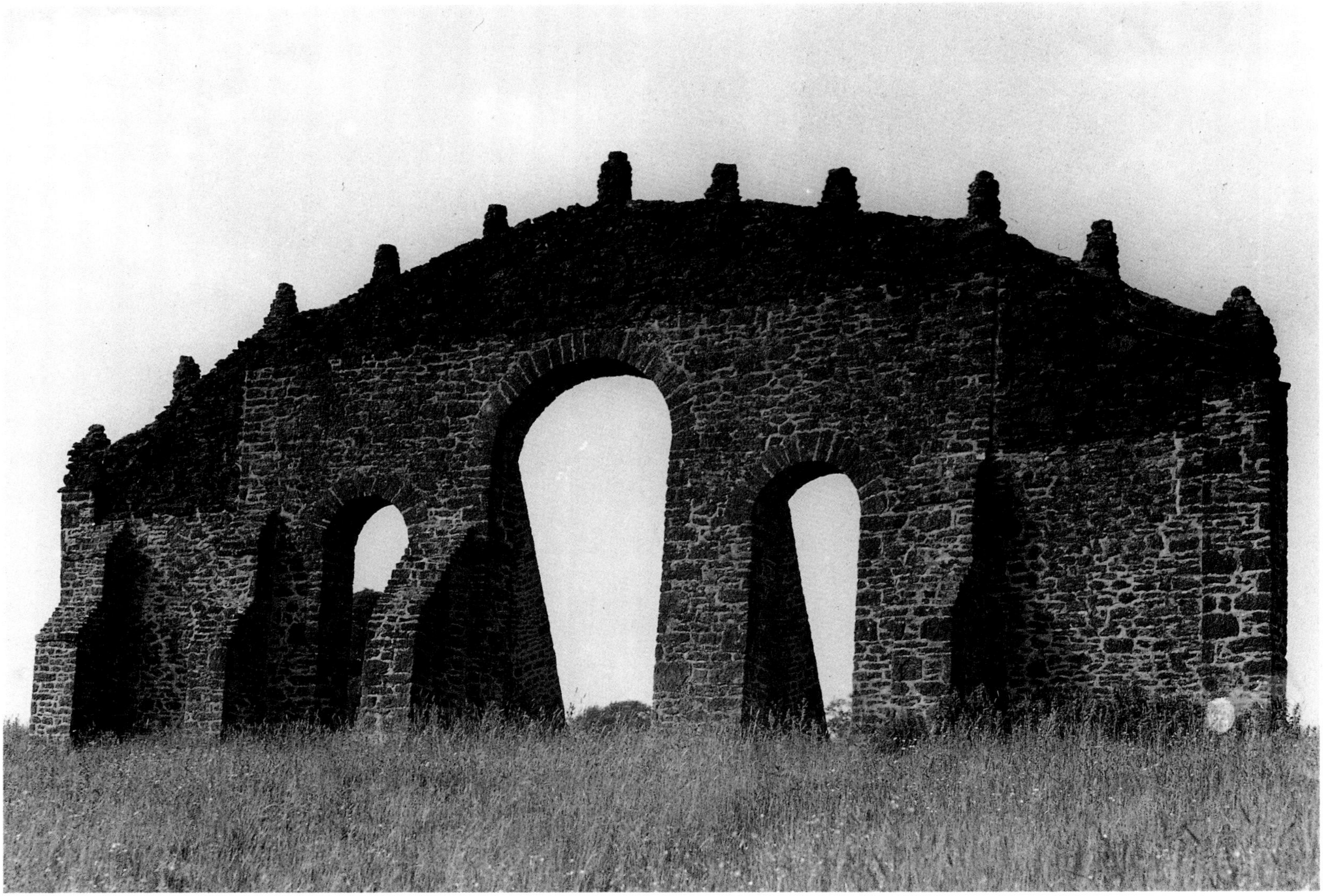

56 William Kent's eyecatcher at Rousham, Oxfordshire, about 1938

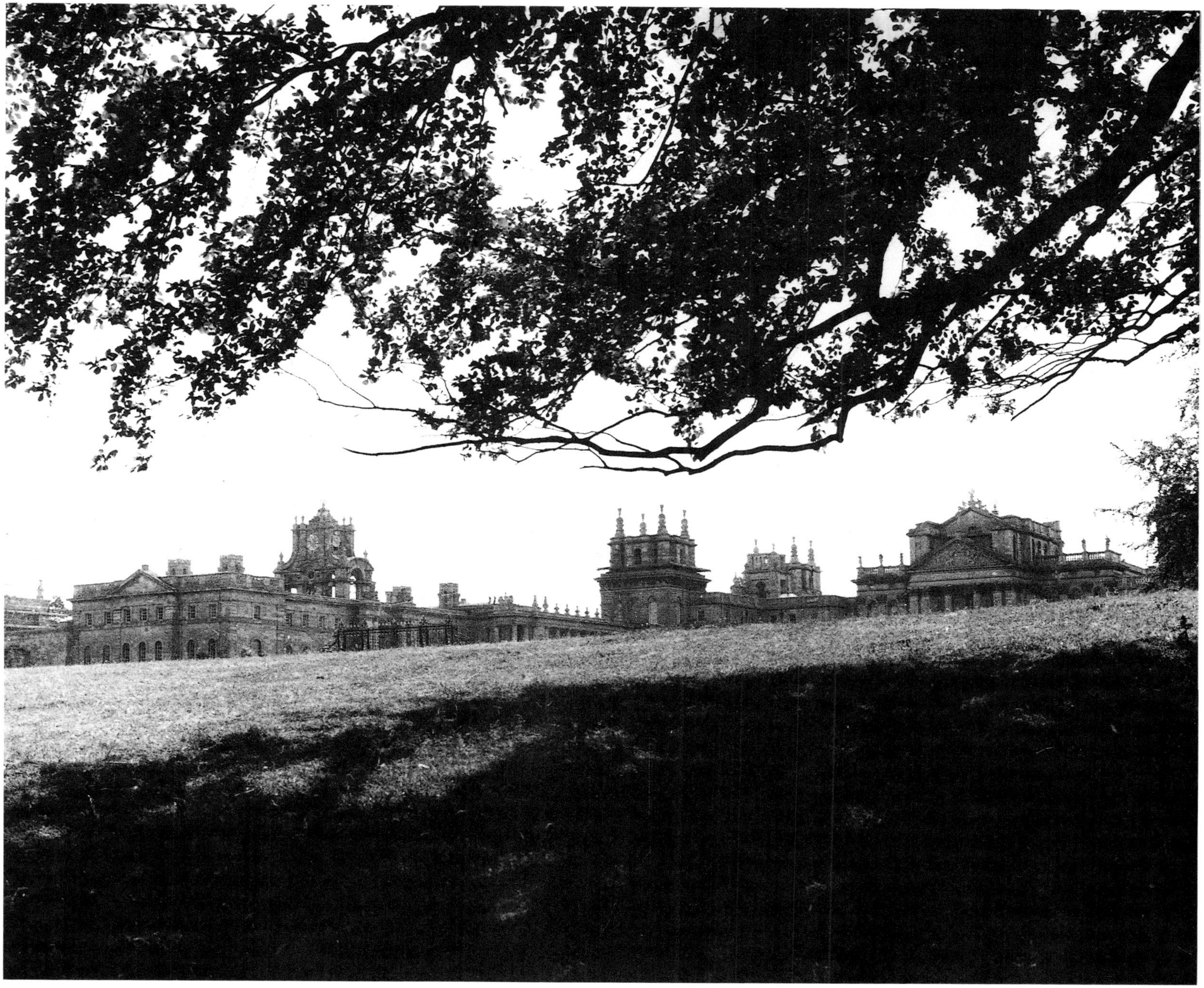

57 Blenheim Palace, Oxfordshire, 1978

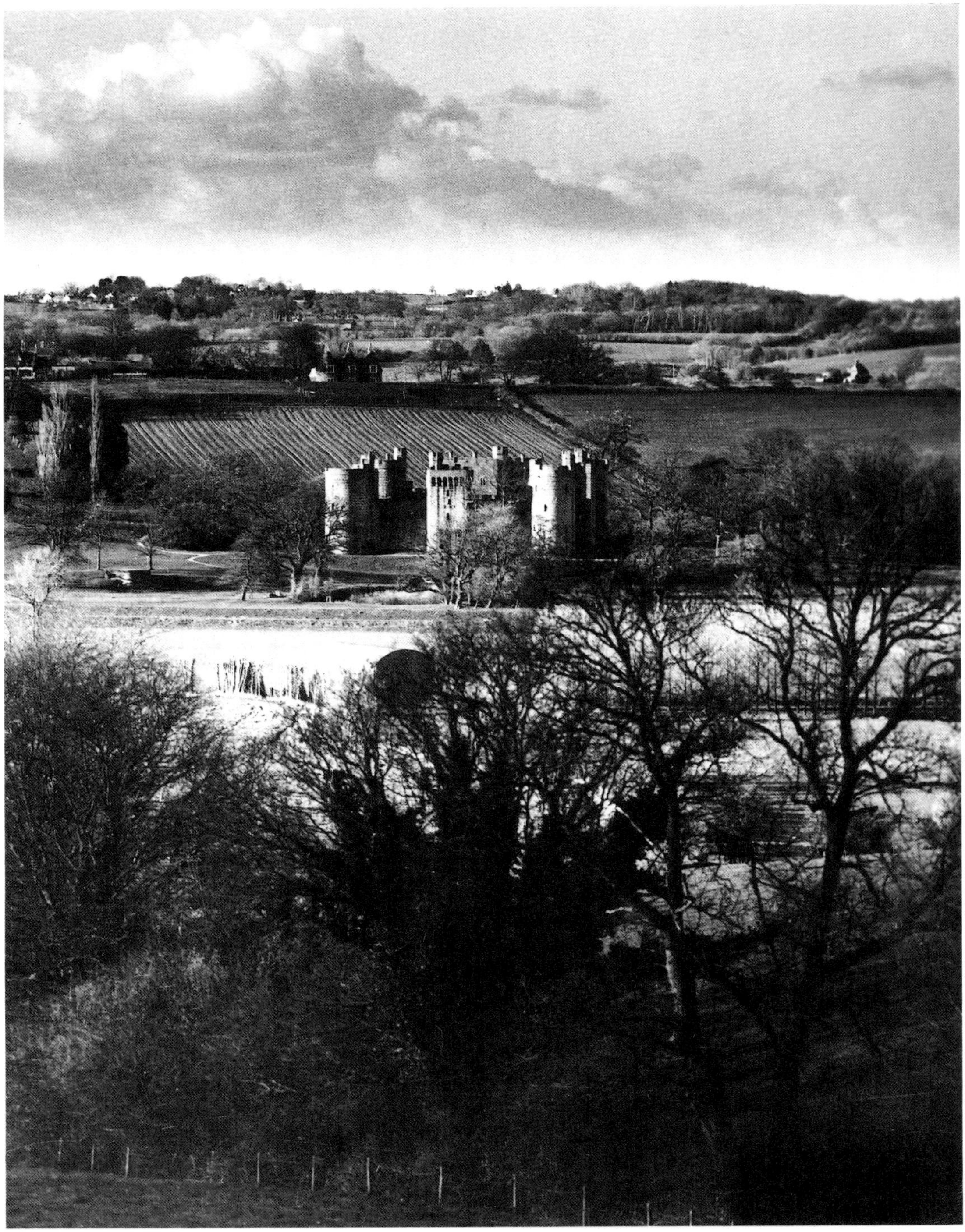

58 Bodiam Castle, East Sussex, 1977

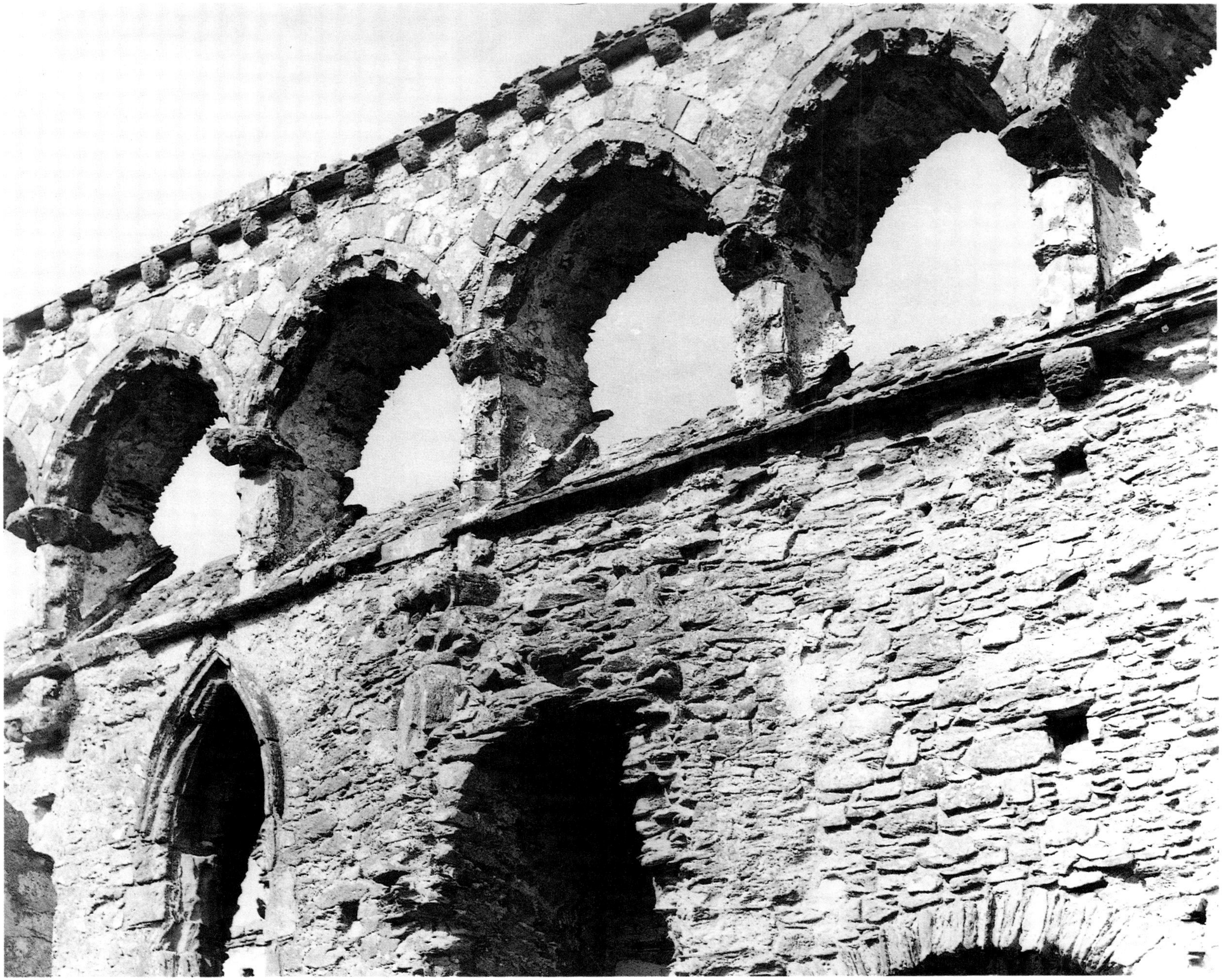

59 Bishop's Palace, St Davids, Dyfed

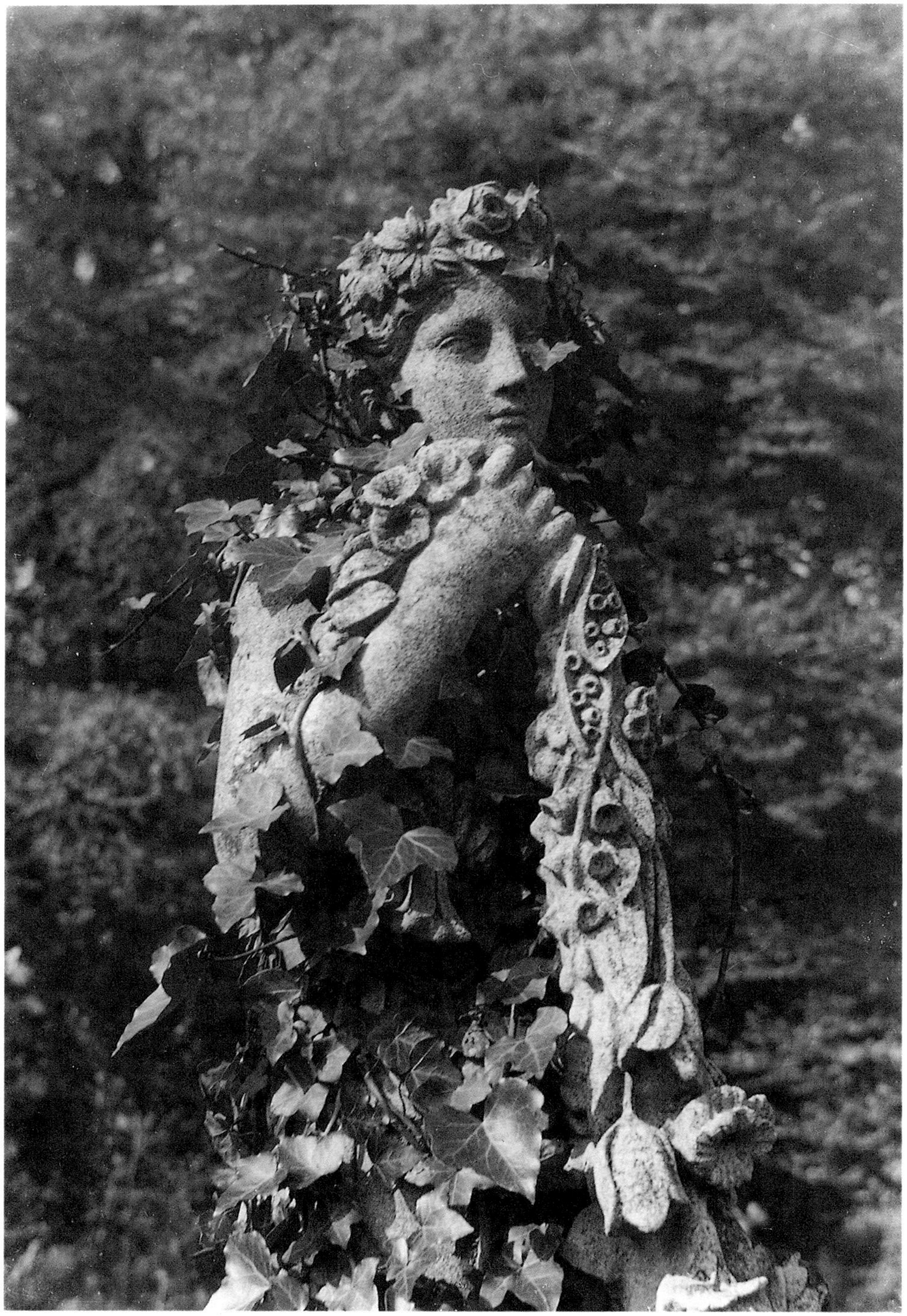

60 Ivied figure at Wotton, Surrey

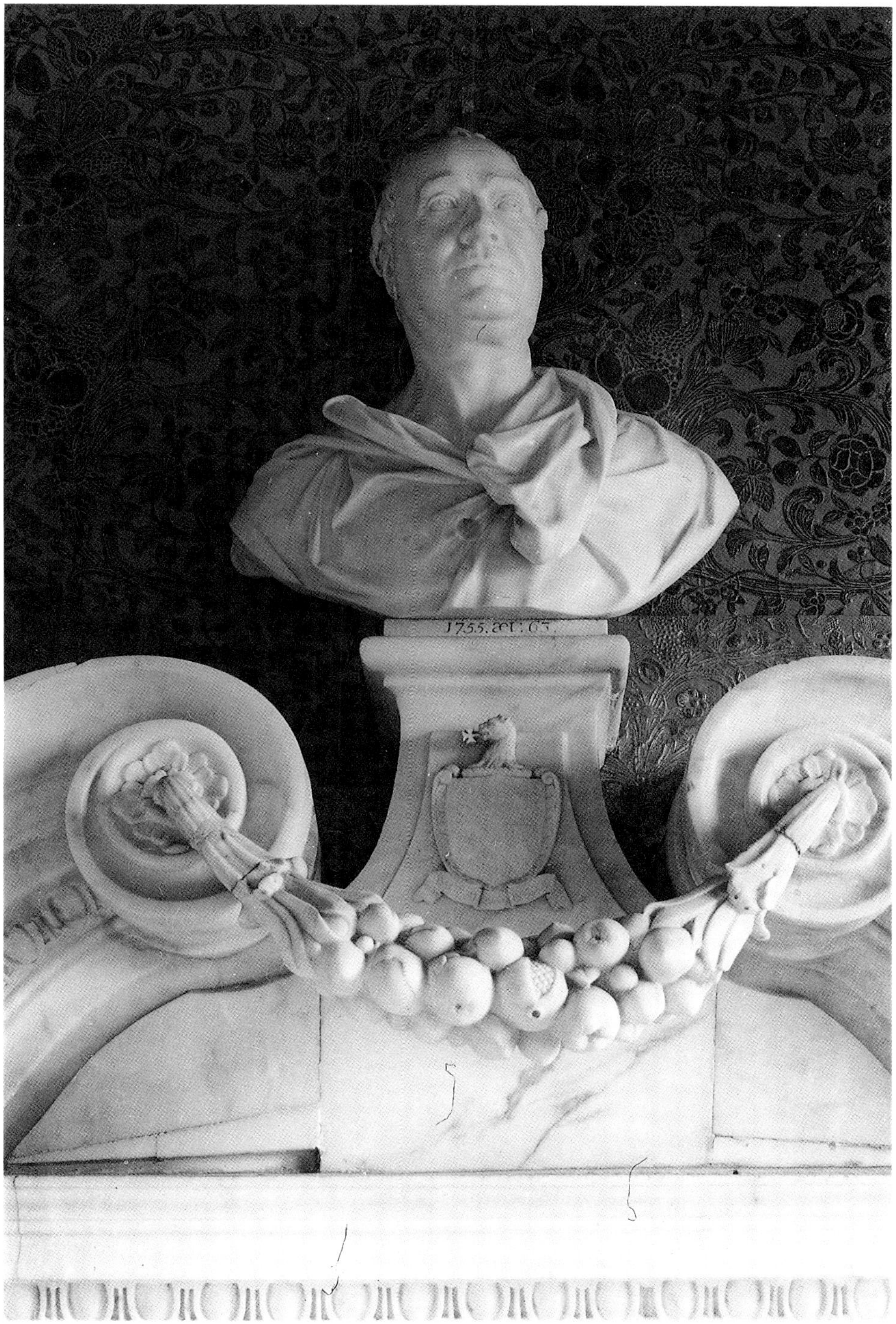

61 Staircase feature at Coleshill, Berkshire

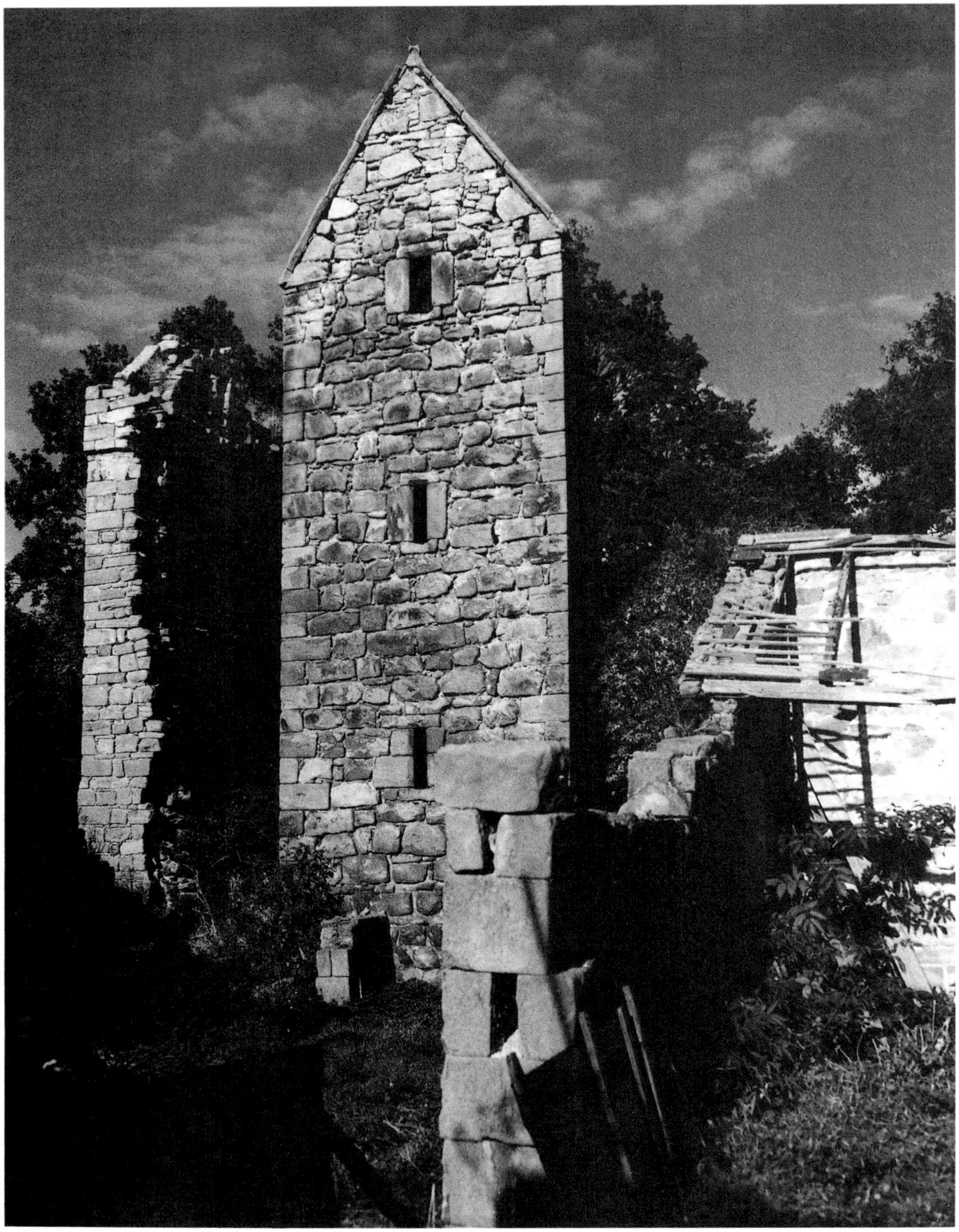

62 Doddington Bastle House, Cumbria, 1975

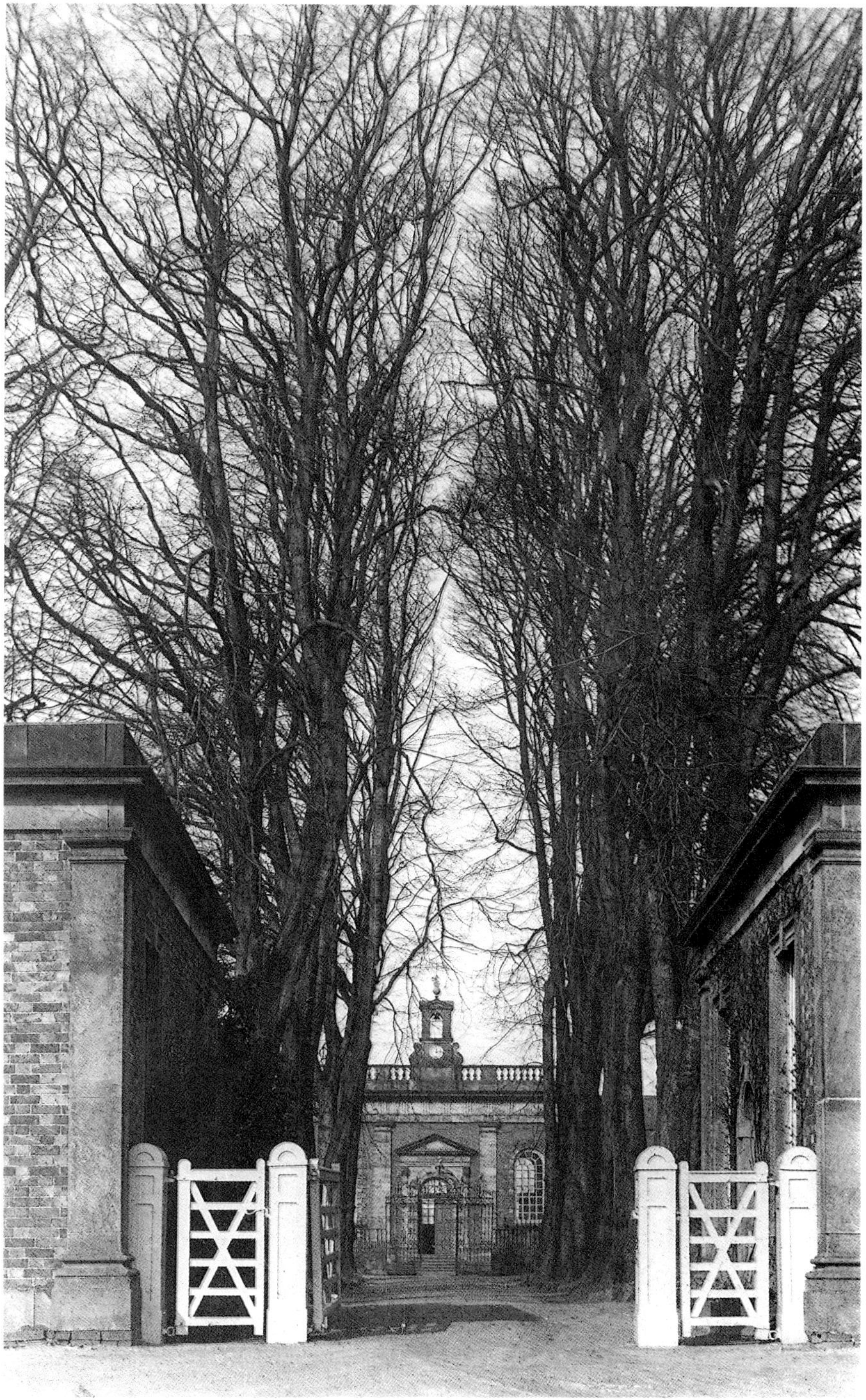

63 Preston on the Weald Moors, Shropshire

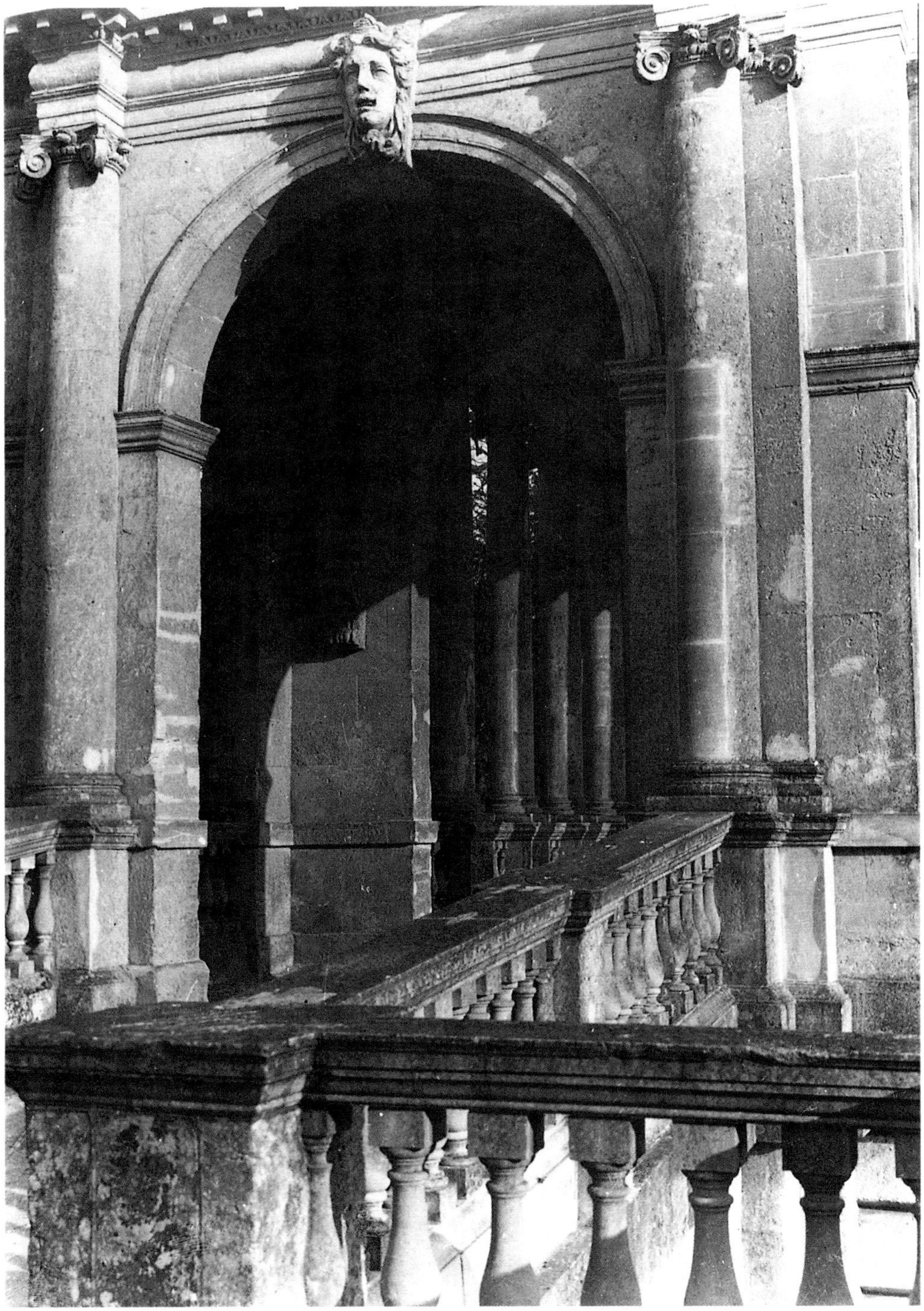

64 Palladian Bridge at Stowe,
Buckinghamshire

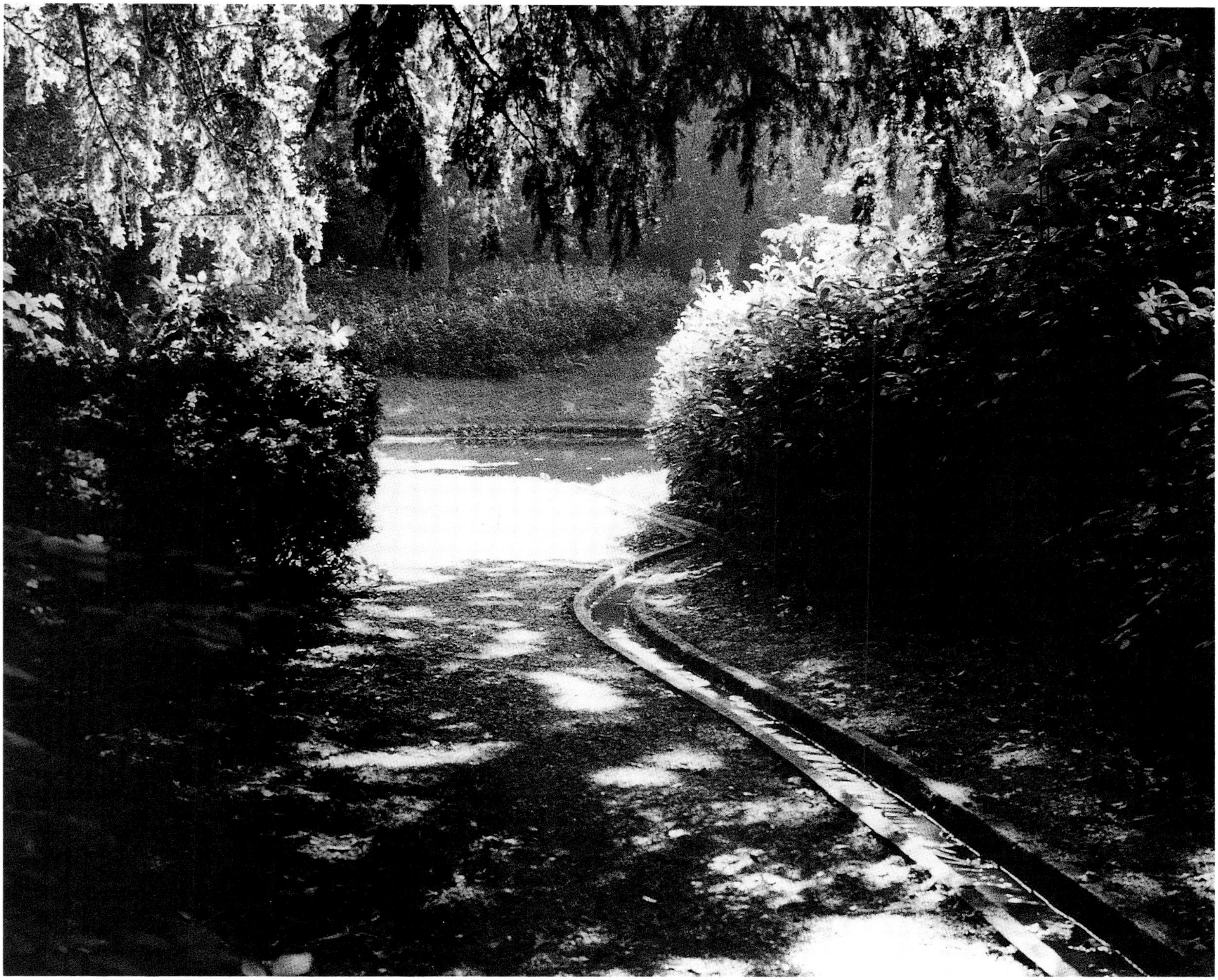

65 William Kent's rill at Rousham, Oxfordshire, 1975

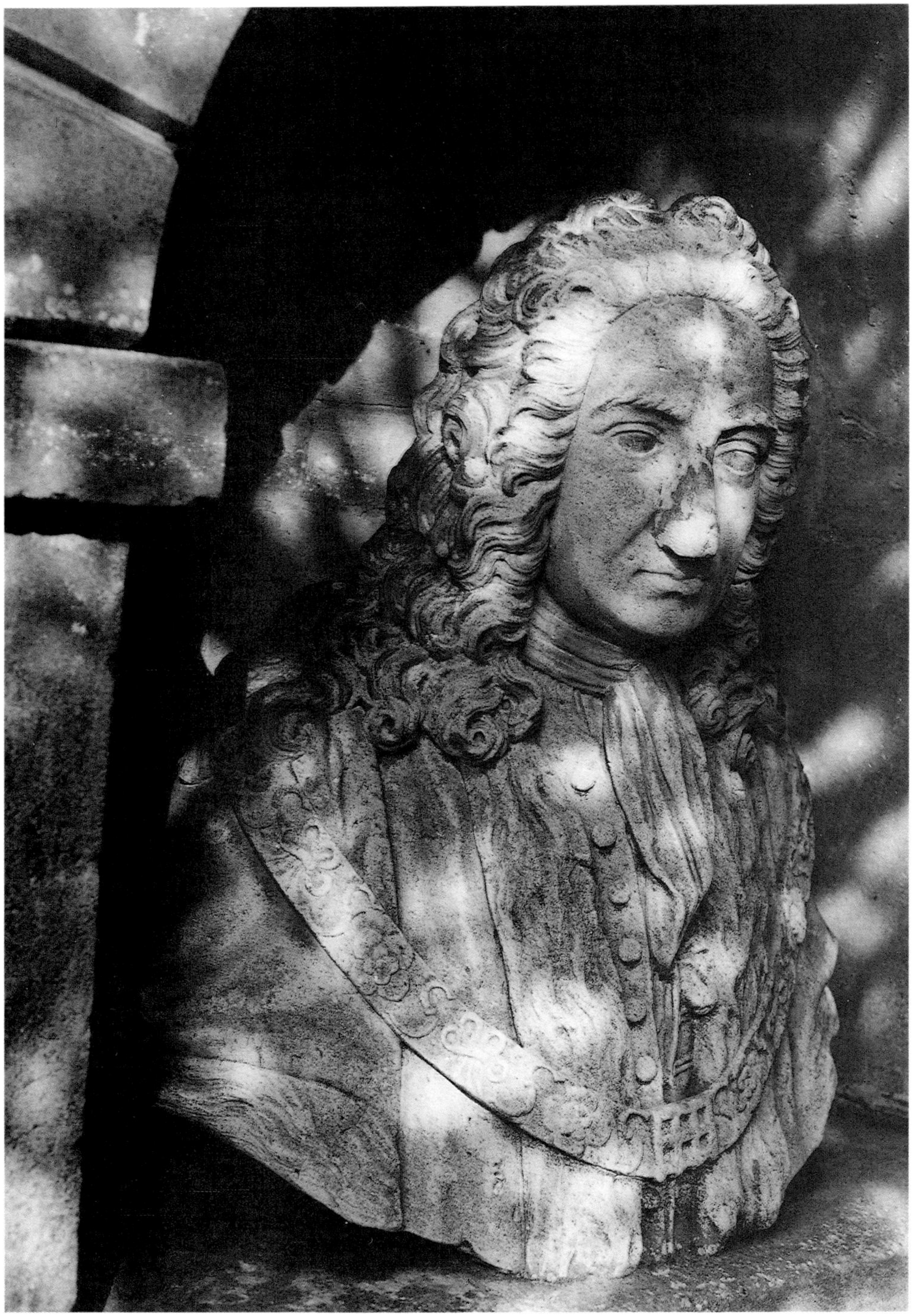

66 Temple of the British Worthies, Stowe, Buckinghamshire, 1950s

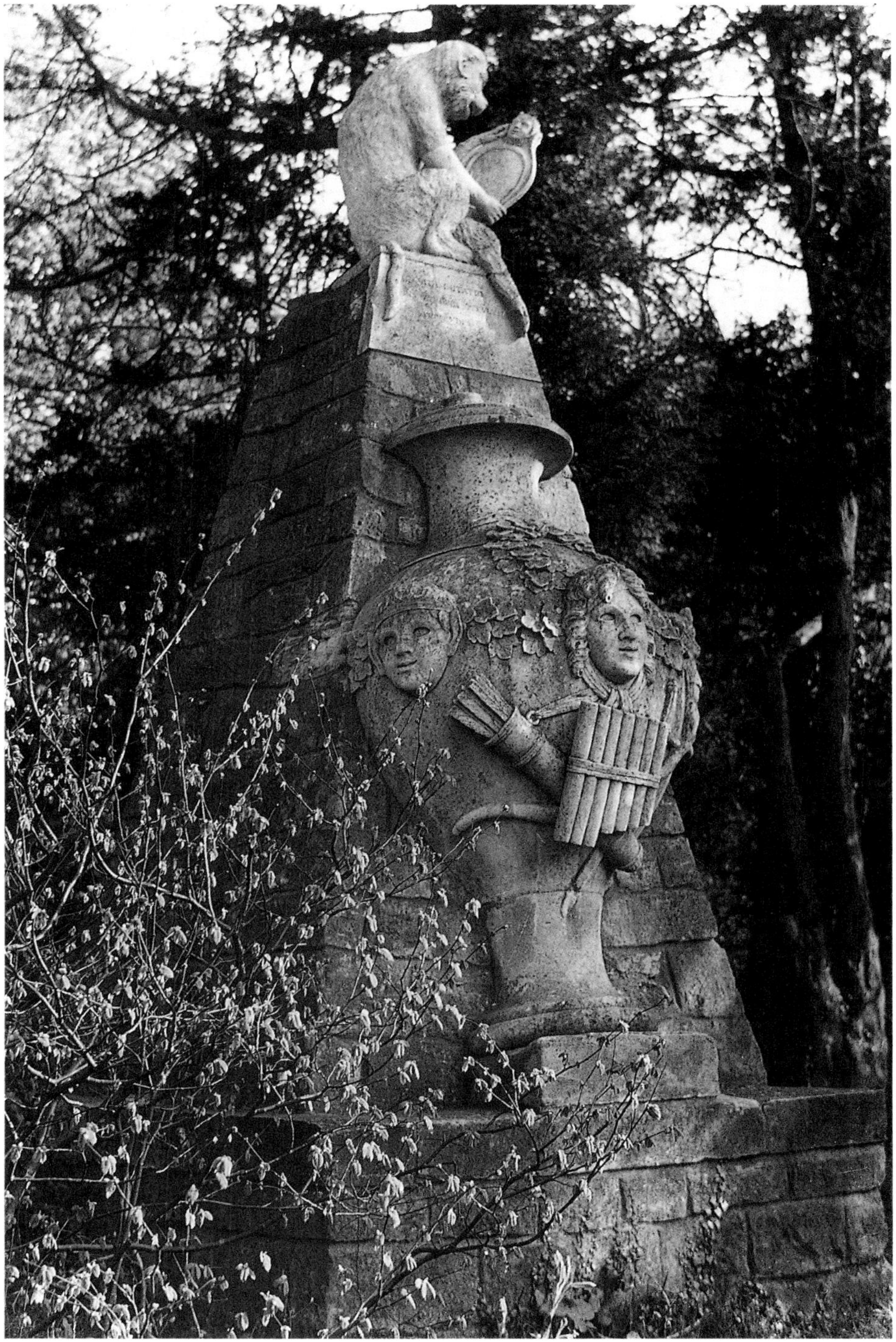

67 Congreve Memorial, Stowe, Buckinghamshire

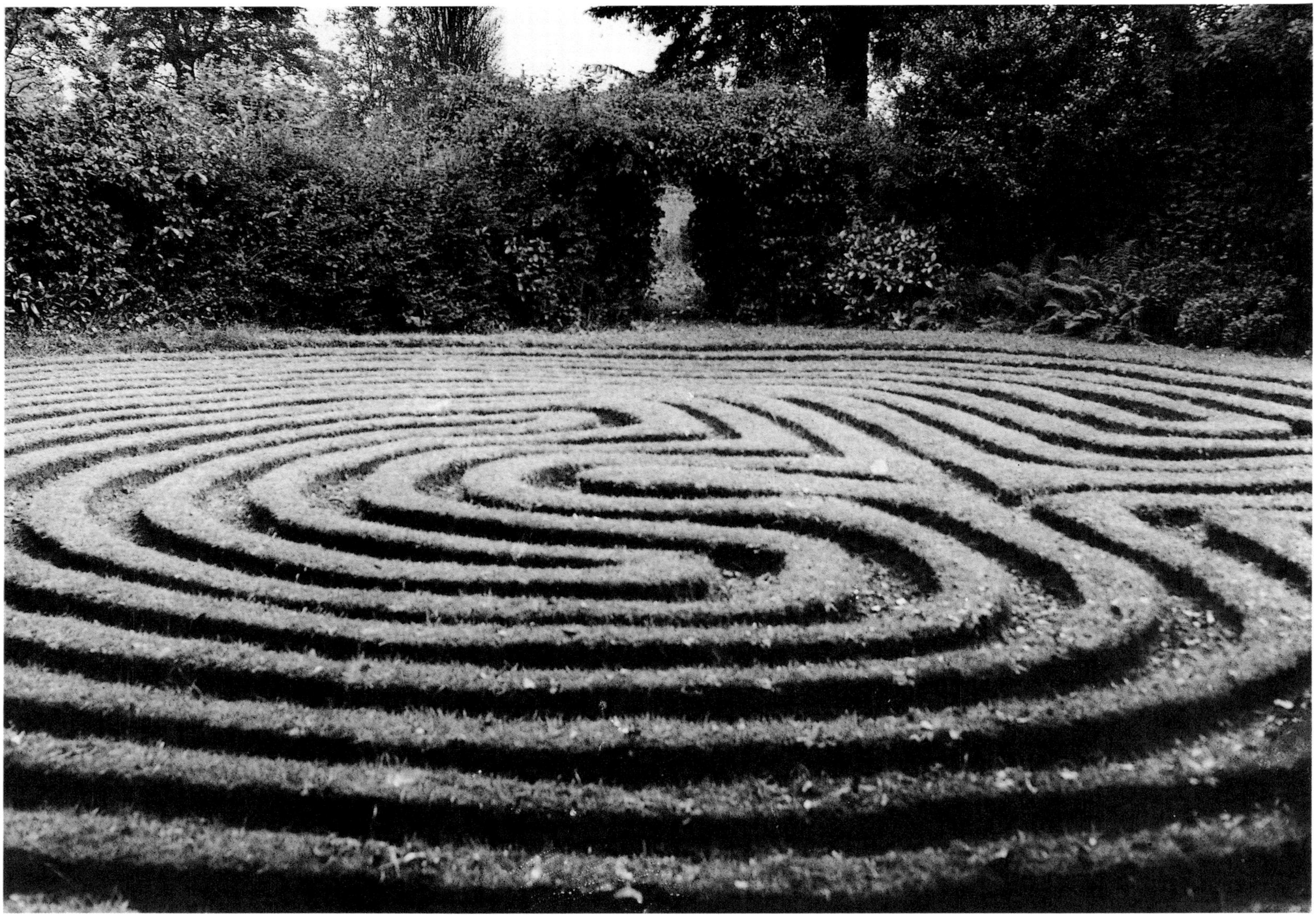

68 Turf maze at Somerton, near Northleach, Oxfordshire, 1930s

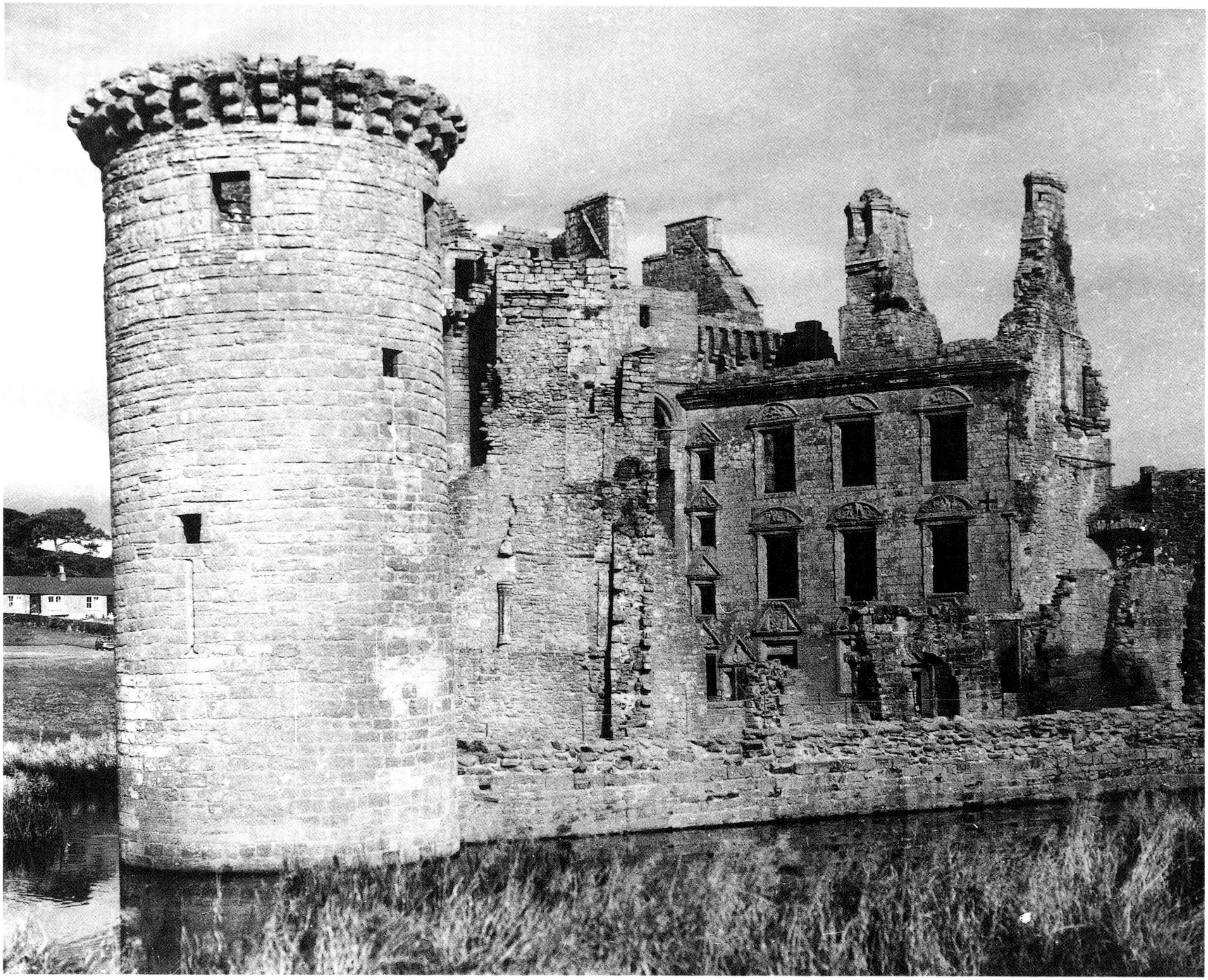

69 Caerlaverock, Dumfriesshire

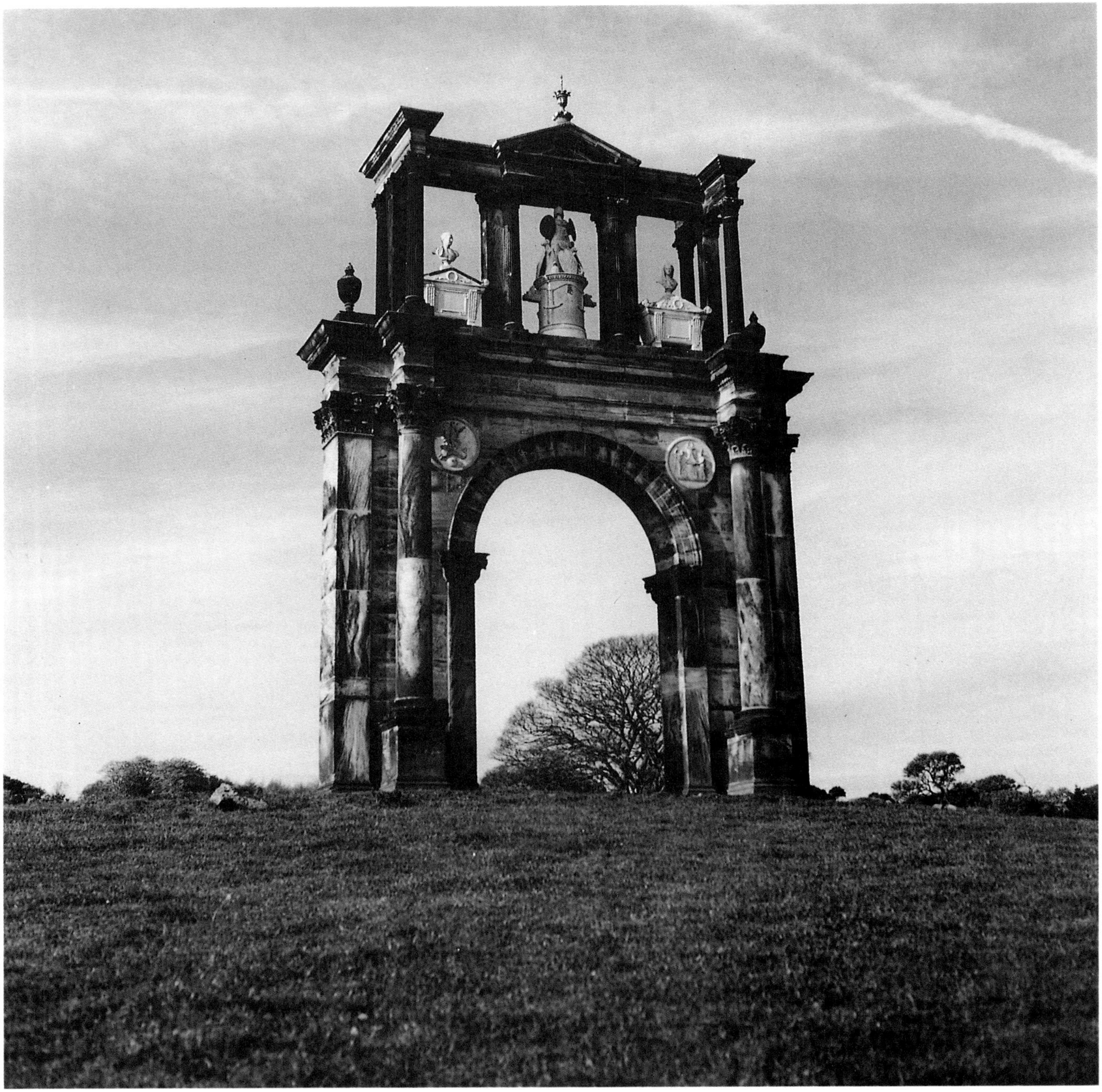

70 The Arch of Hadrian, Shugborough, Staffordshire

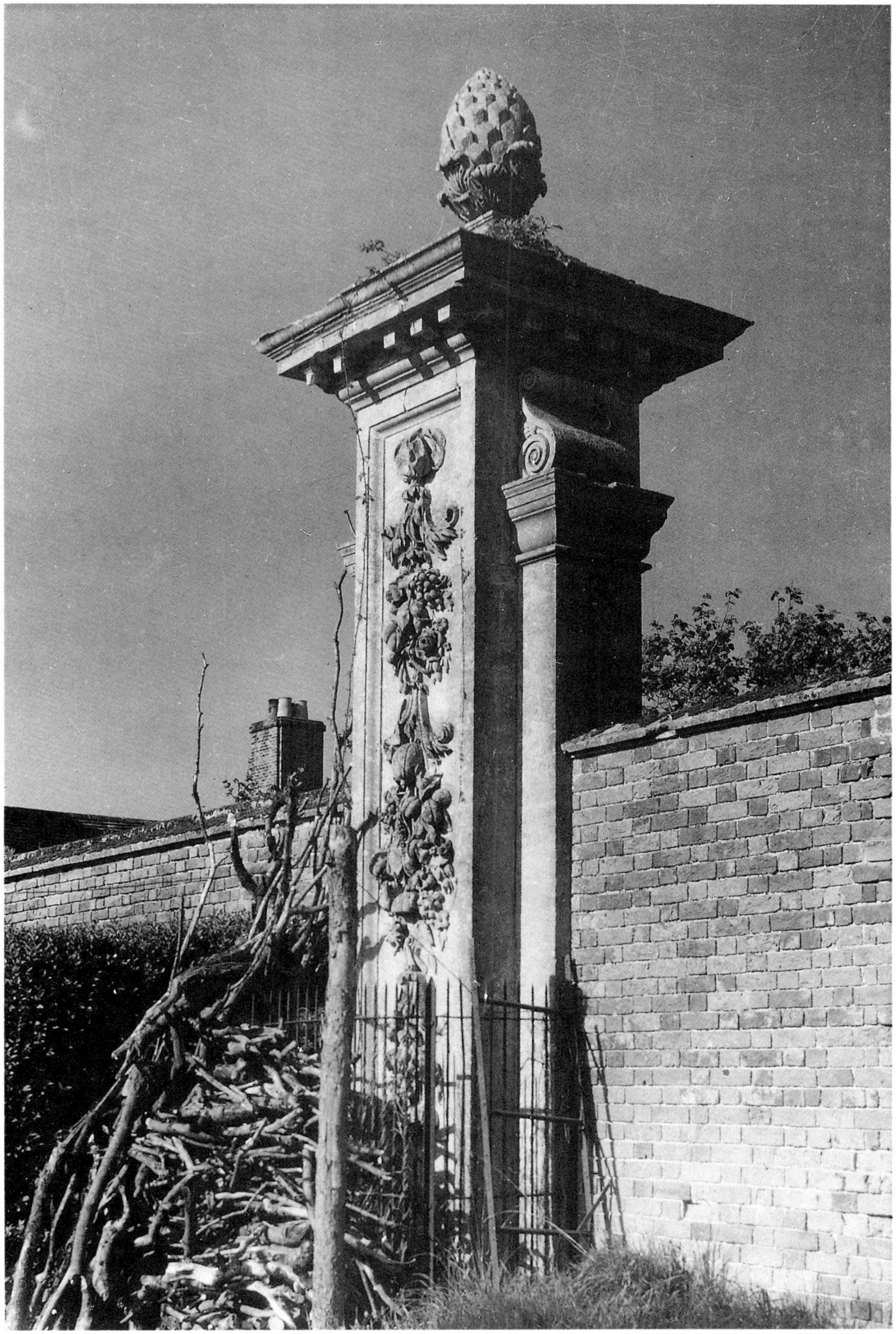

71 Hamstead Marshall, Buckinghamshire, 1960s

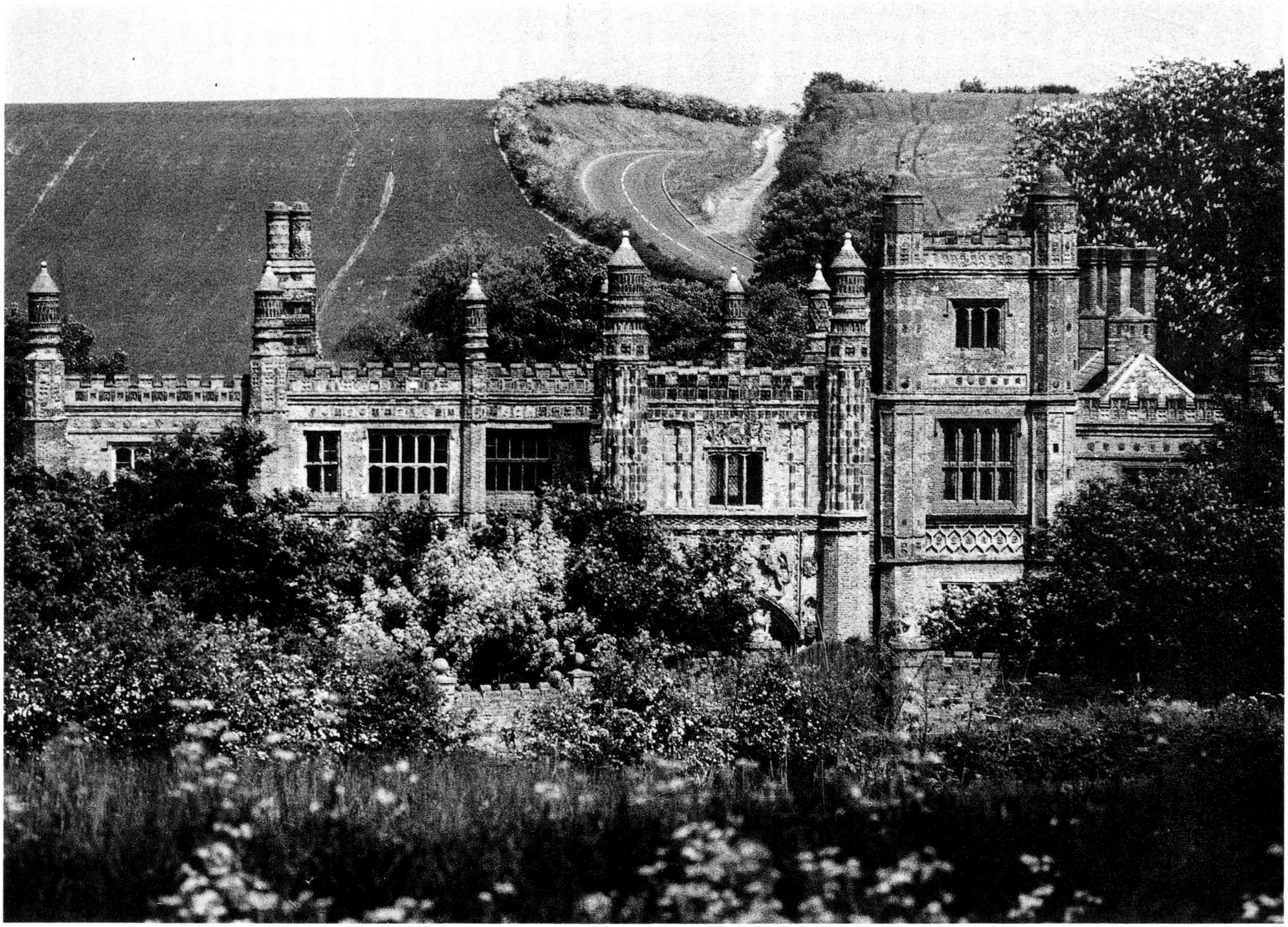

72 East Barsham manor house, Norfolk

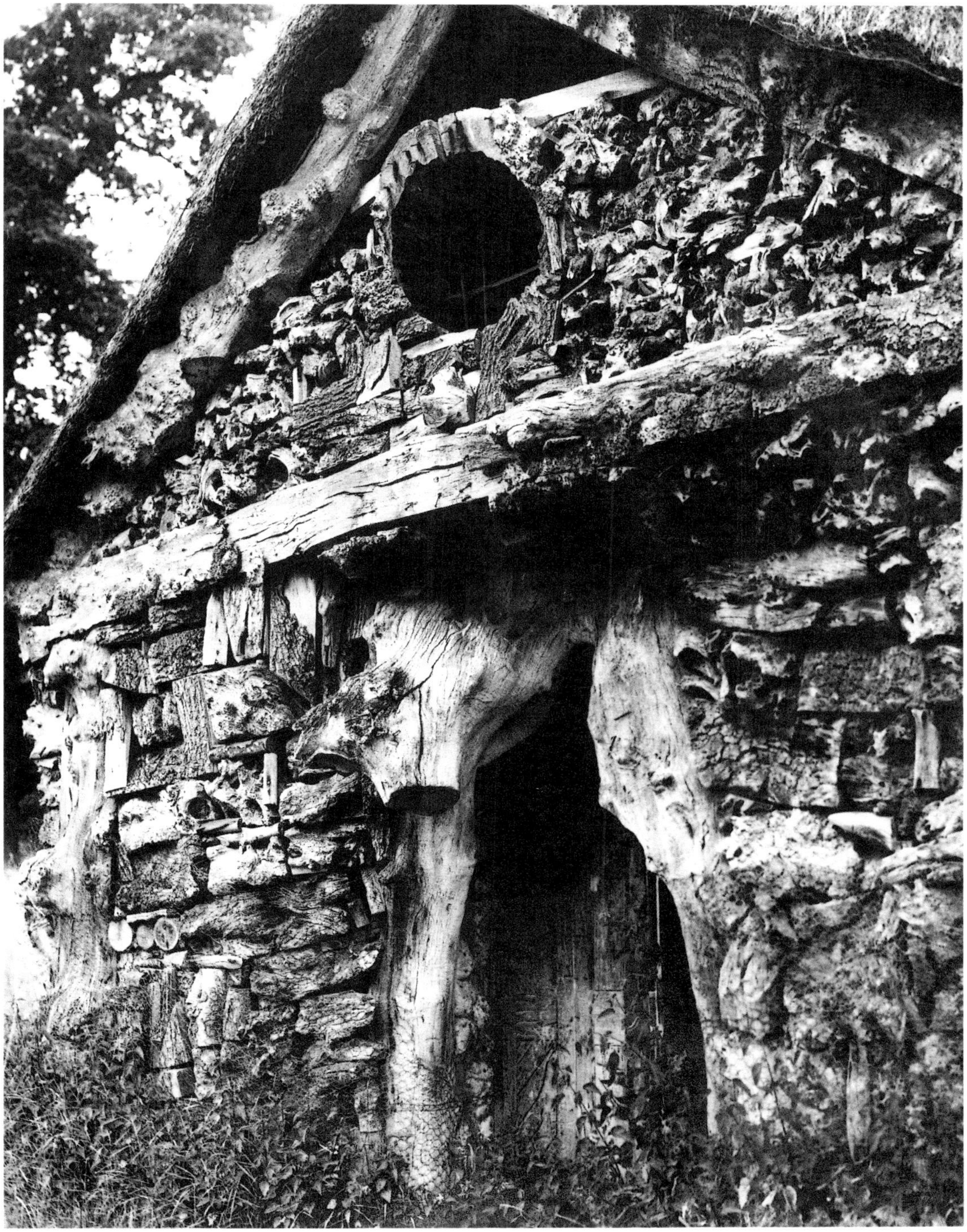

73 The Root-house, Badminton, Wiltshire, about 1974

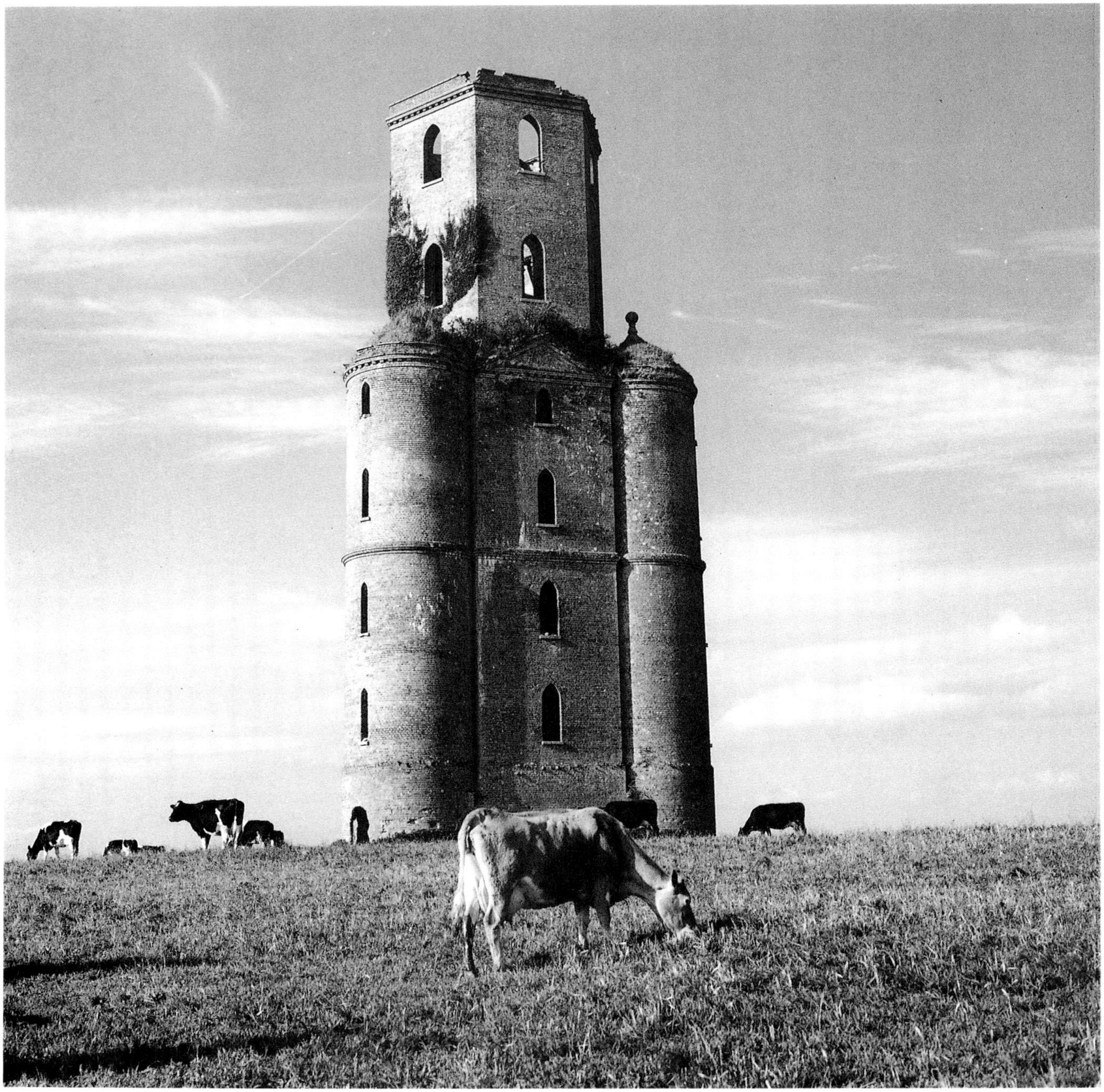

74 Horton Tower, Dorset

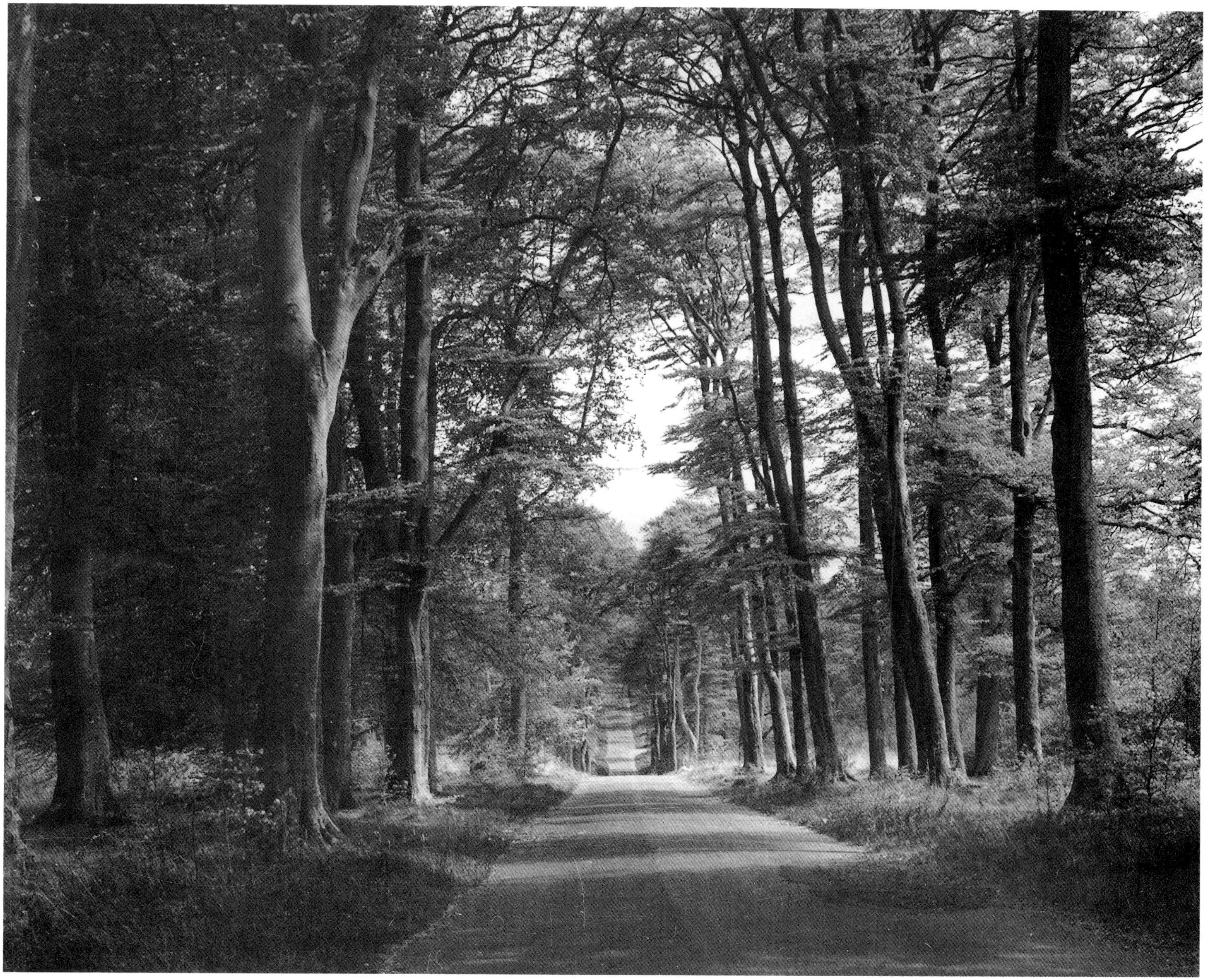

75 In the park at Castle Howard, Yorkshire

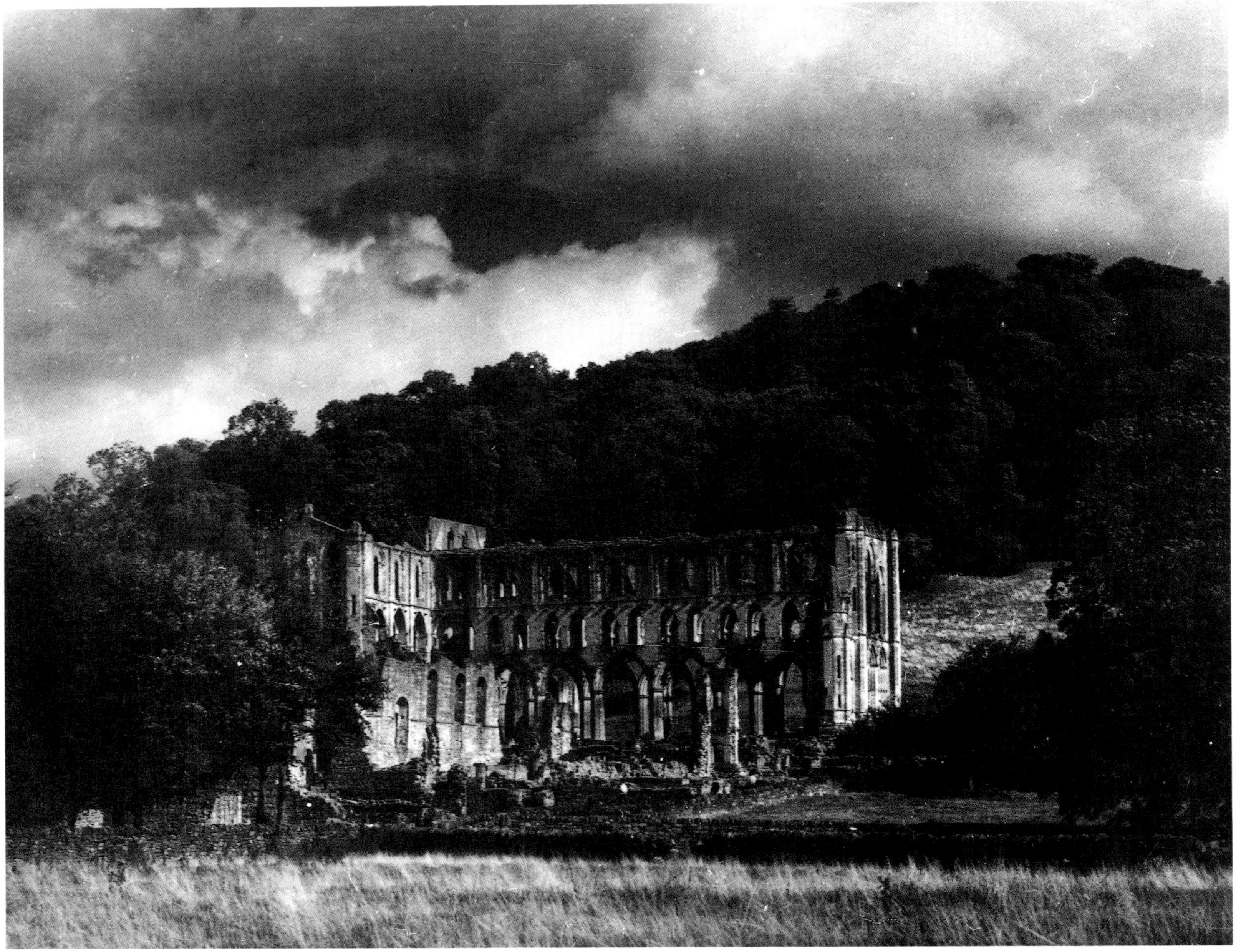

76 Rievaulx Abbey, Yorkshire

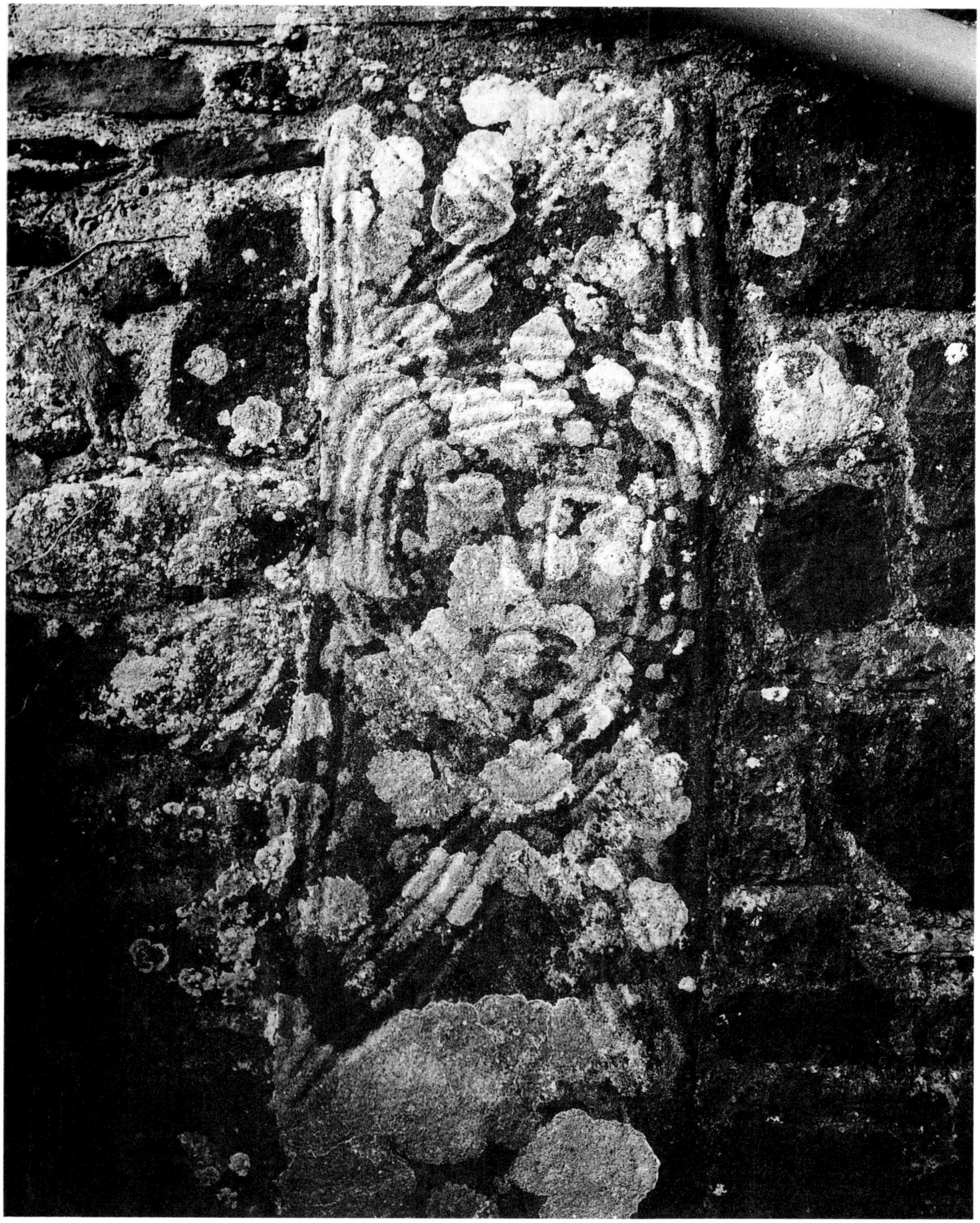

77 Sculptured stone, Llanwnda, Dyfed

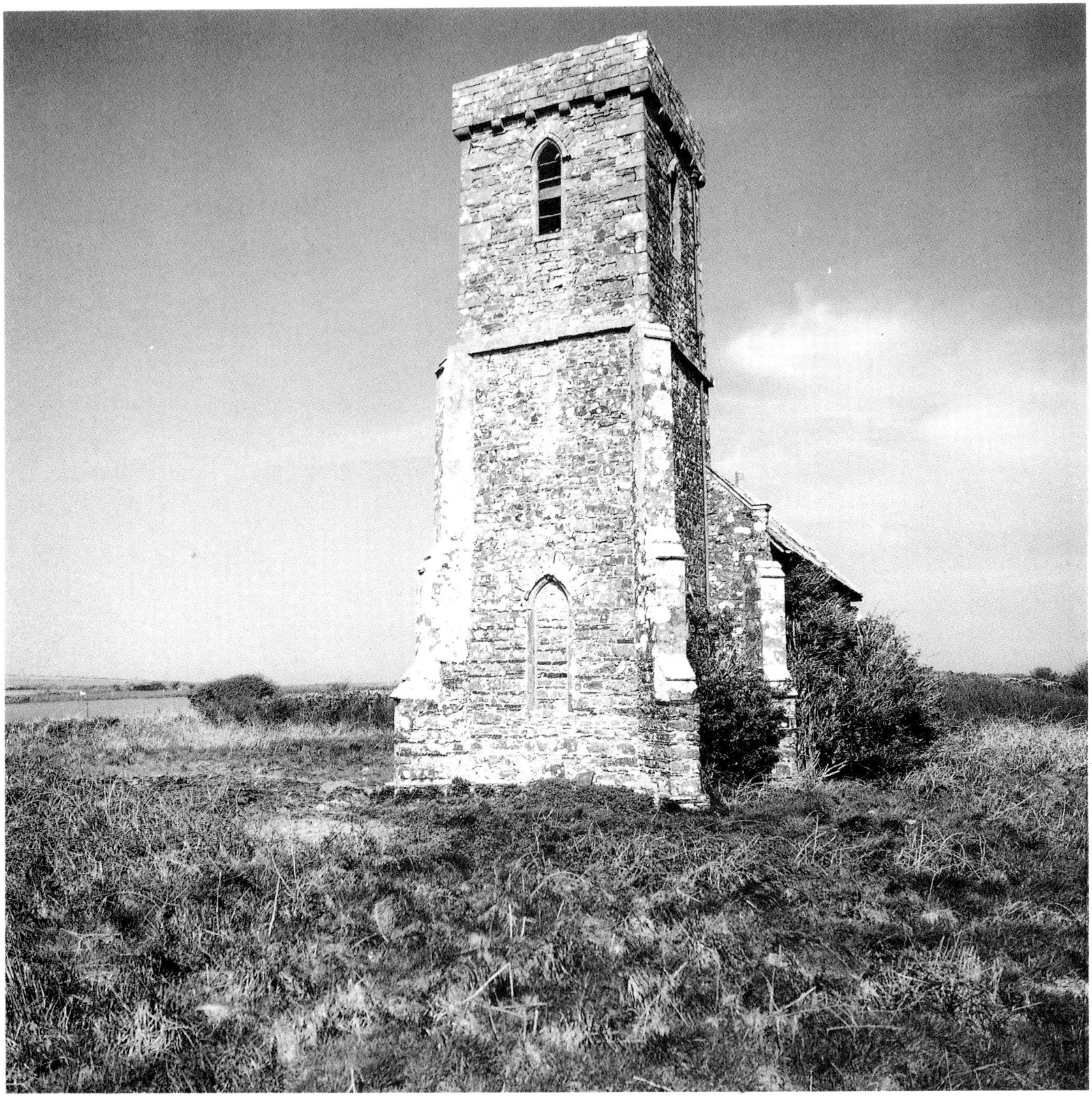

78 St Edrens, Dyfed

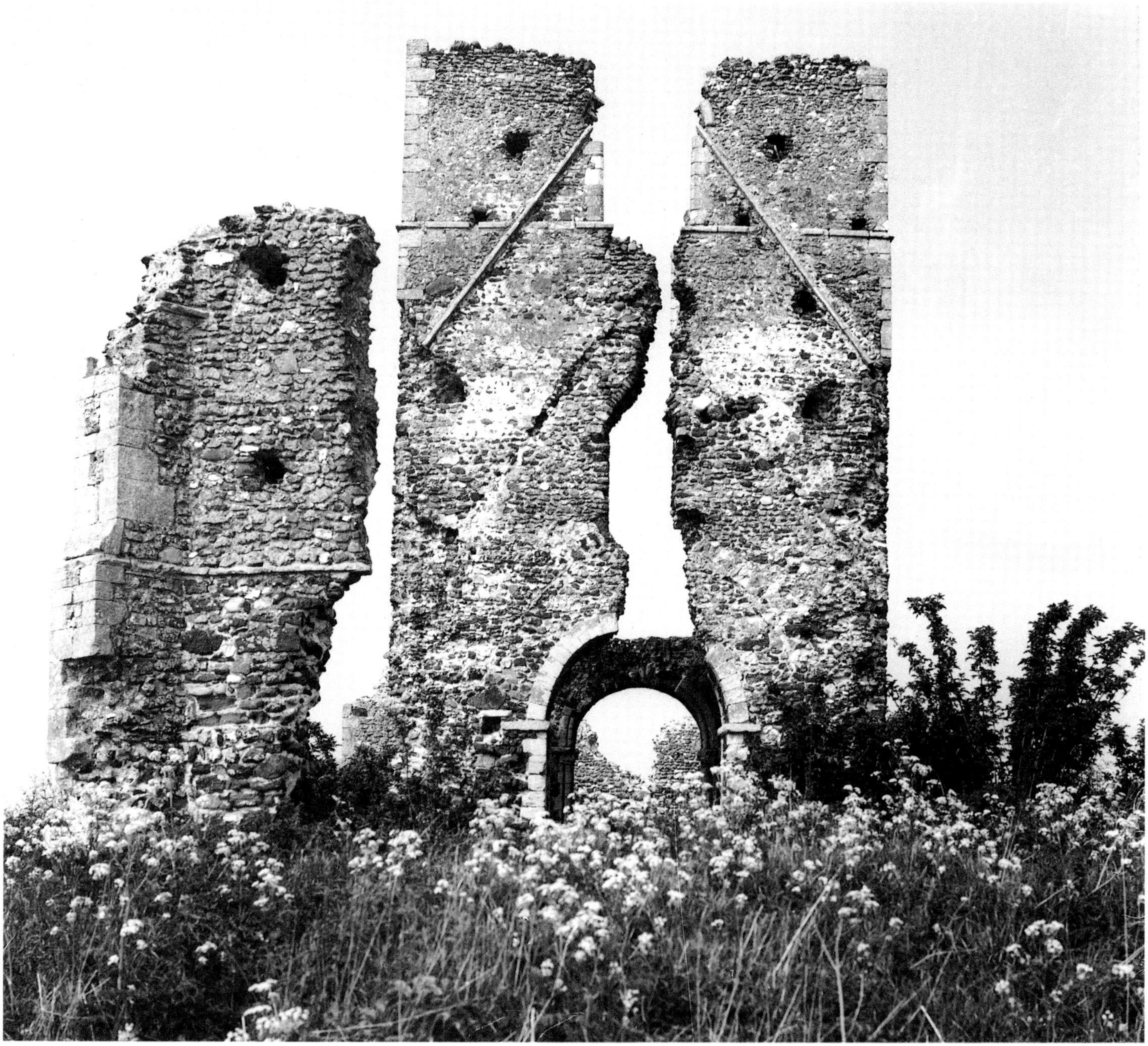

79 Bawsey, Norfolk

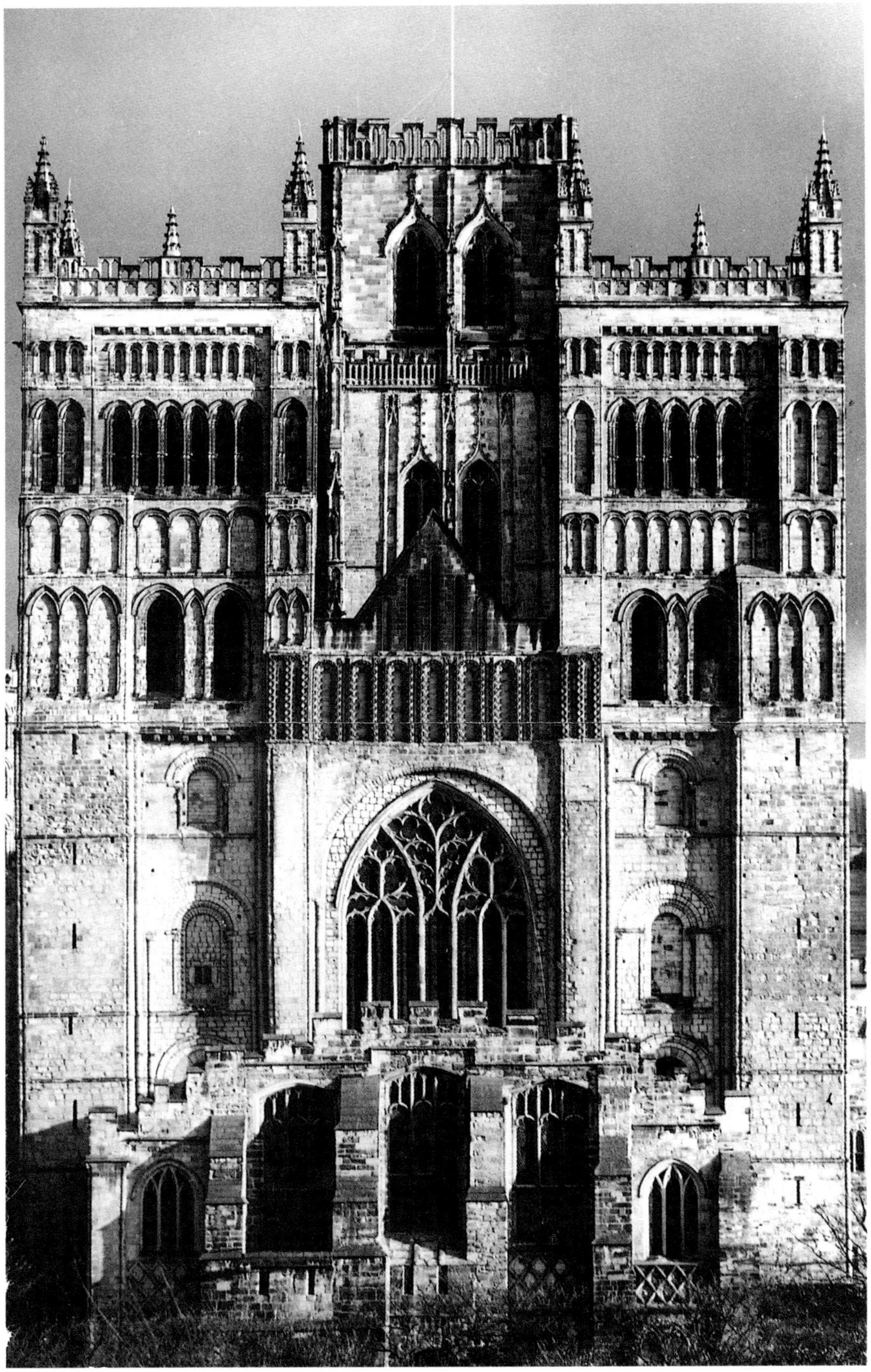

80 West front of Durham Cathedral

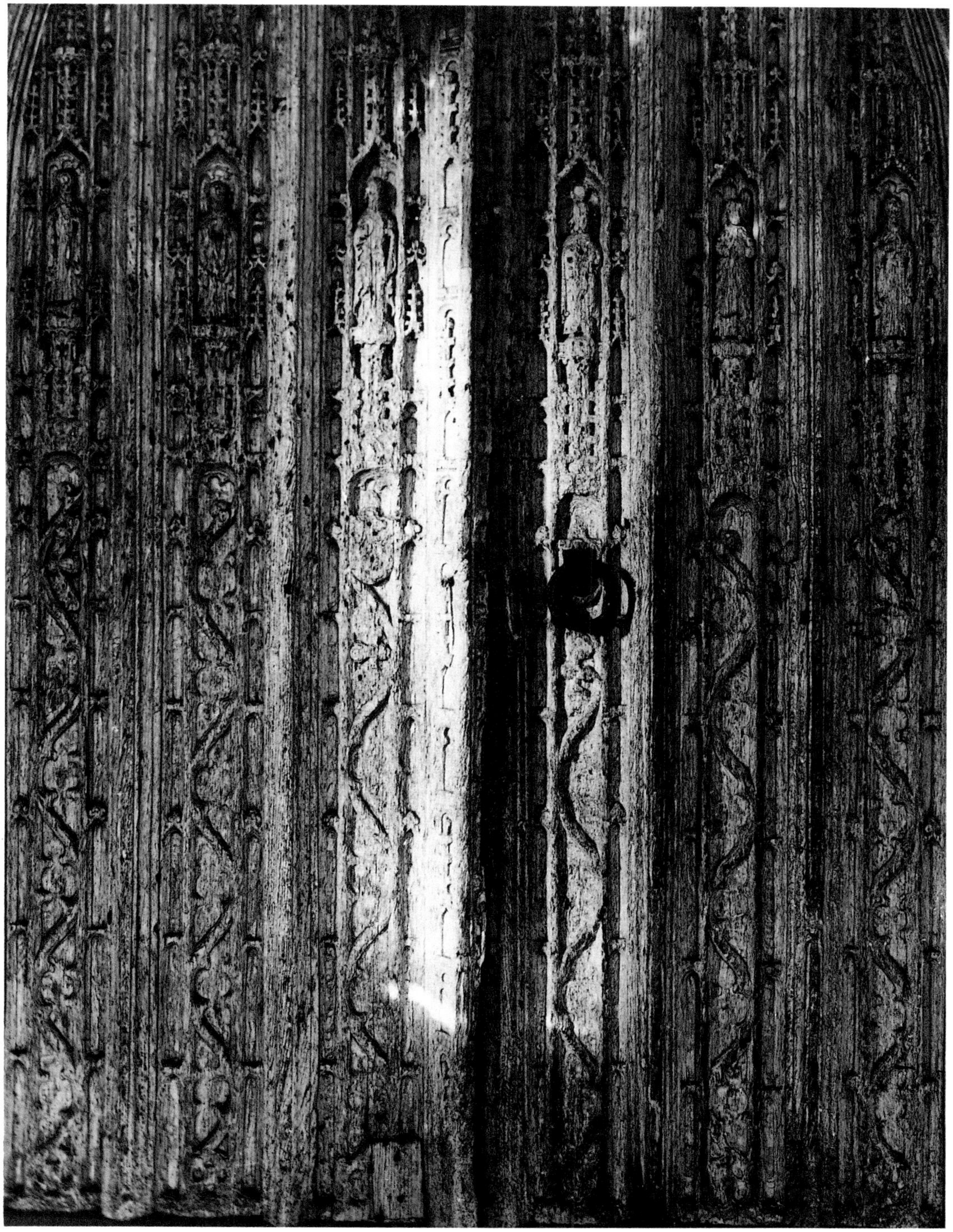

81 Detail of South door,
Stoke-by-Nayland, Suffolk

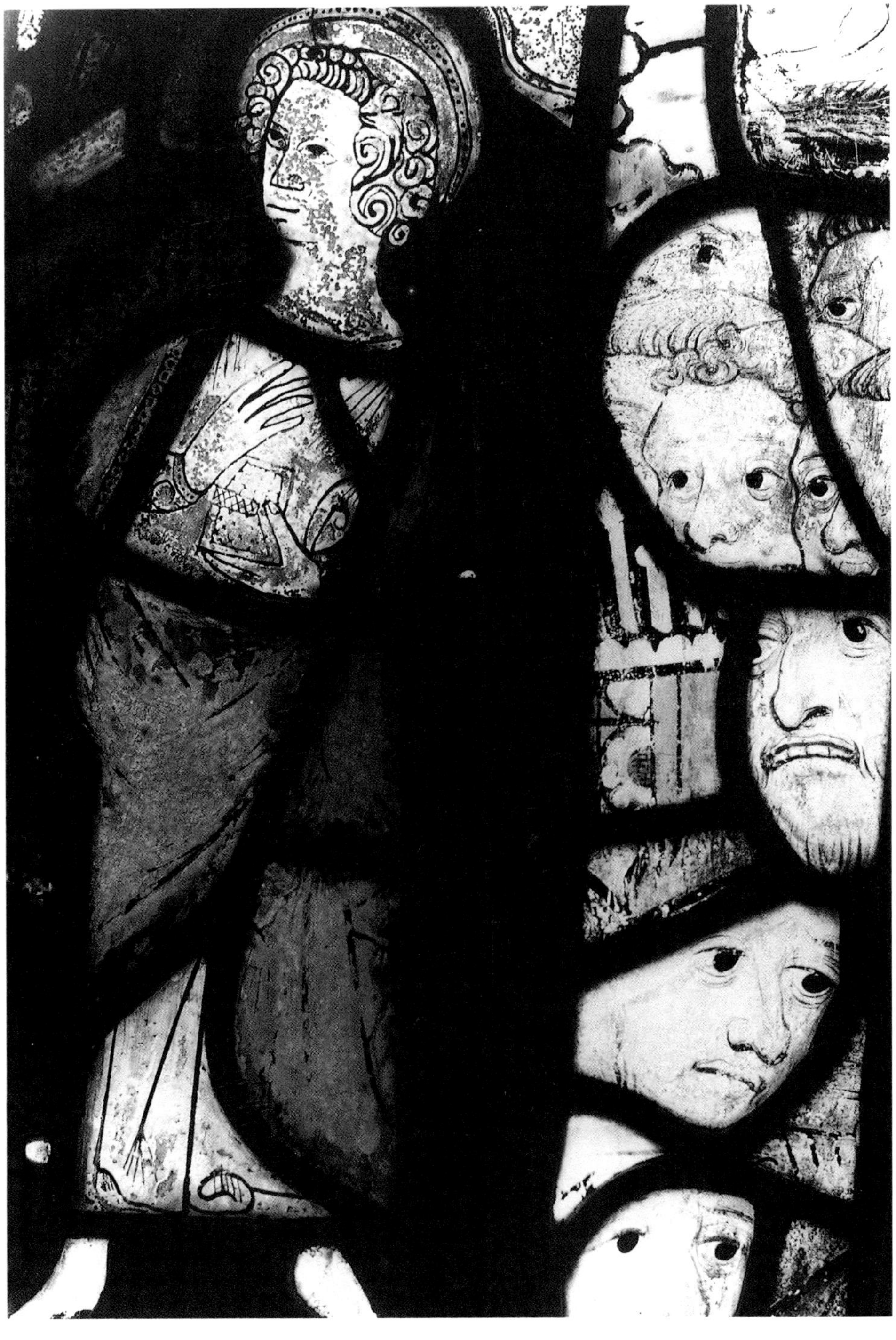

82 Glass at Cherington, Warwickshire

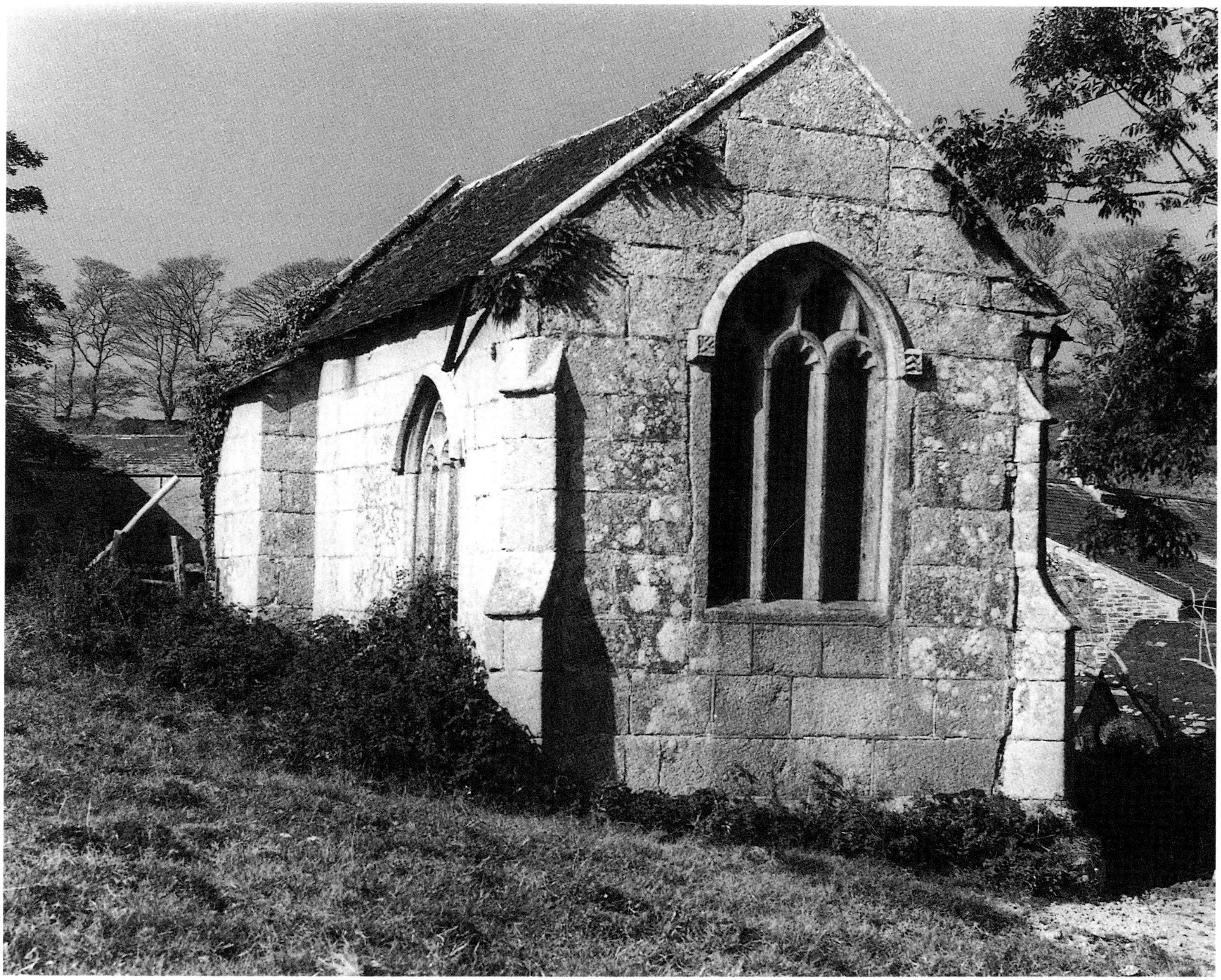

83 Ruined chapel, Trecarrel, Cornwall, 1941

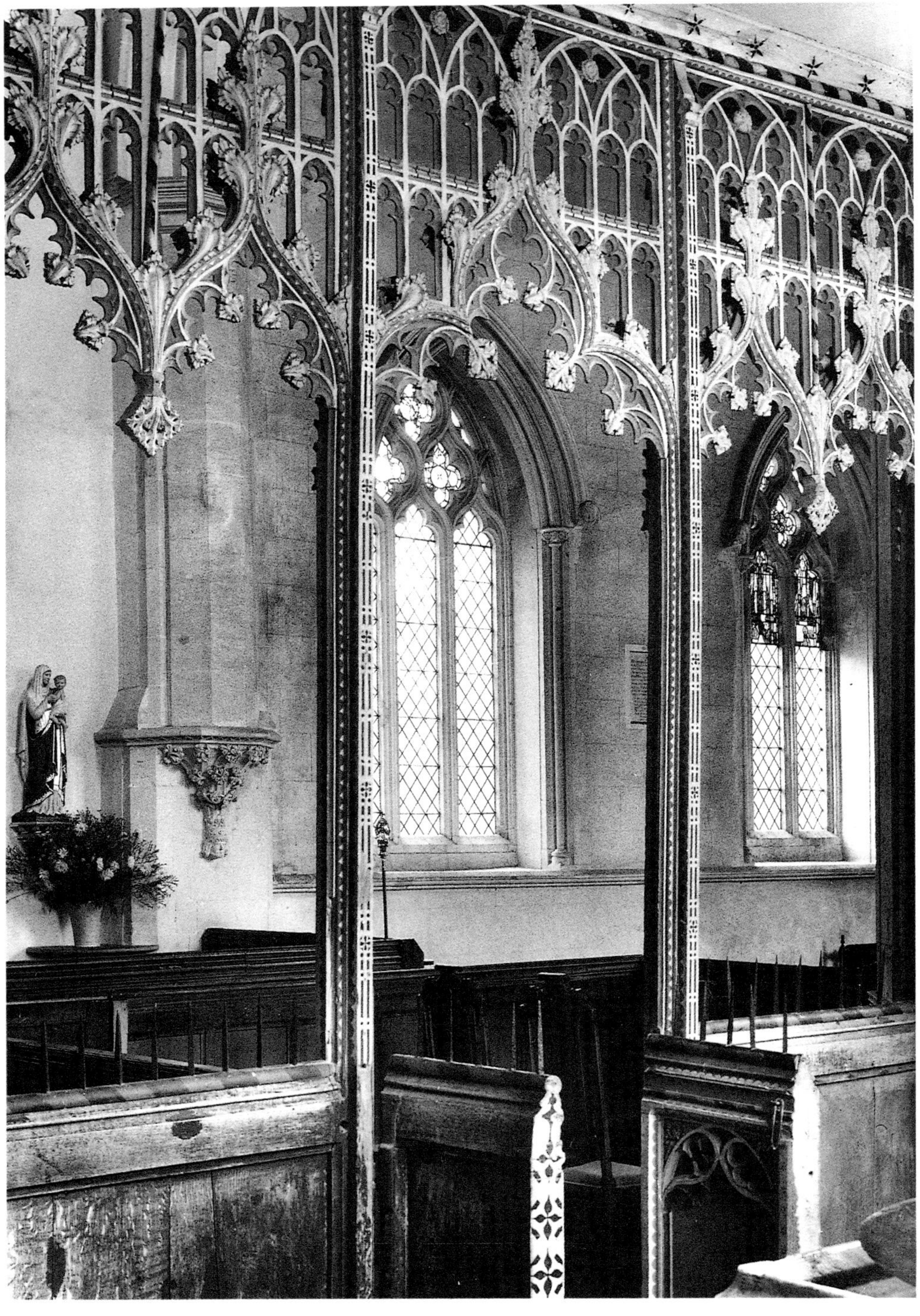

84 Screen at Dennington, Suffolk

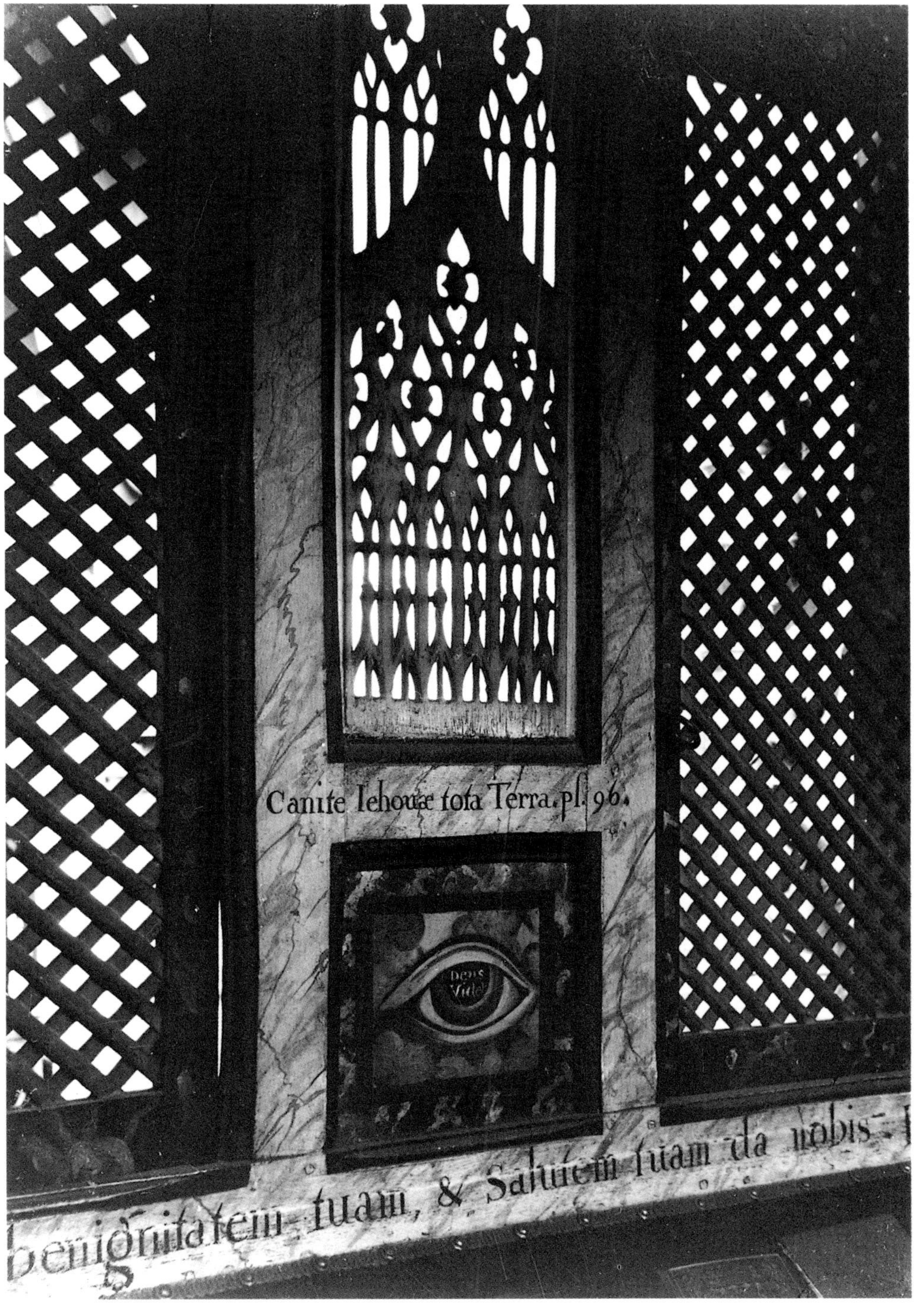

85 Kederminster pew, Langley Marish, Buckinghamshire

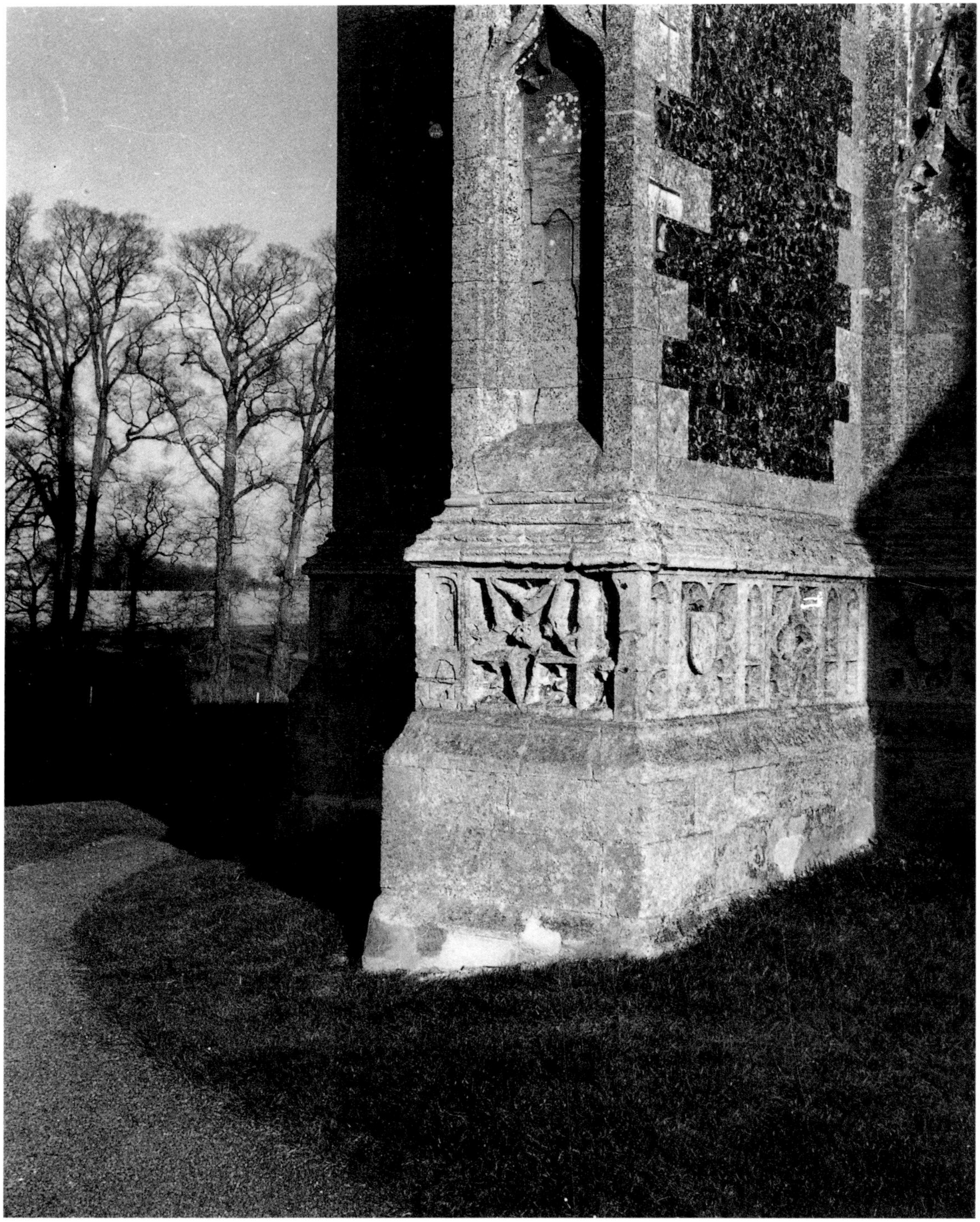

86 Foot of the Tower at Lavenham, Suffolk

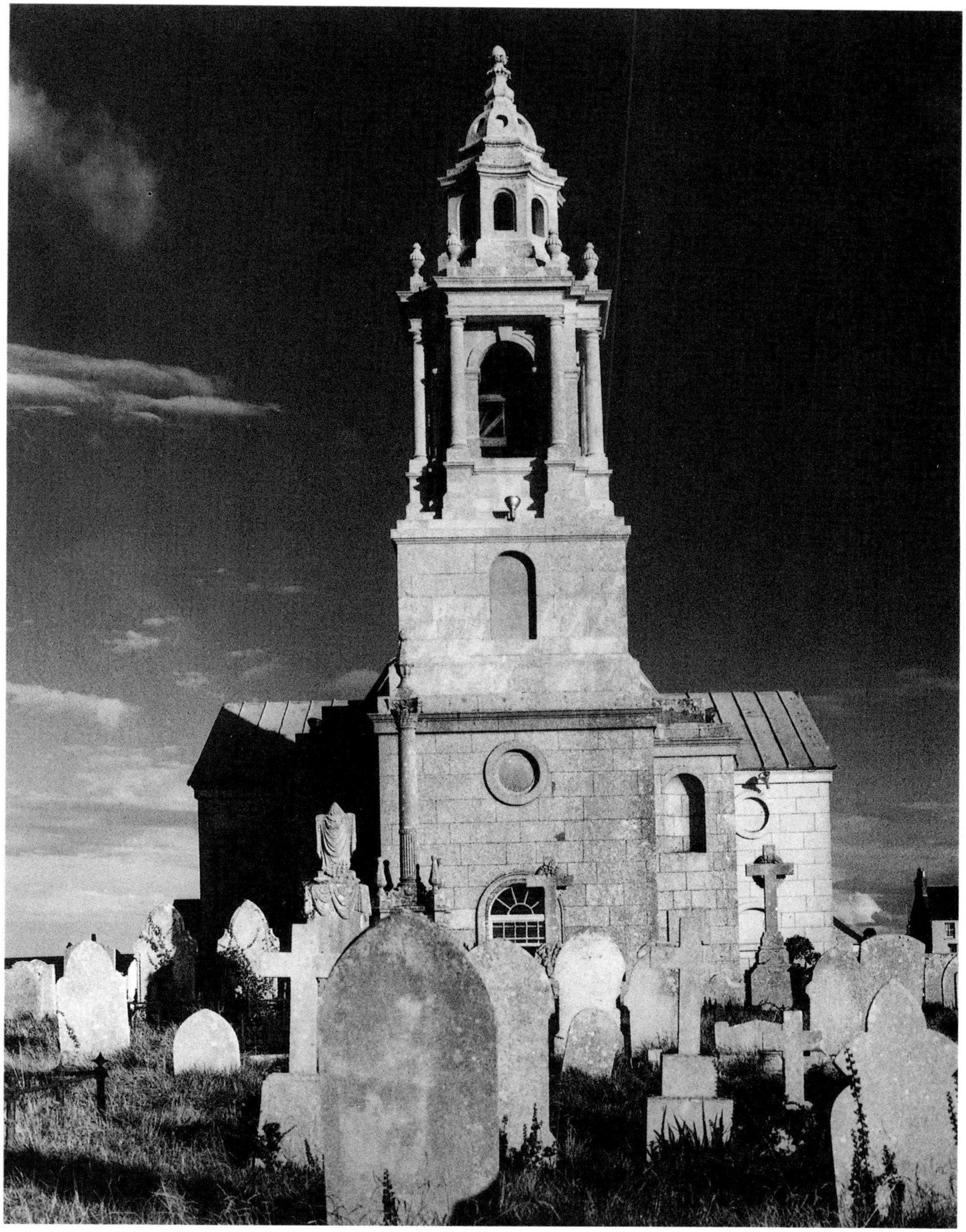

87 St George Reforne, Portland, Dorset, about 1970

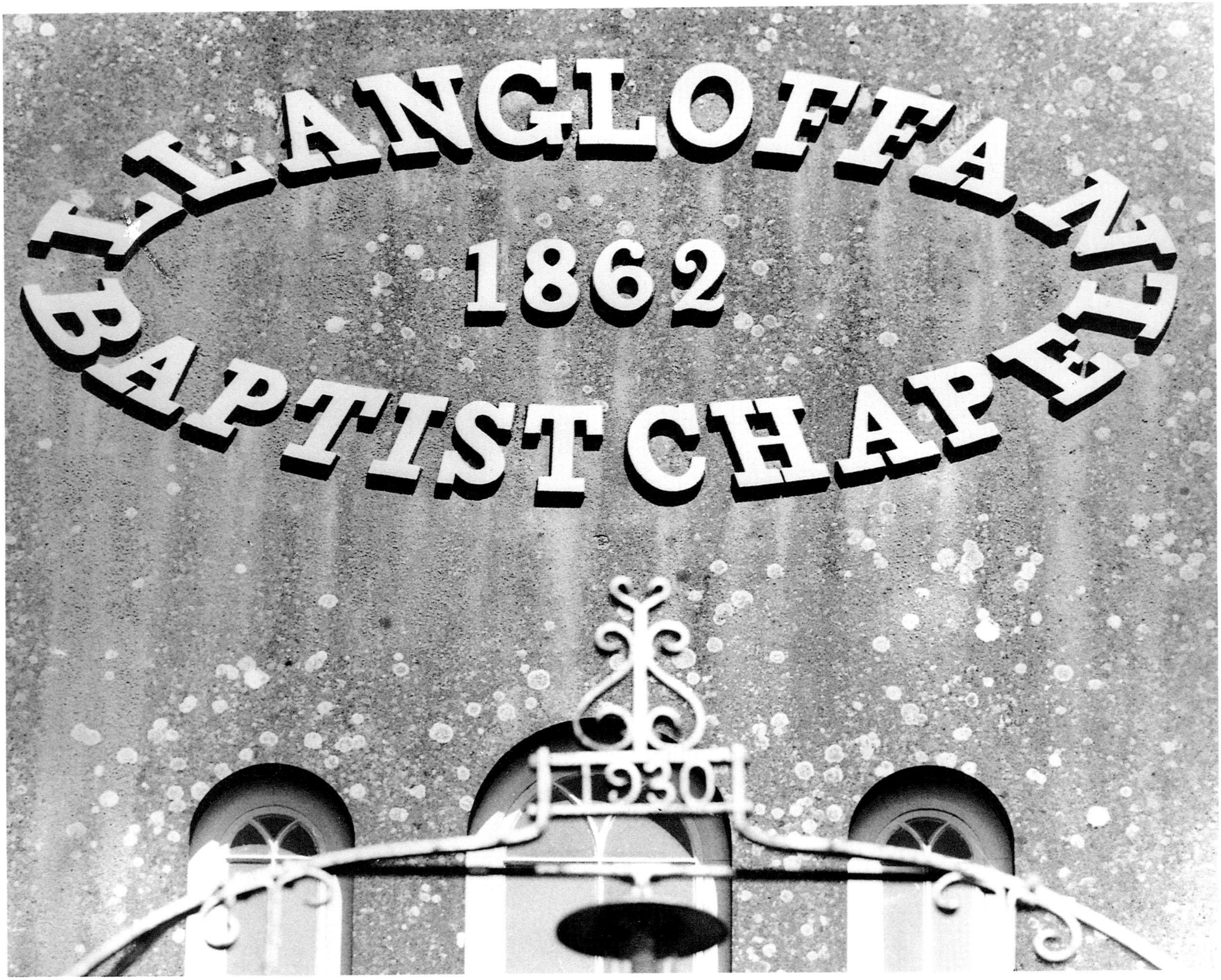

88 Baptist Chapel, Llangloffan, Dyfed

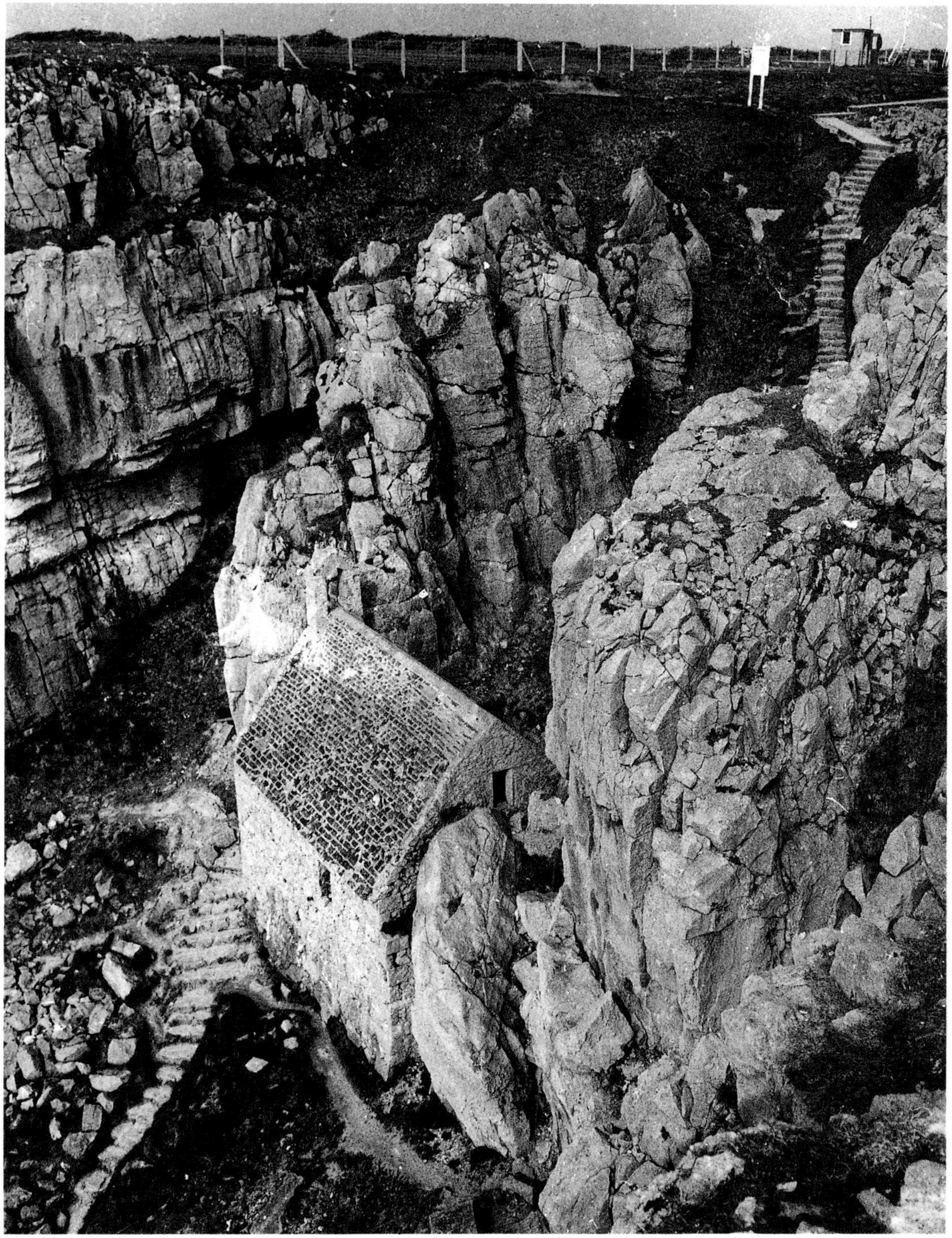

89 St Govans Chapel, Pembrokeshire, 1970

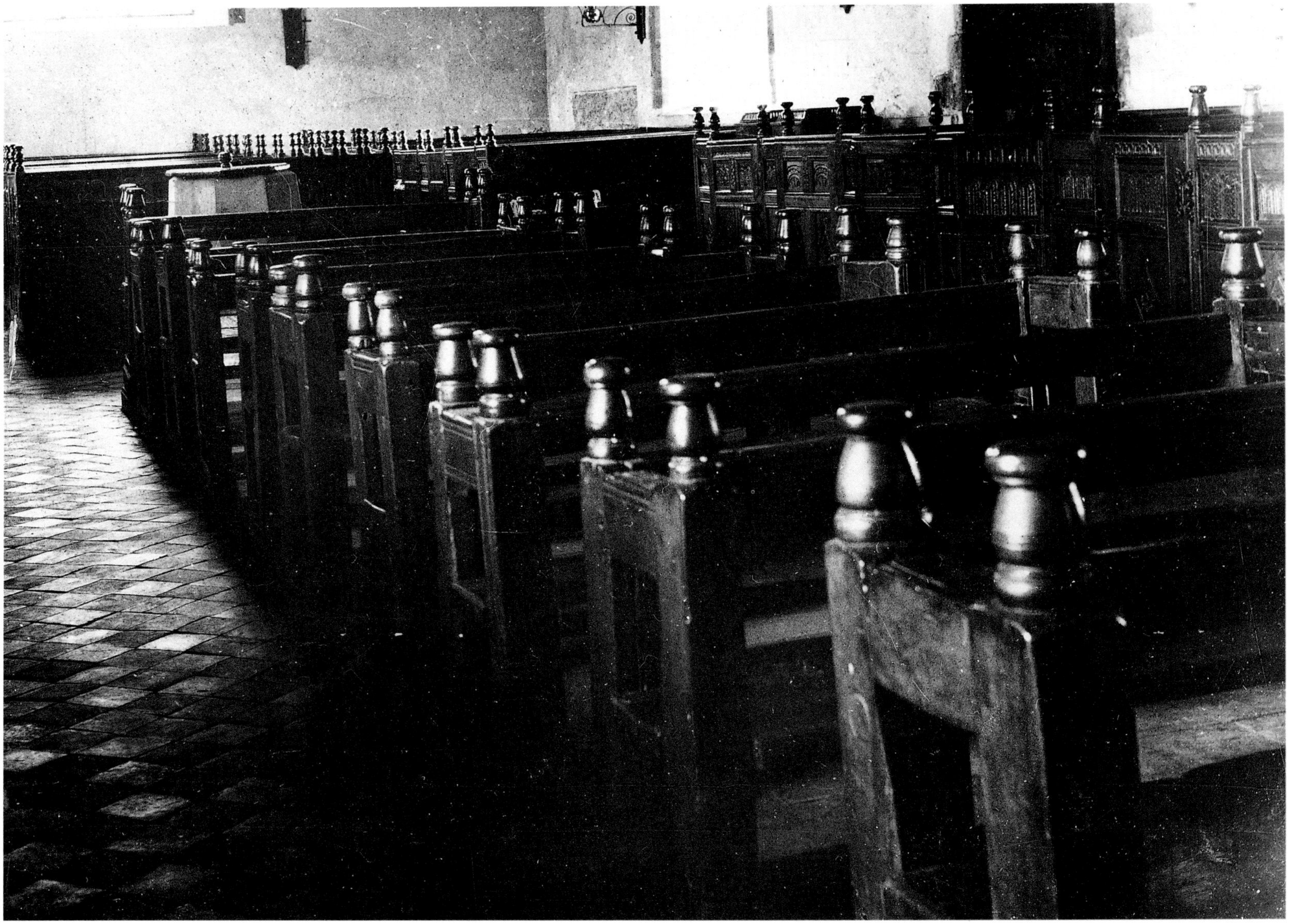

90 Interior at Worthen, Shropshire, 1939

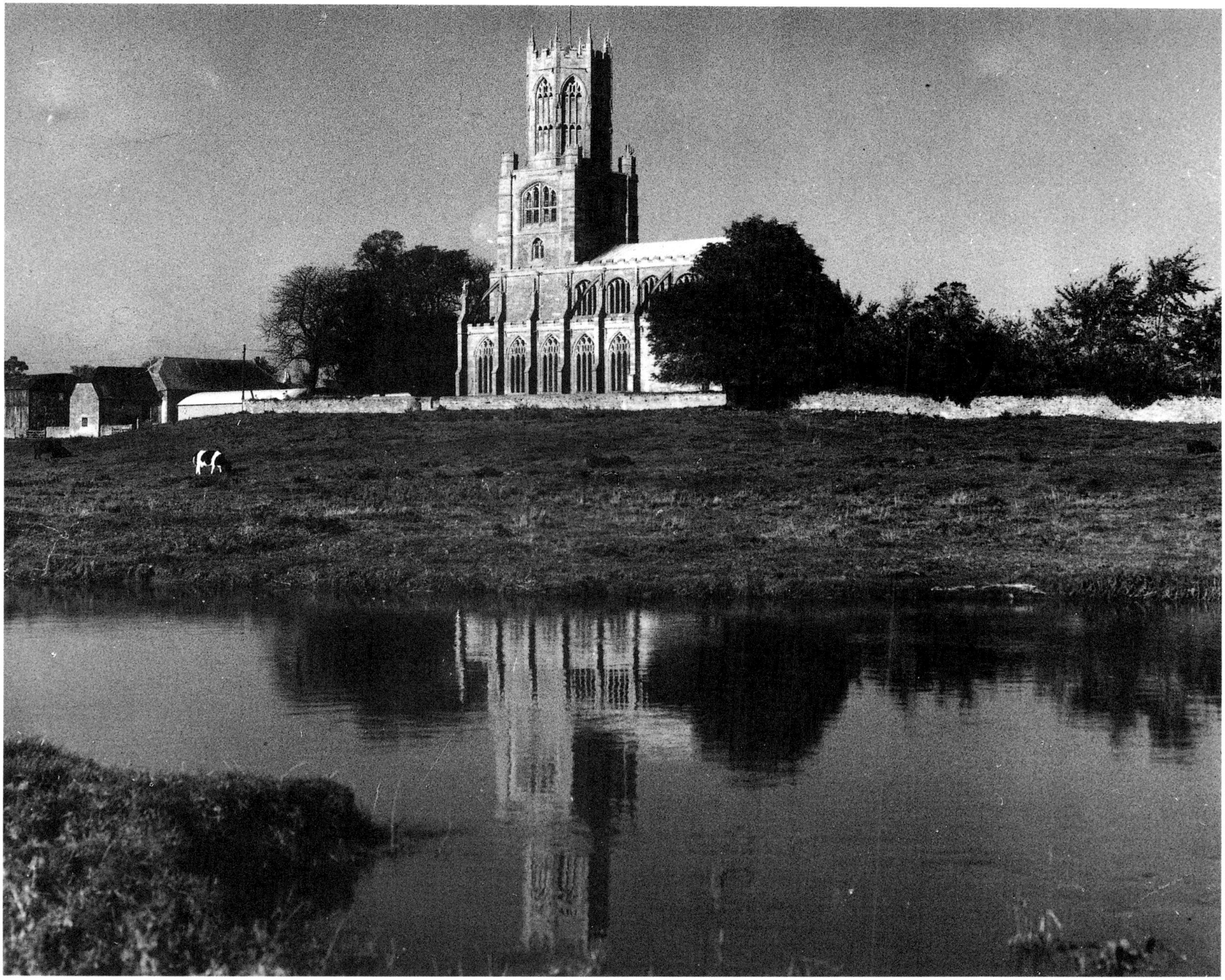

91 Fortheringhay, Northamptonshire

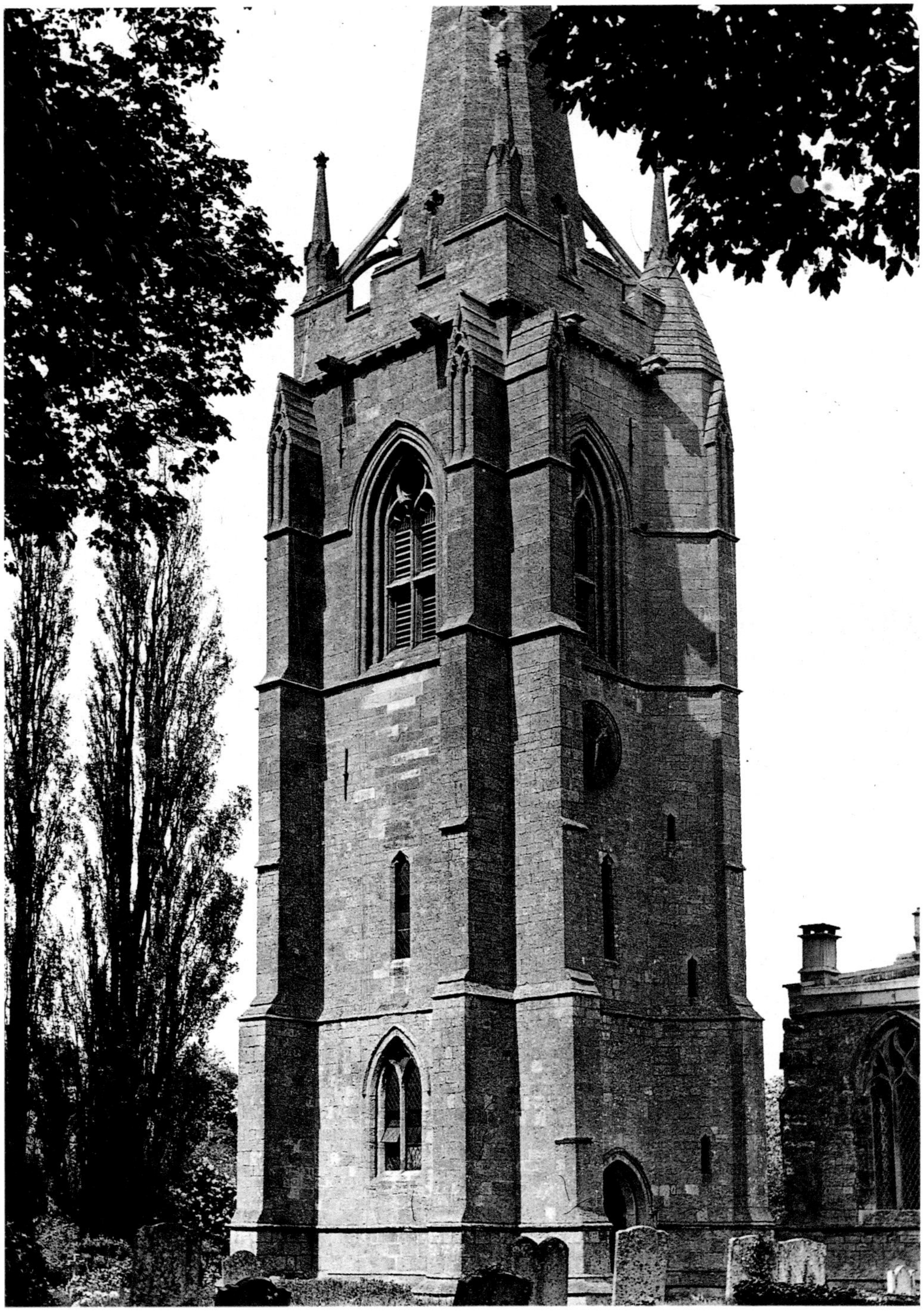

92 Spire of Fleet, Lincolnshire

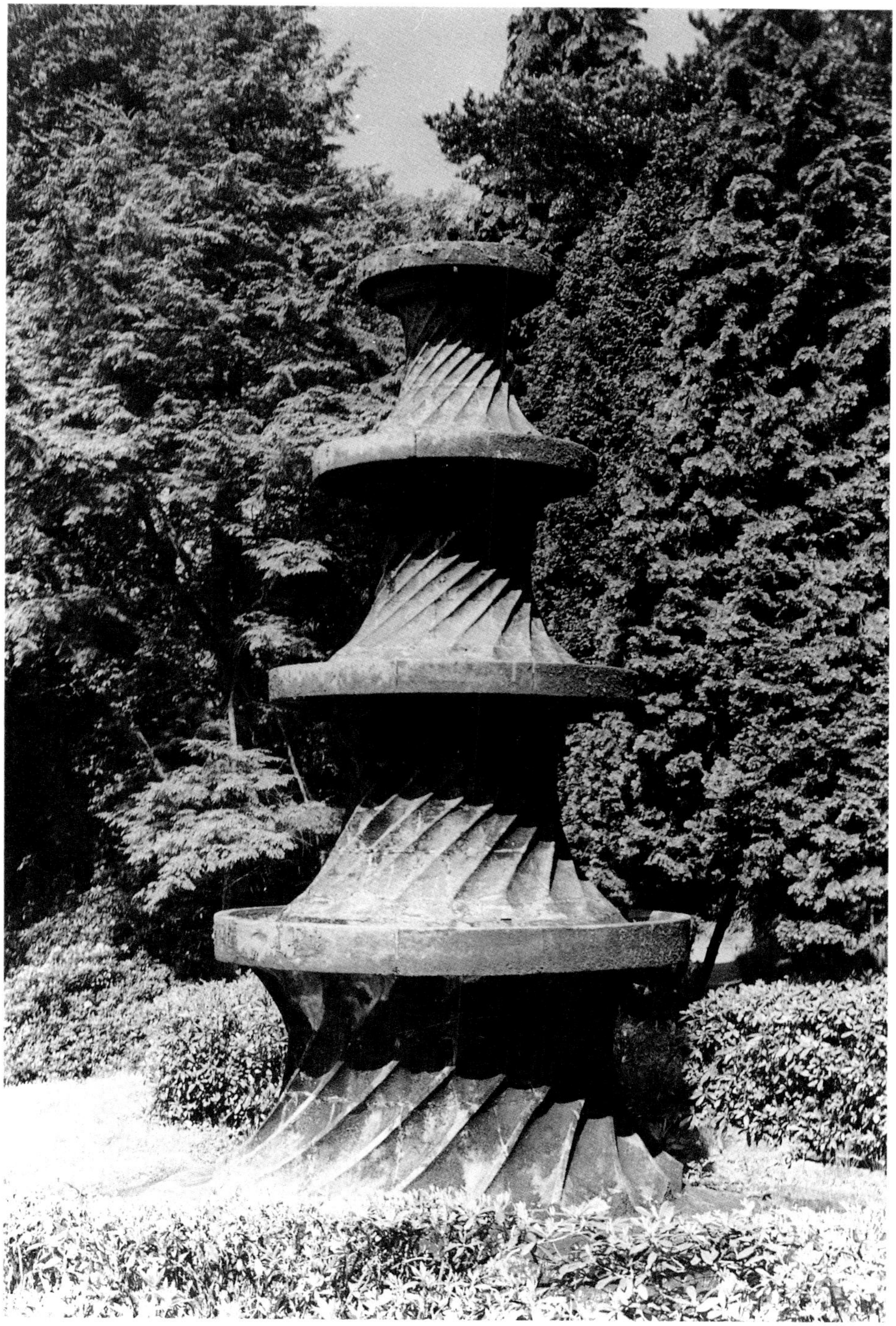

93 Fountain at Alton Towers, Staffordshire

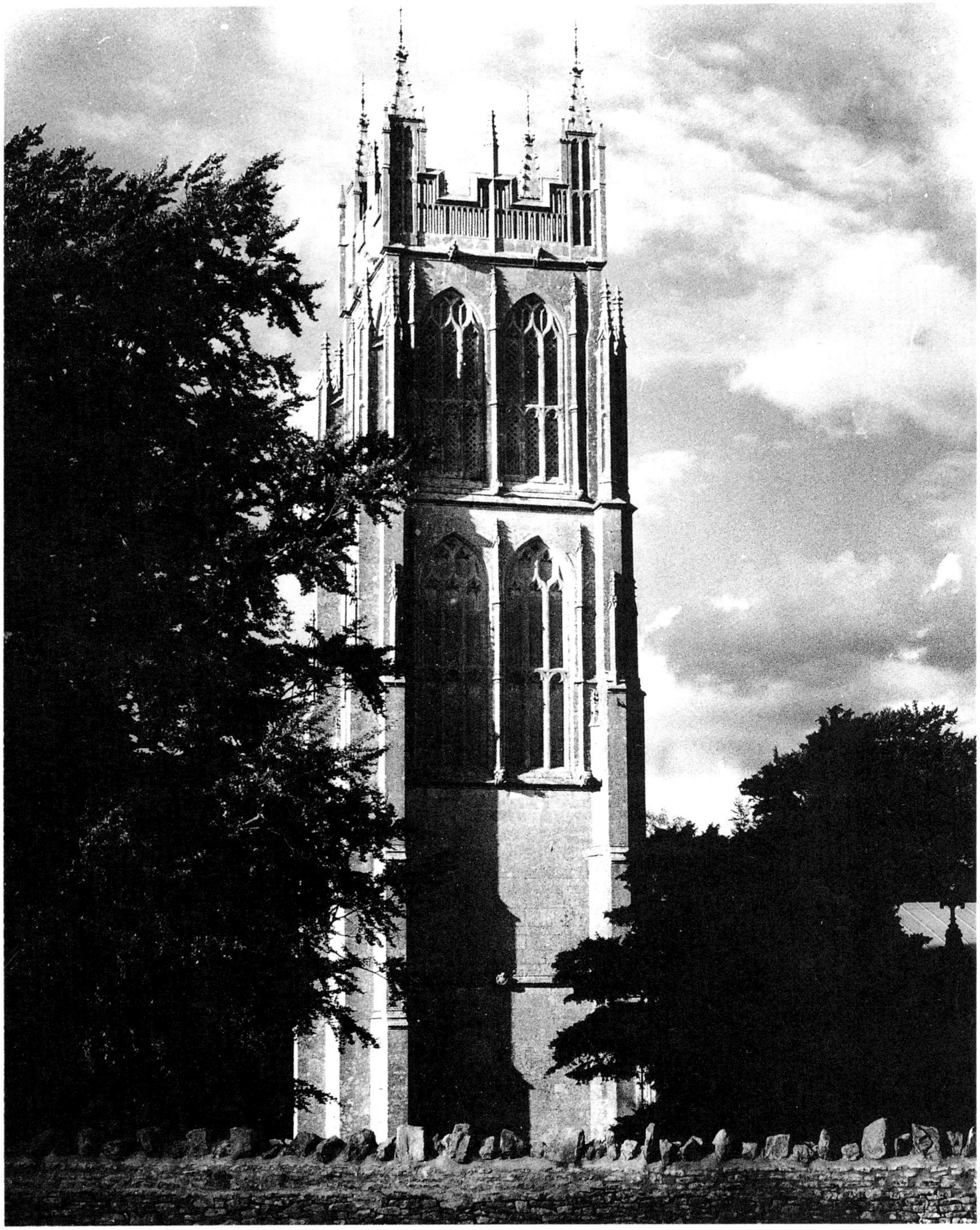

94 Tower of Chewton Mendip, Somerset

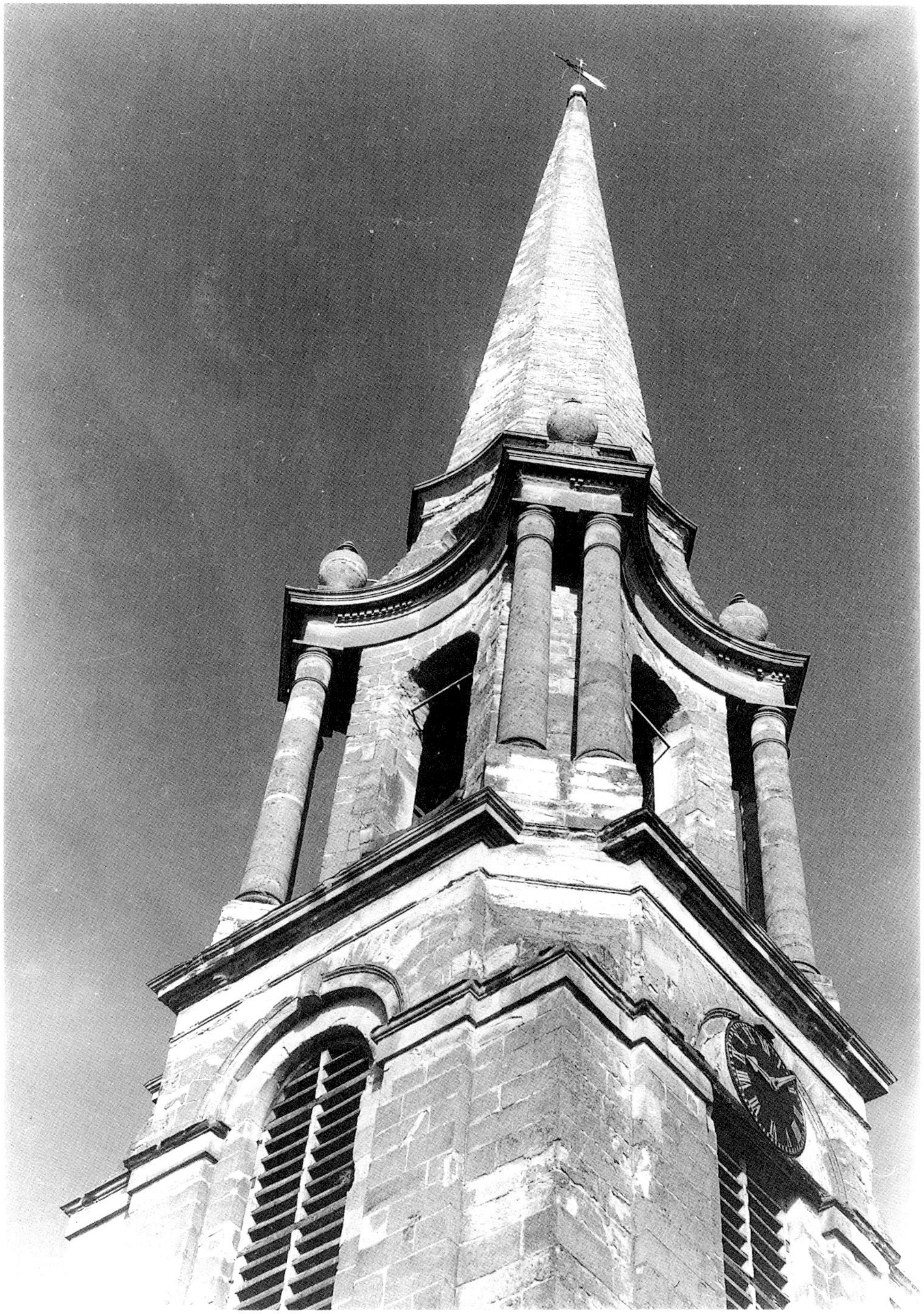

95 Tower at Tardebigge, Hereford and Worcester, about 1950

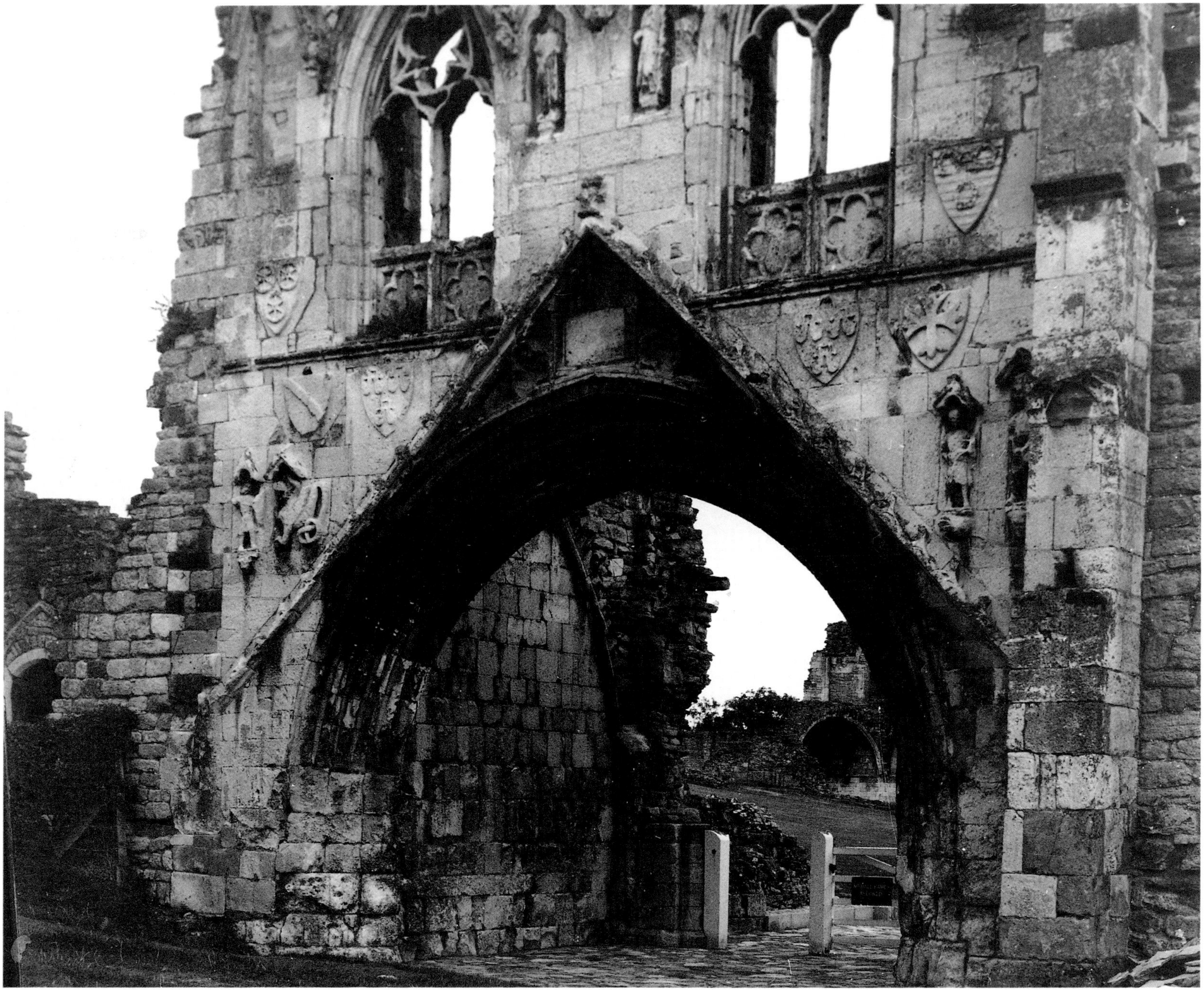

96 Kirkham Priory, Yorkshire, about 1950

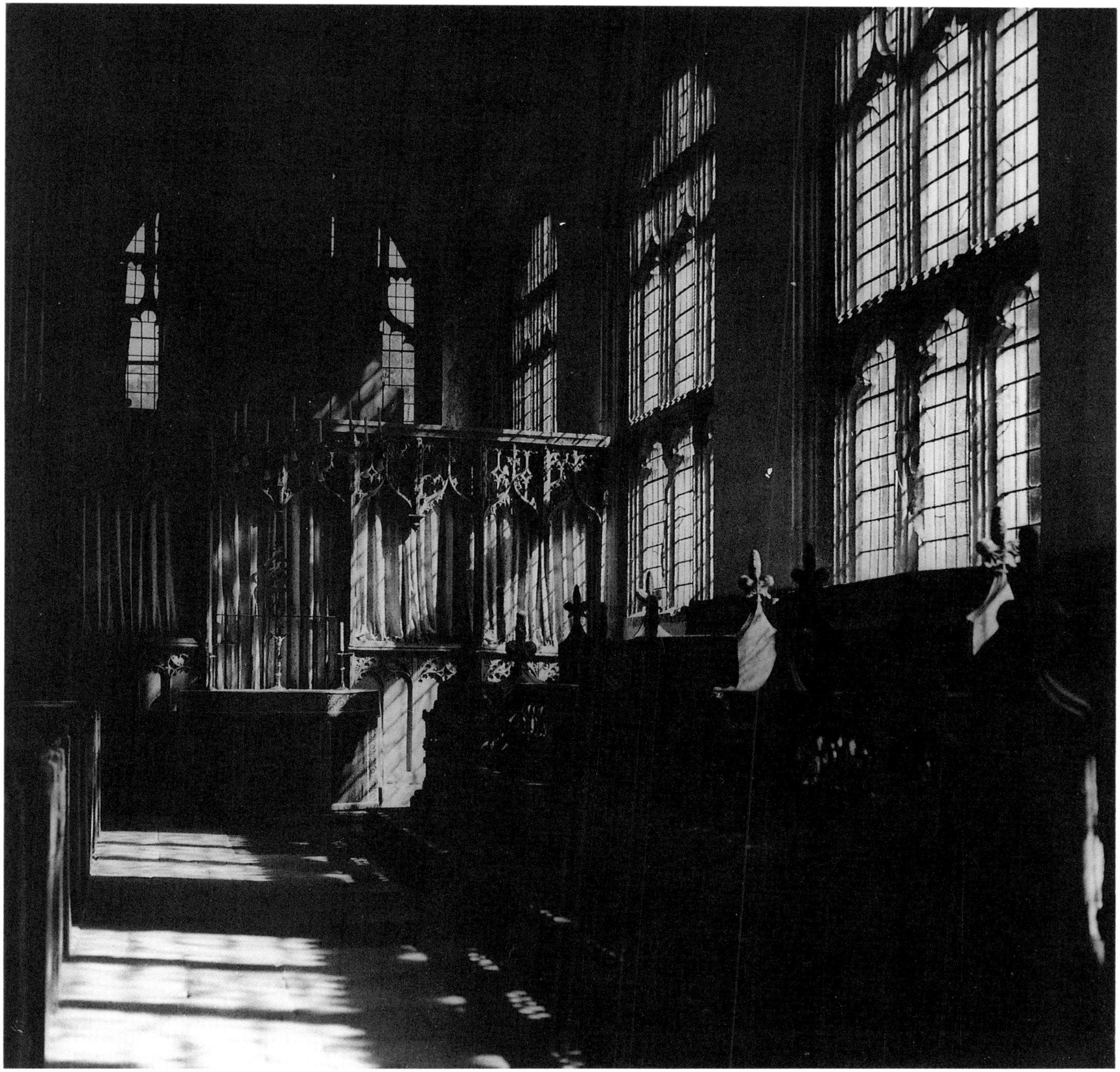

97 Walpole St Peter, Norfolk

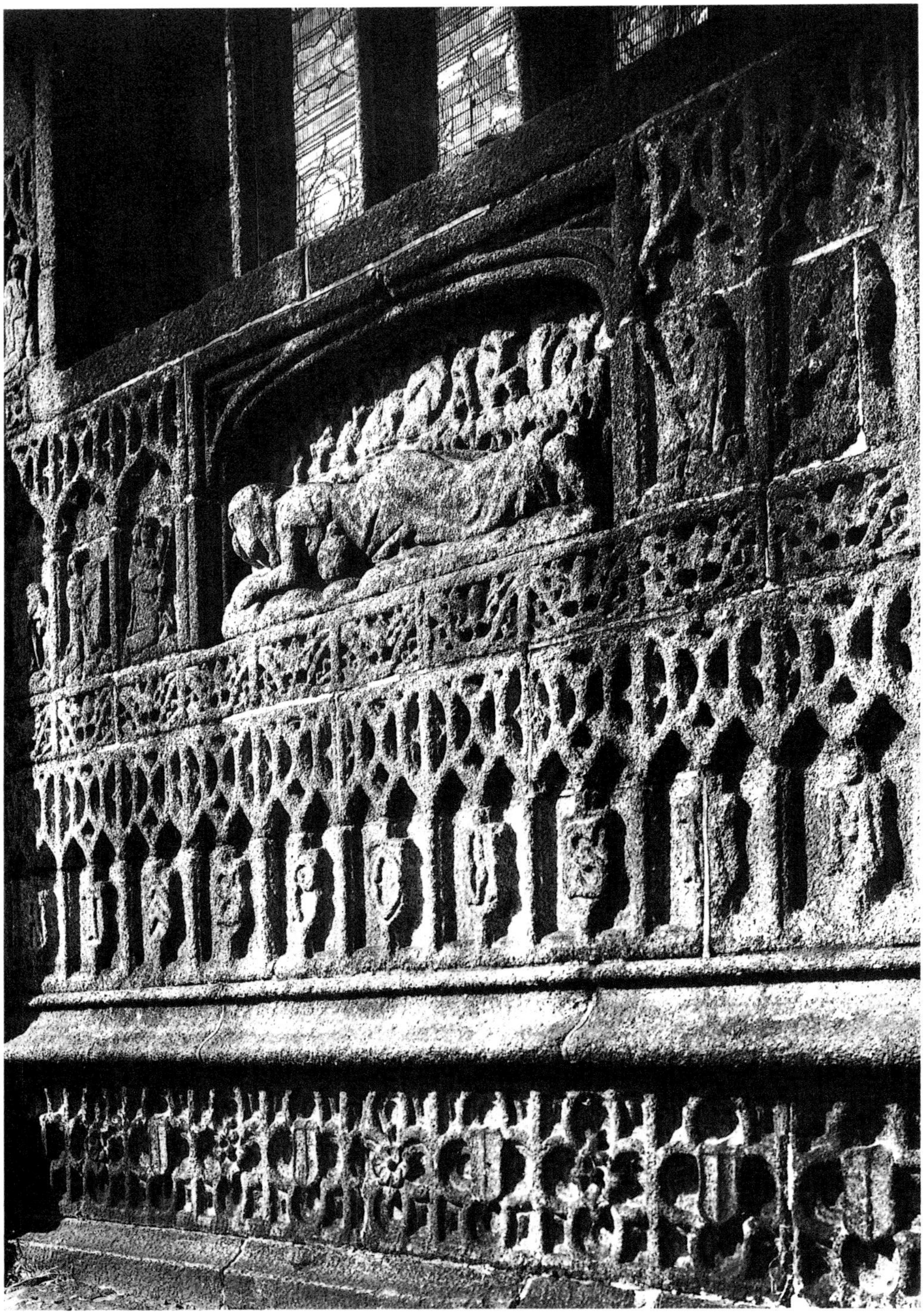

98 Interior, Launceston, Cornwall

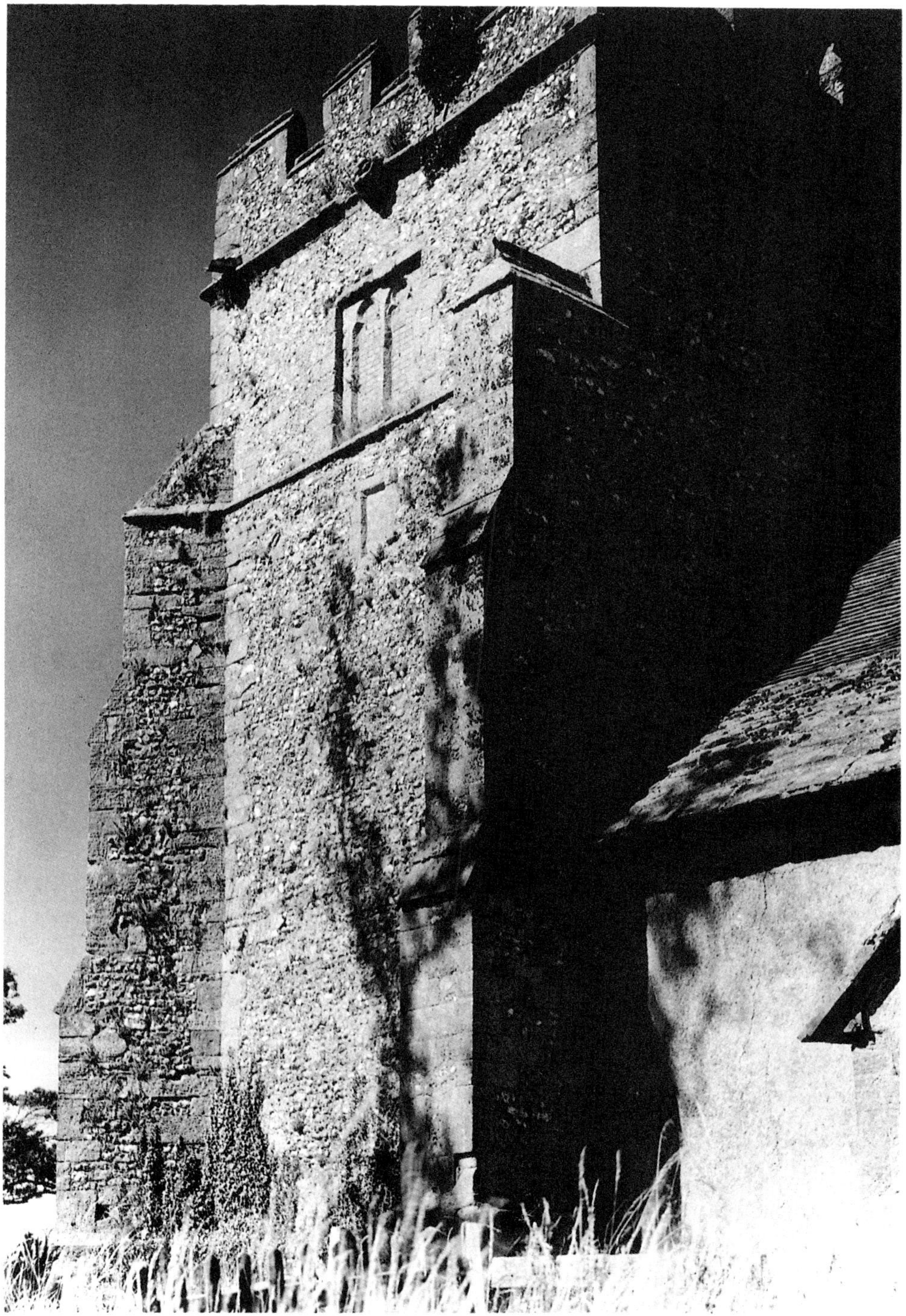

99 Tower of Hamsey, Sussex, 1939

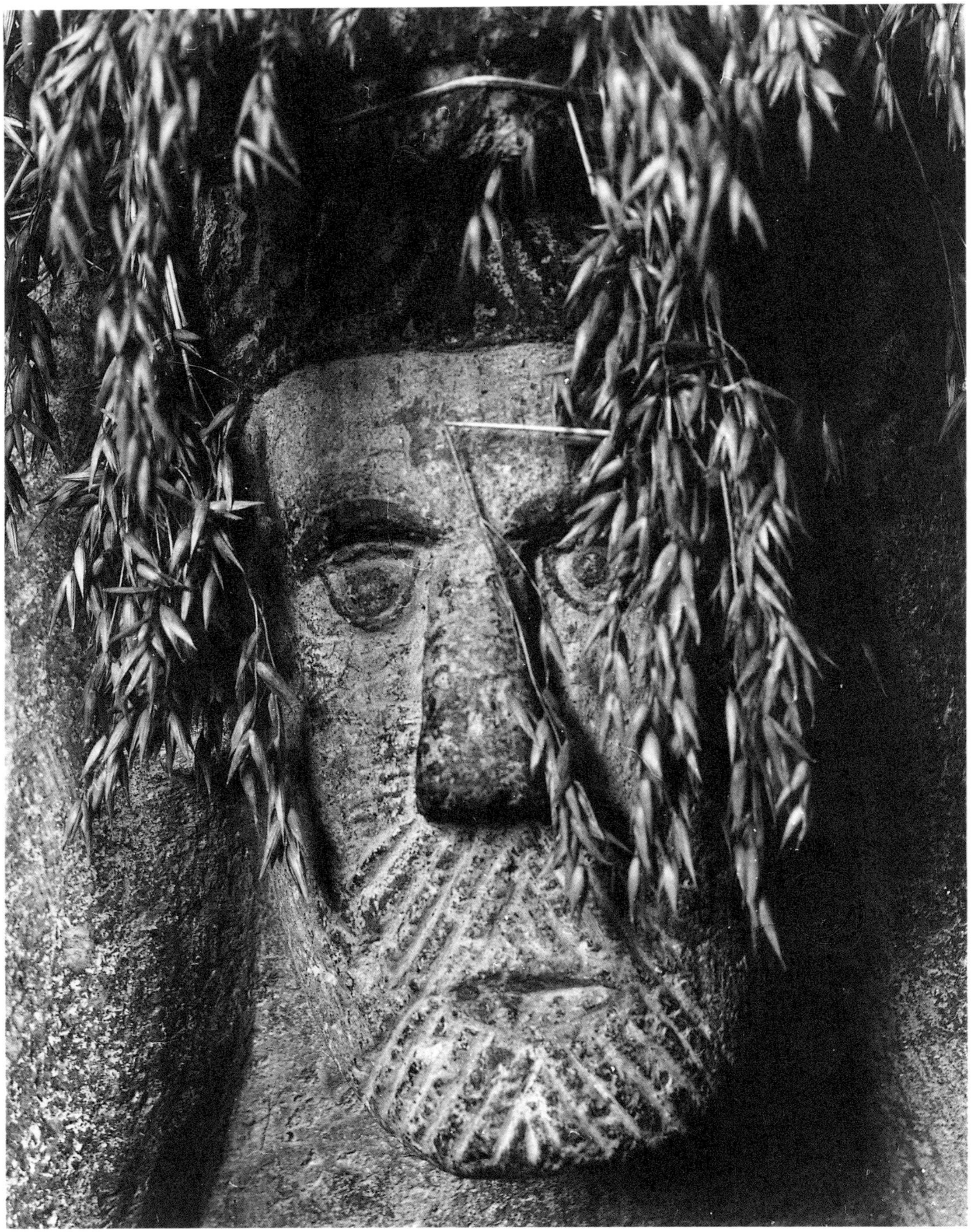

100 Harvest festival

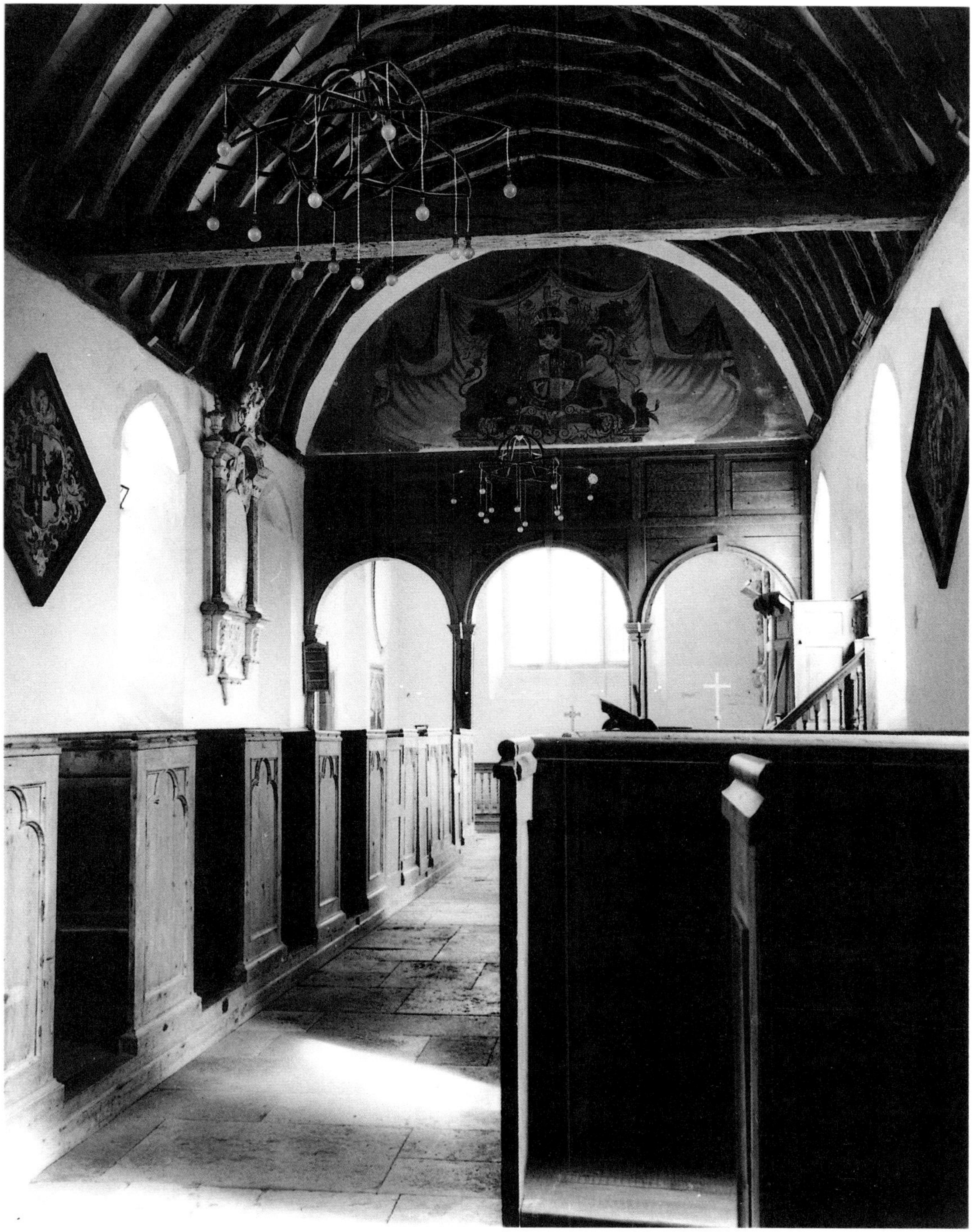

101 Interior of Warminghurst, West Sussex

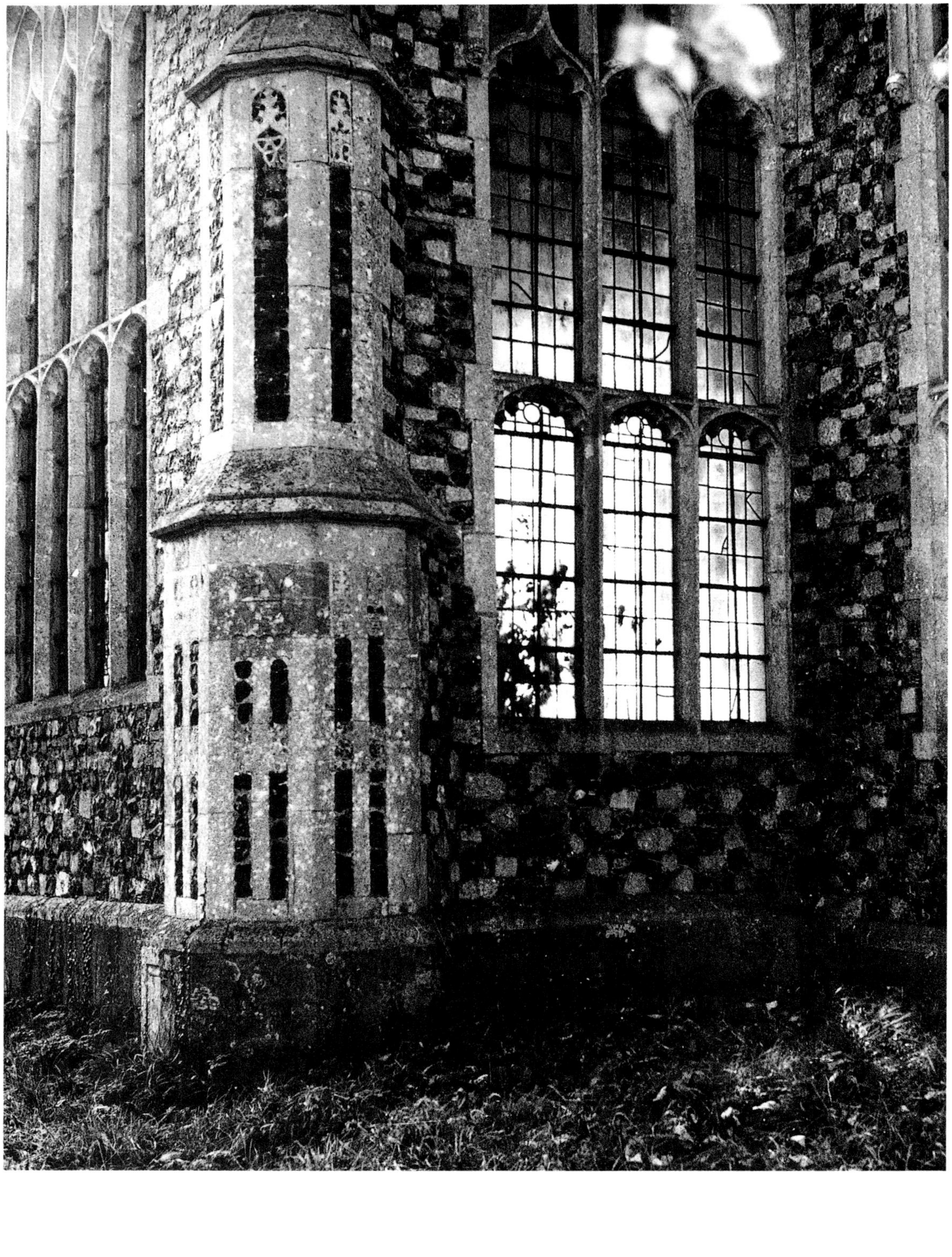

102 Window at Gipping, Suffolk, 1968

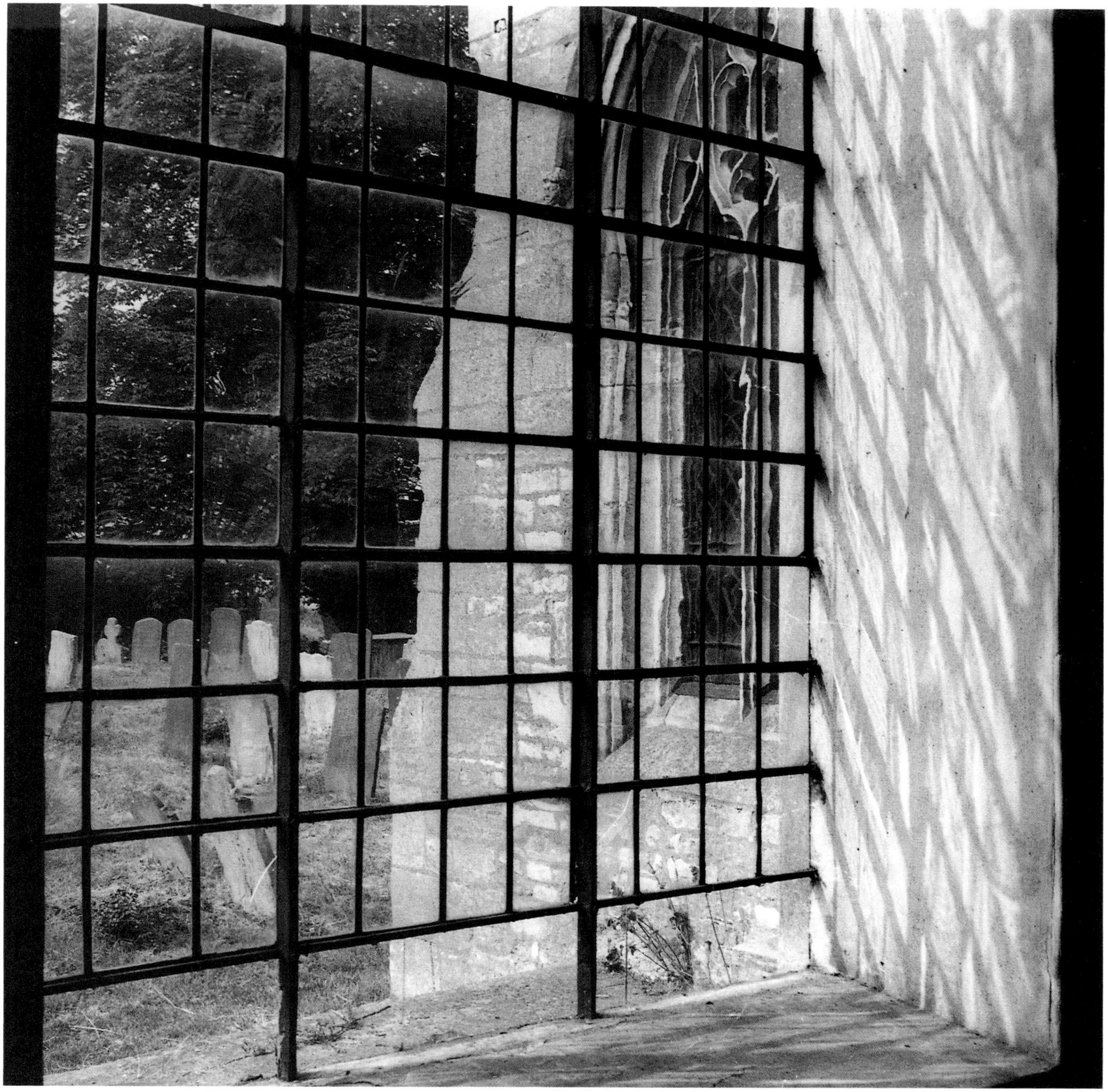

103 Hougham, Lincolnshire

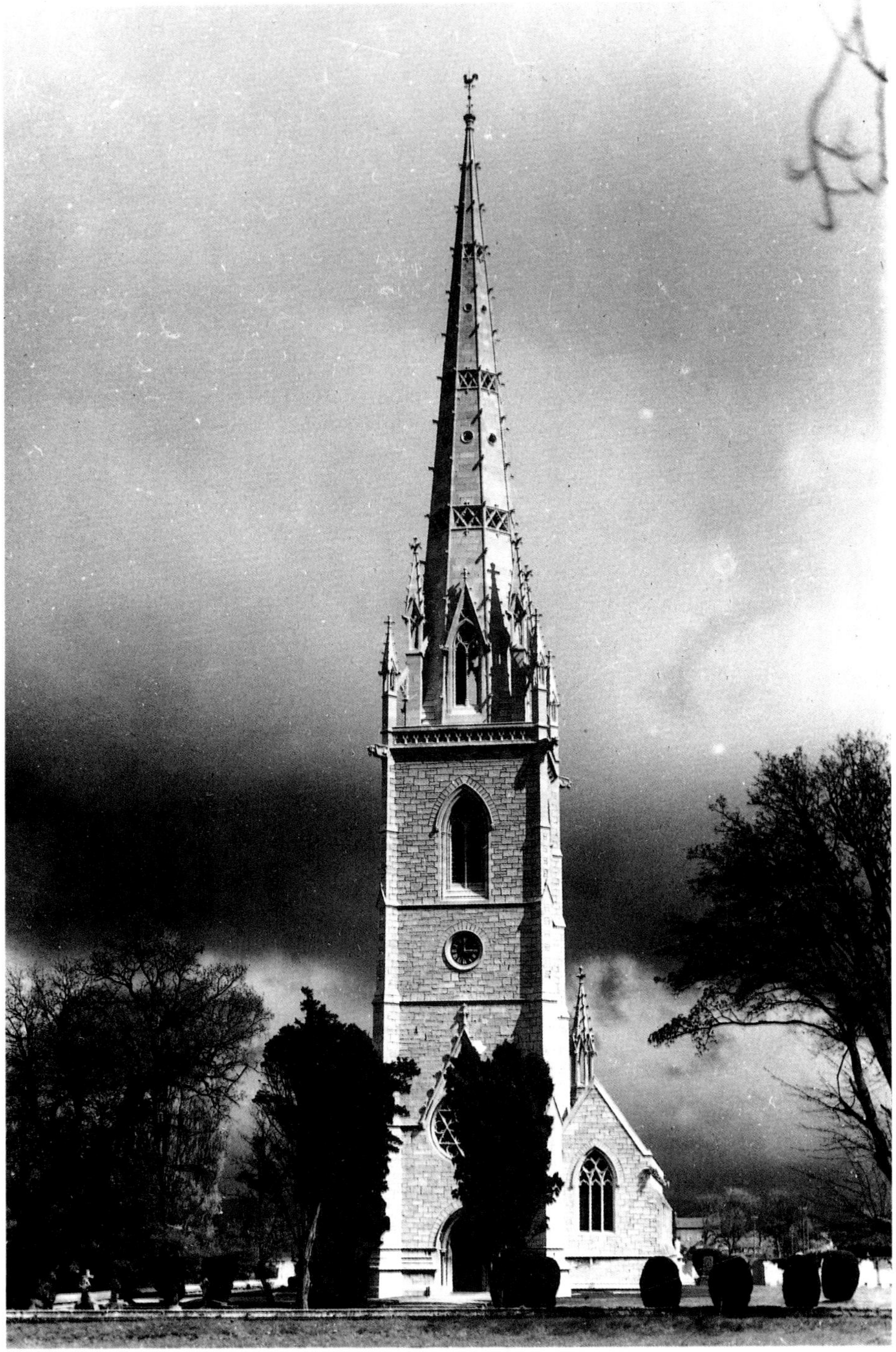

104 The 'marble church', Bodelwyddan, Flintshire

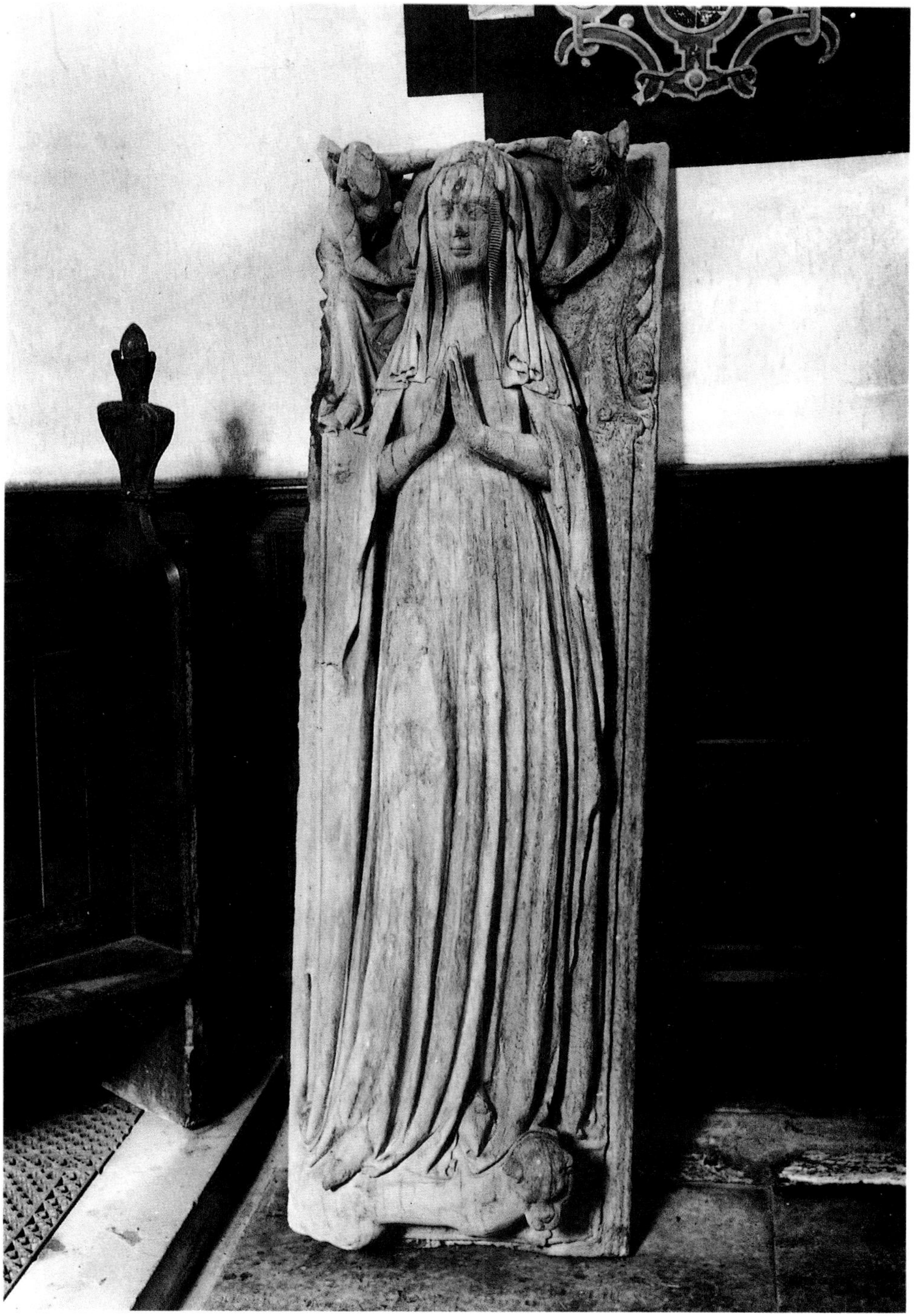

105 Monument at Sparsholt, Oxfordshire

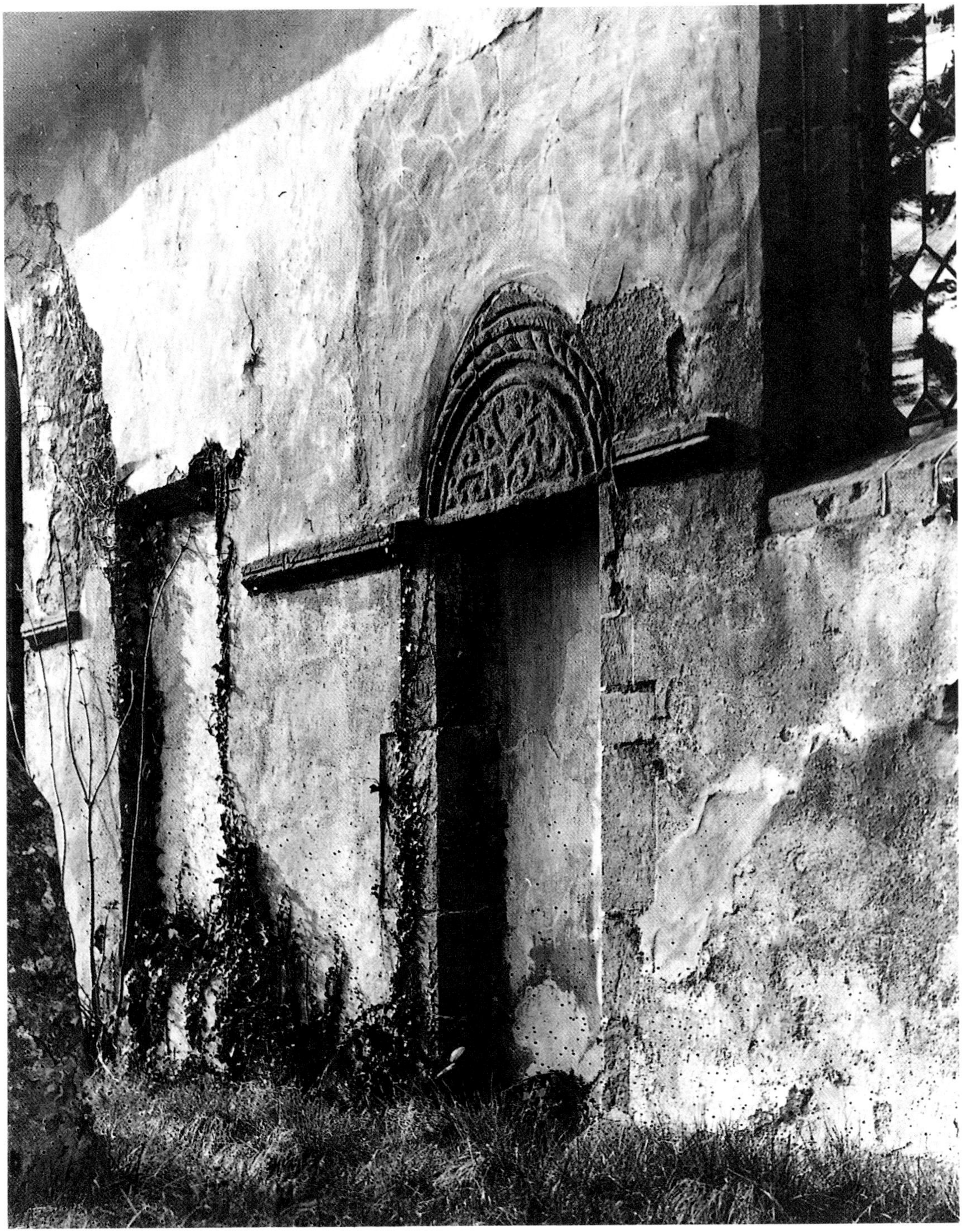

106 Doorway at Tugford, Shropshire

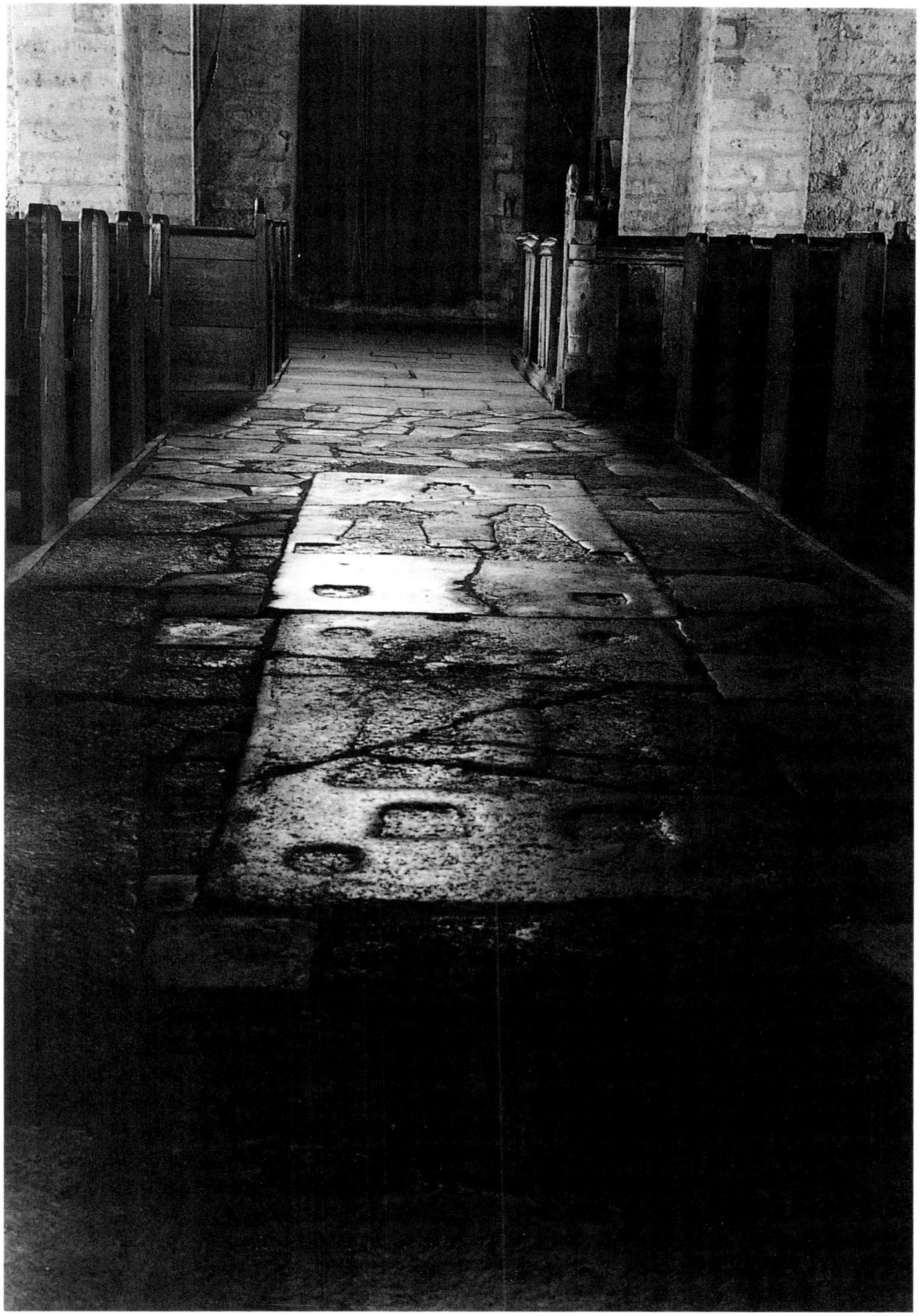

107 Nave floor, Whitchurch, Buckinghamshire

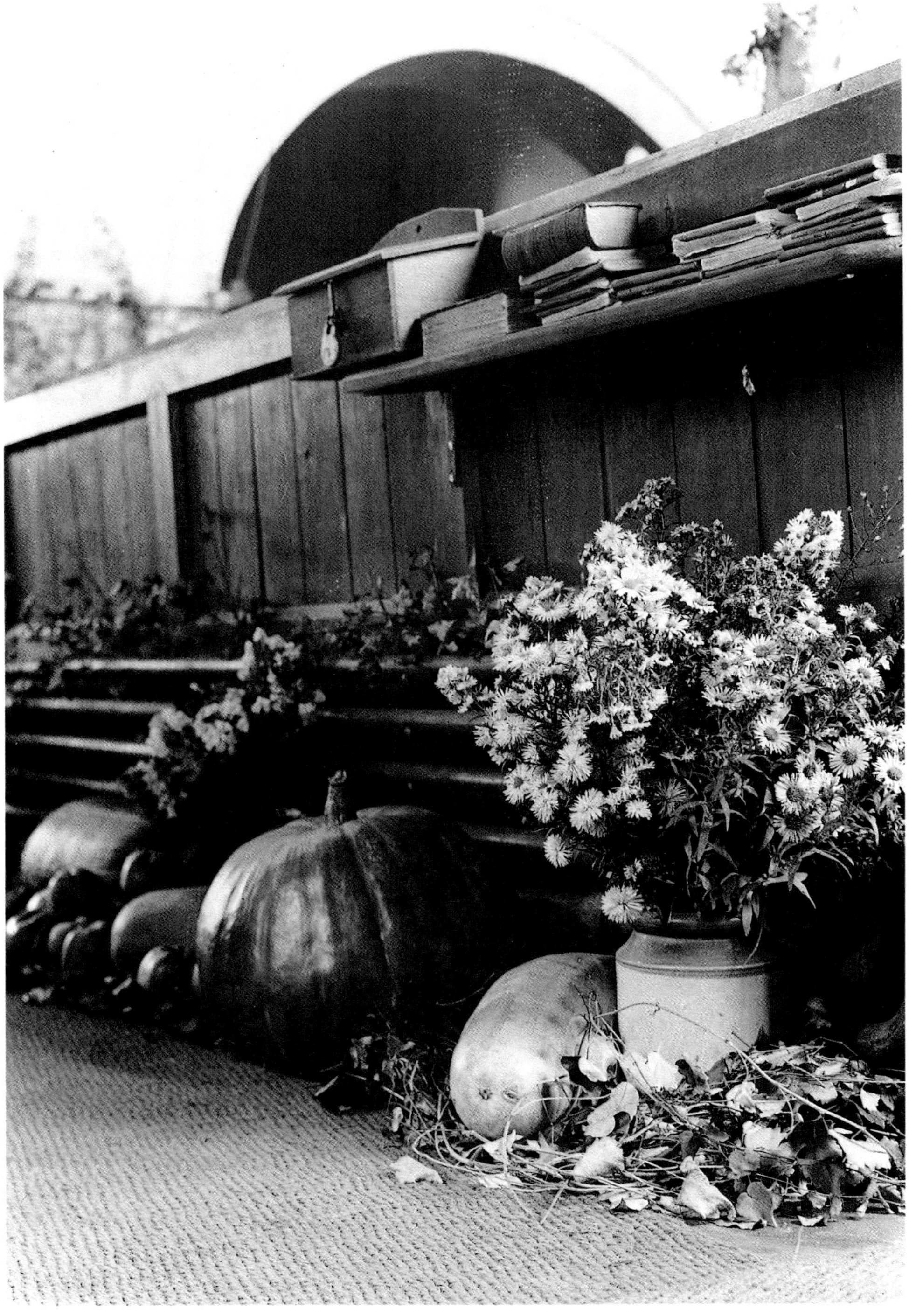

108 Harvest festival at Charlbury, Oxfordshire

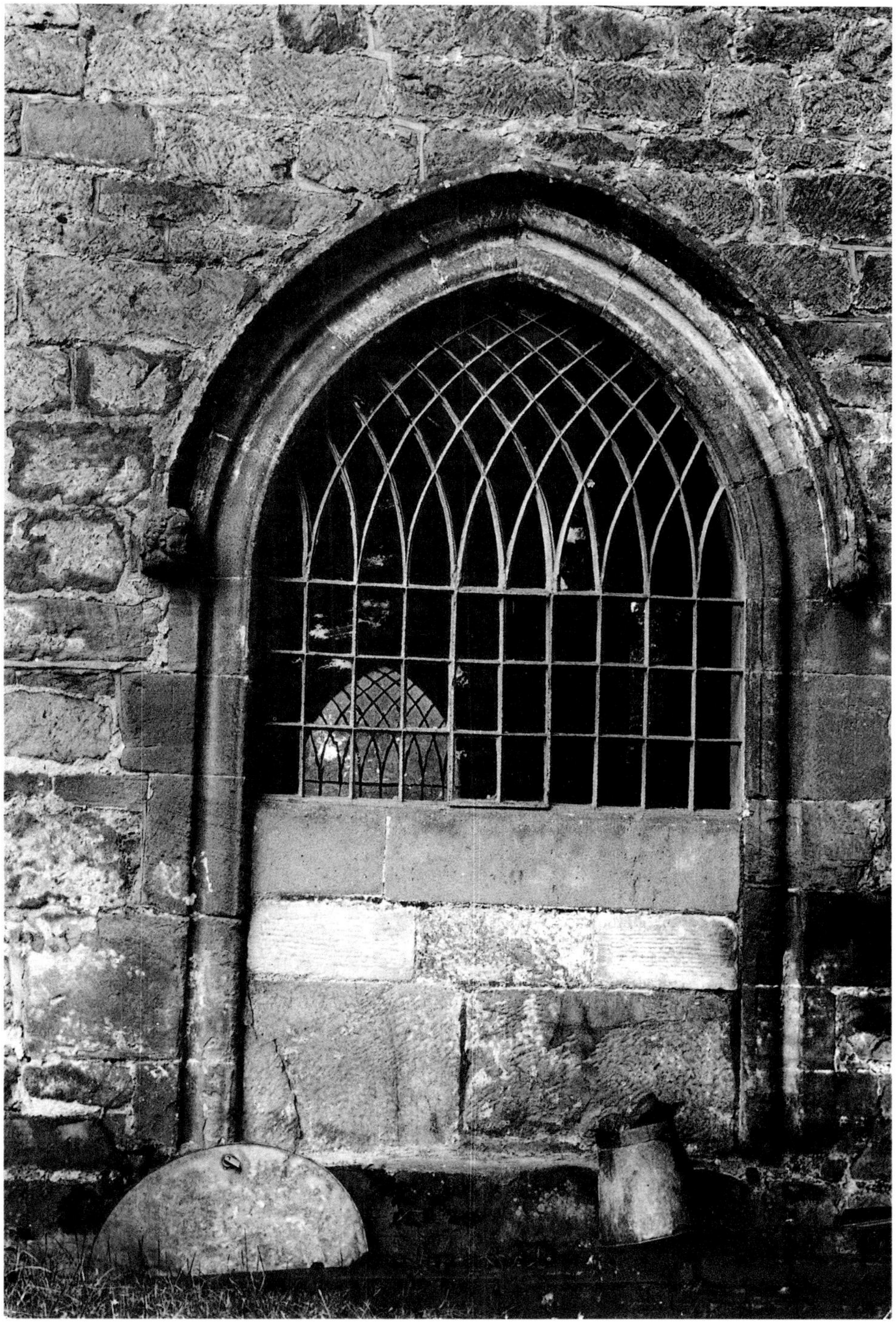

109 Cast iron tracery at Longnor, Shropshire

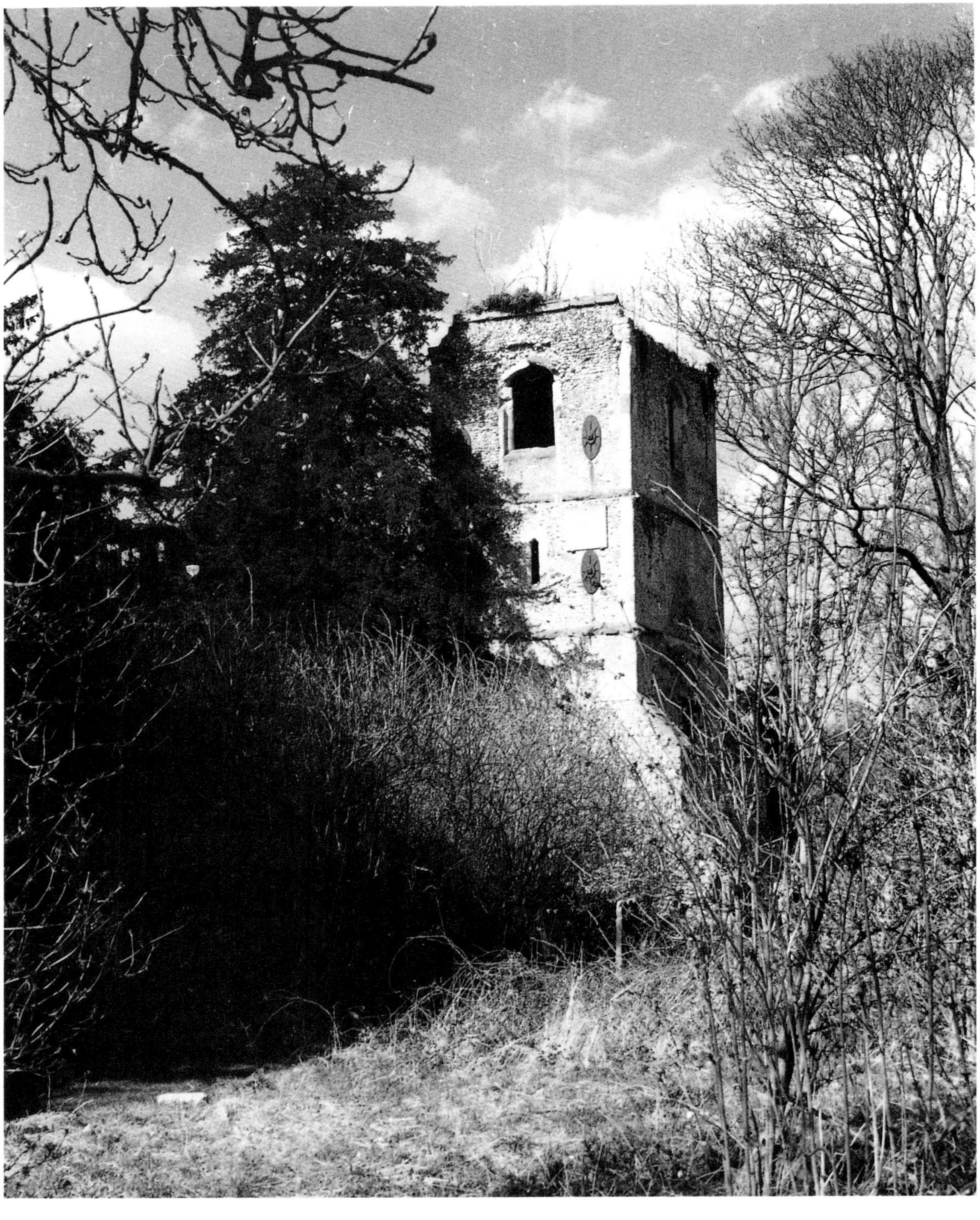

110 Tower at Thundrige, Hertfordshire

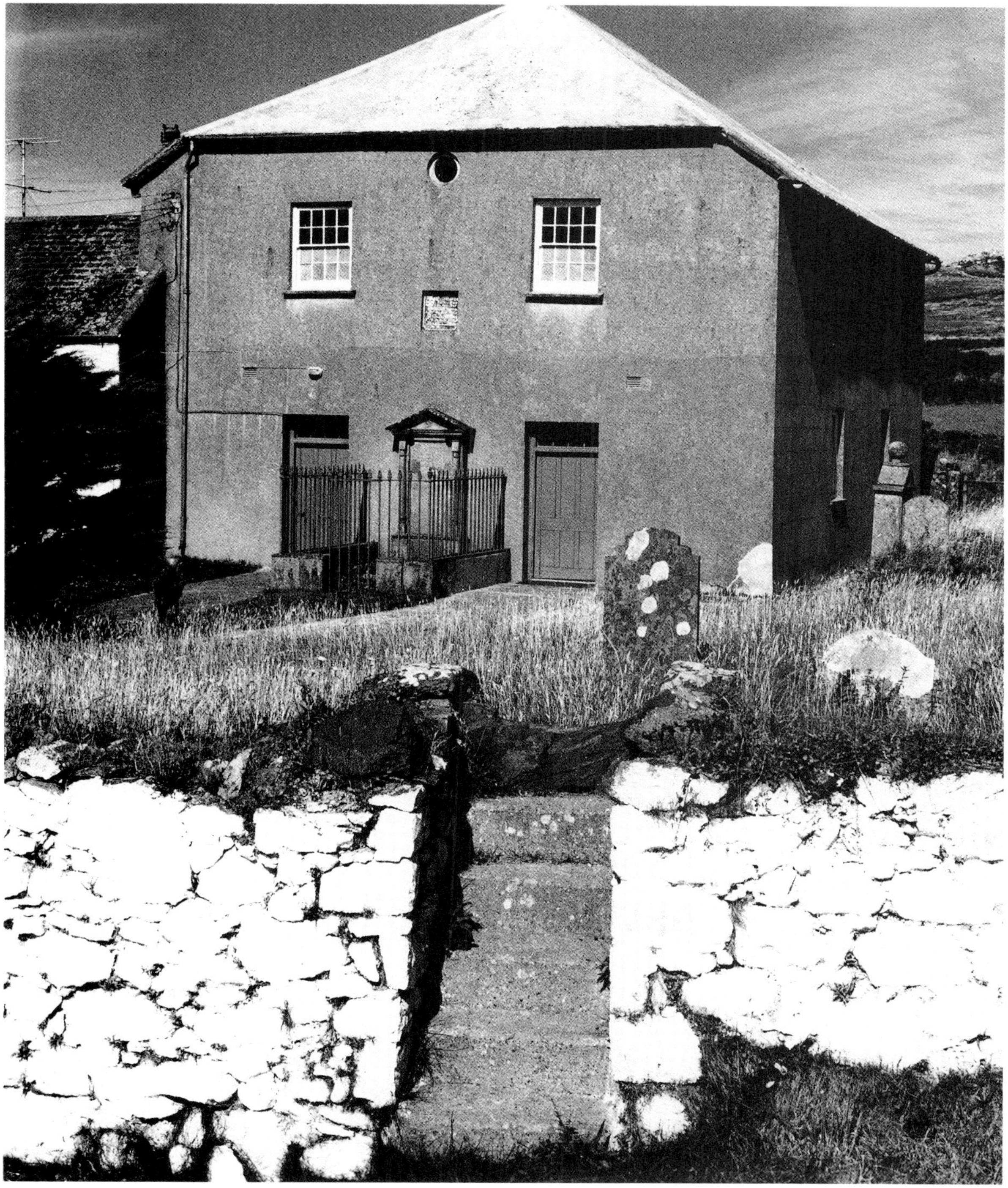

111 Rhosycaerau, near Fishguard, Dyfed, 1970

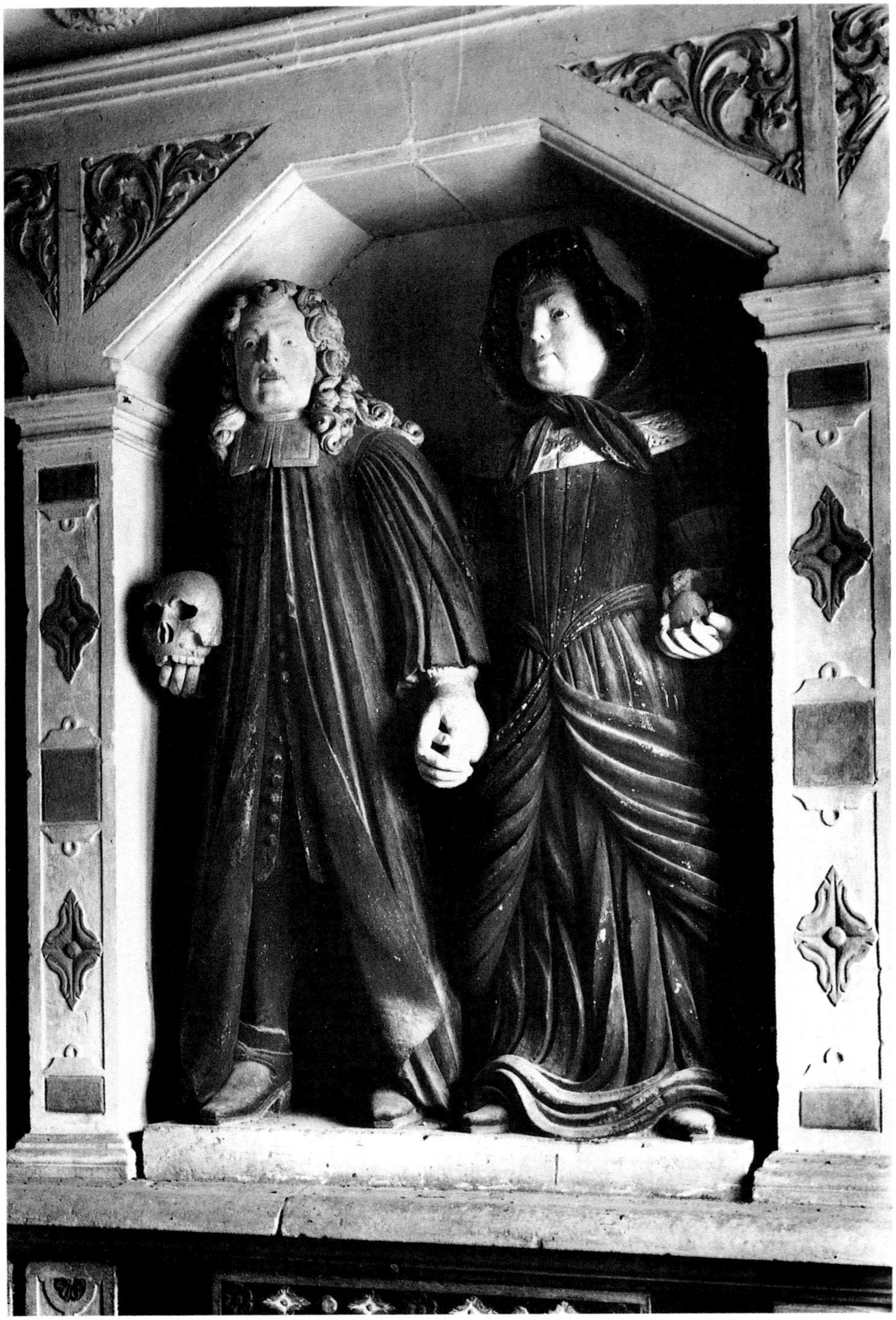

112 Howard monument, Rudbaxton, near Haverfordwest, Dyfed

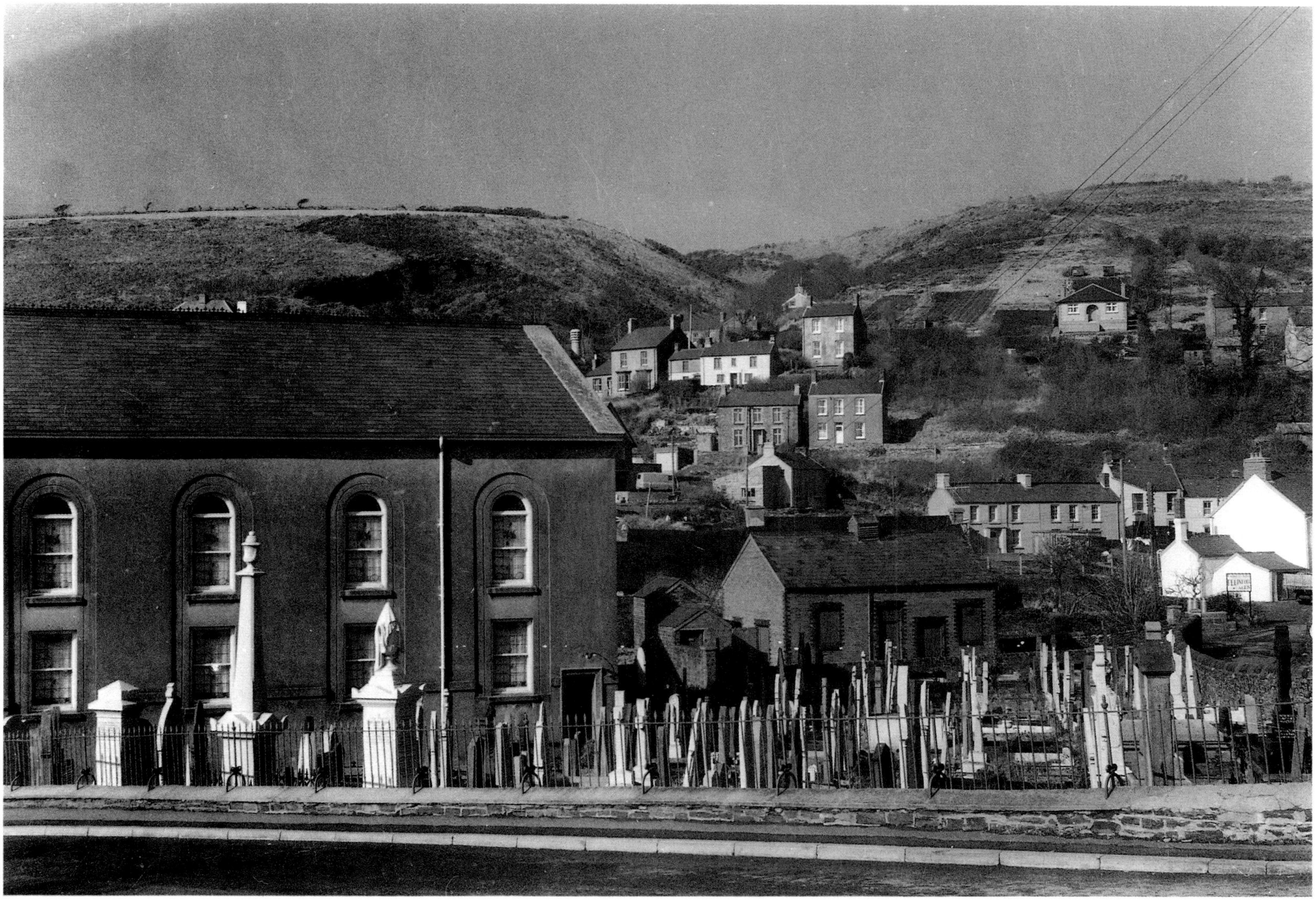

113 Chapel at Pembrey, Dyfed

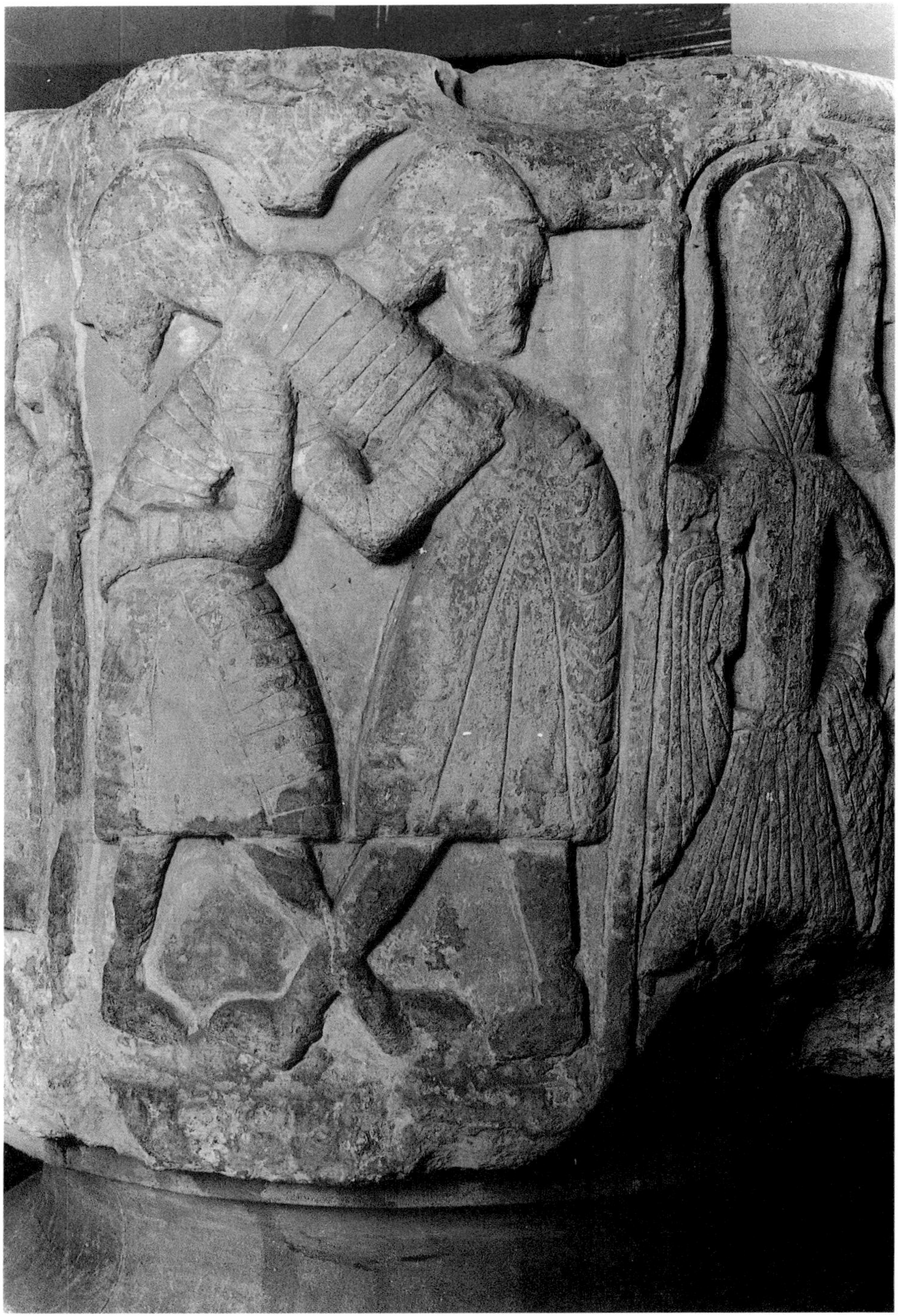

114 Font at Cowlam, Yorkshire

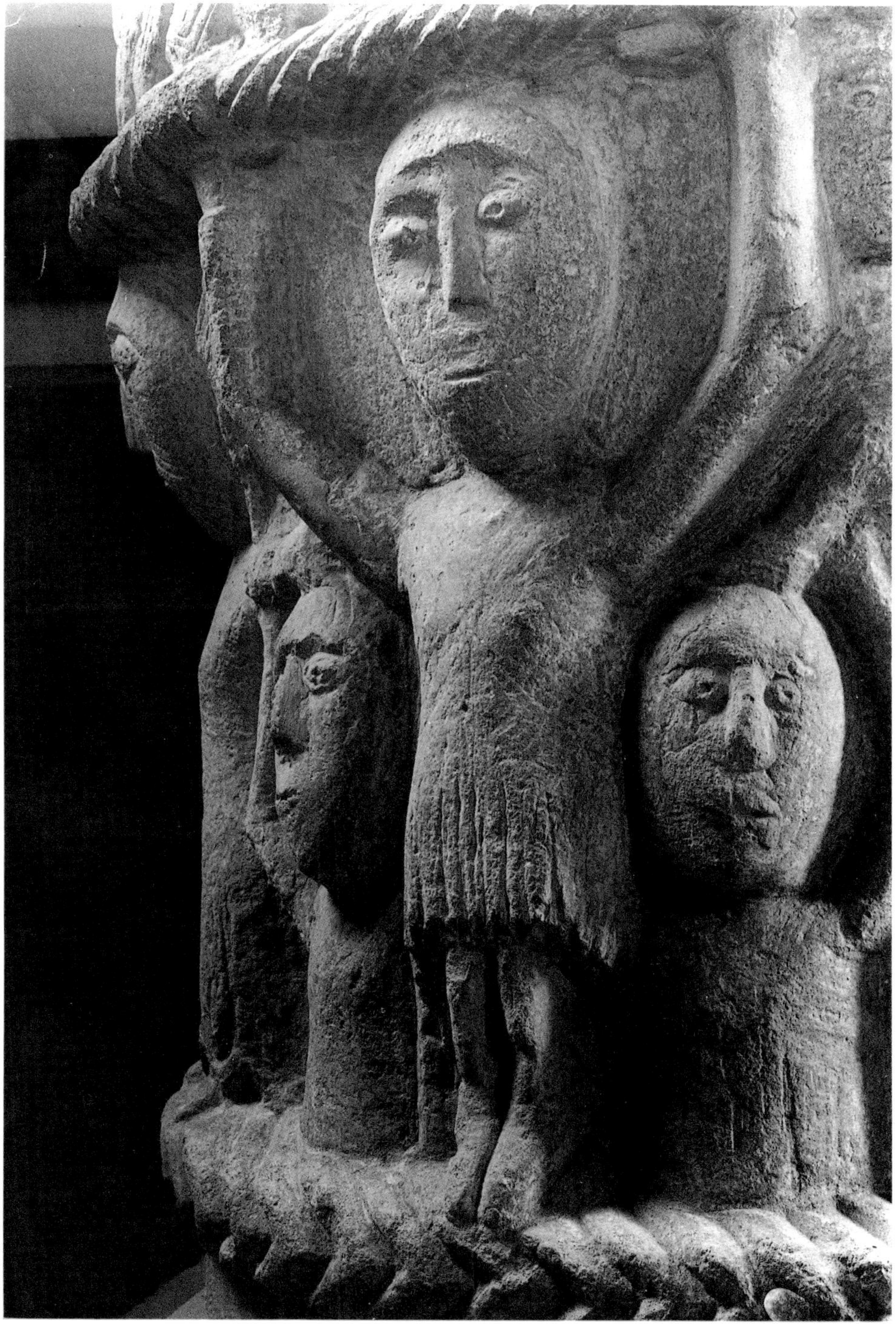

115 Font at Toller Fratrum, Dorset

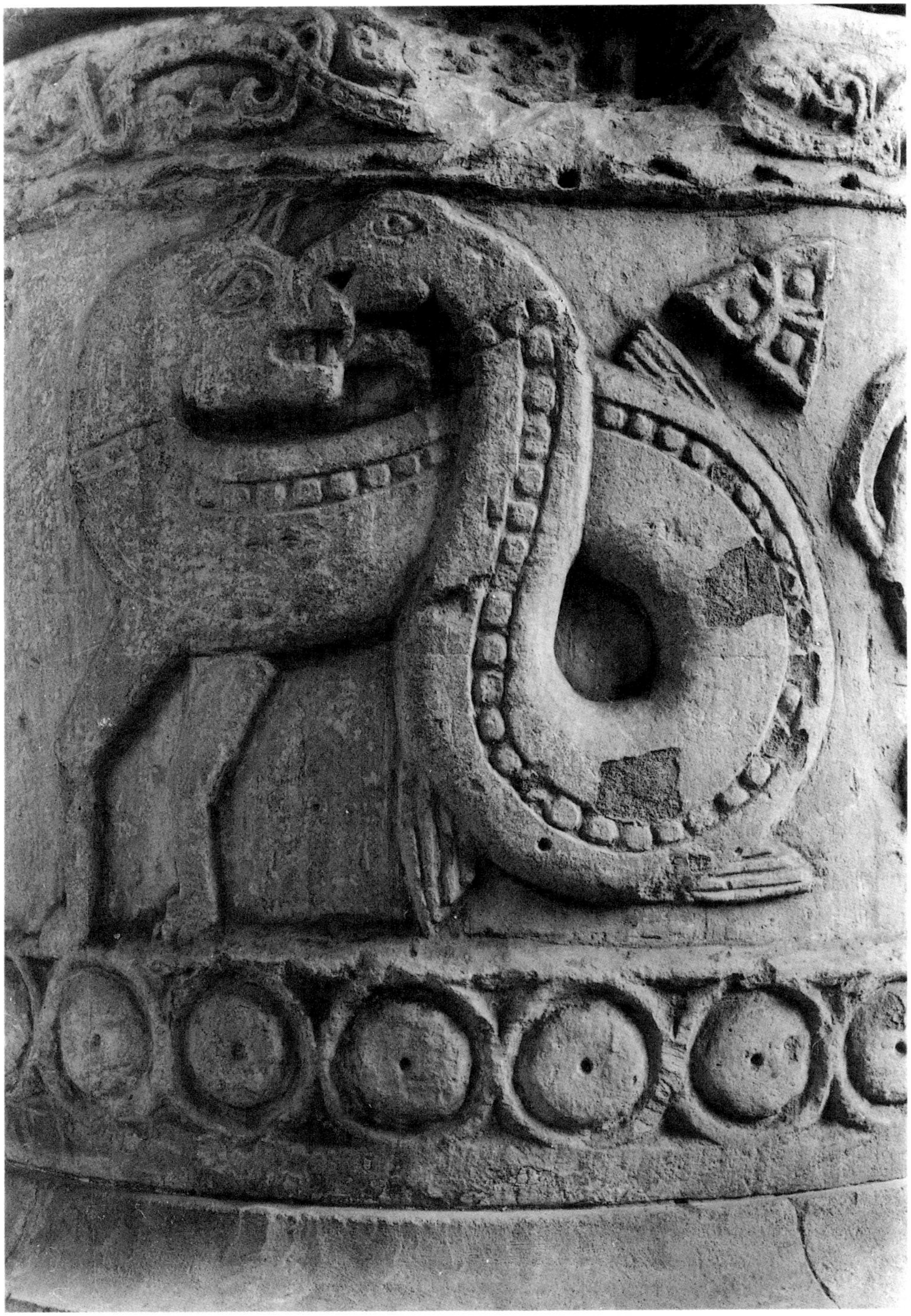

116 Font at Hook Norton, Oxfordshire

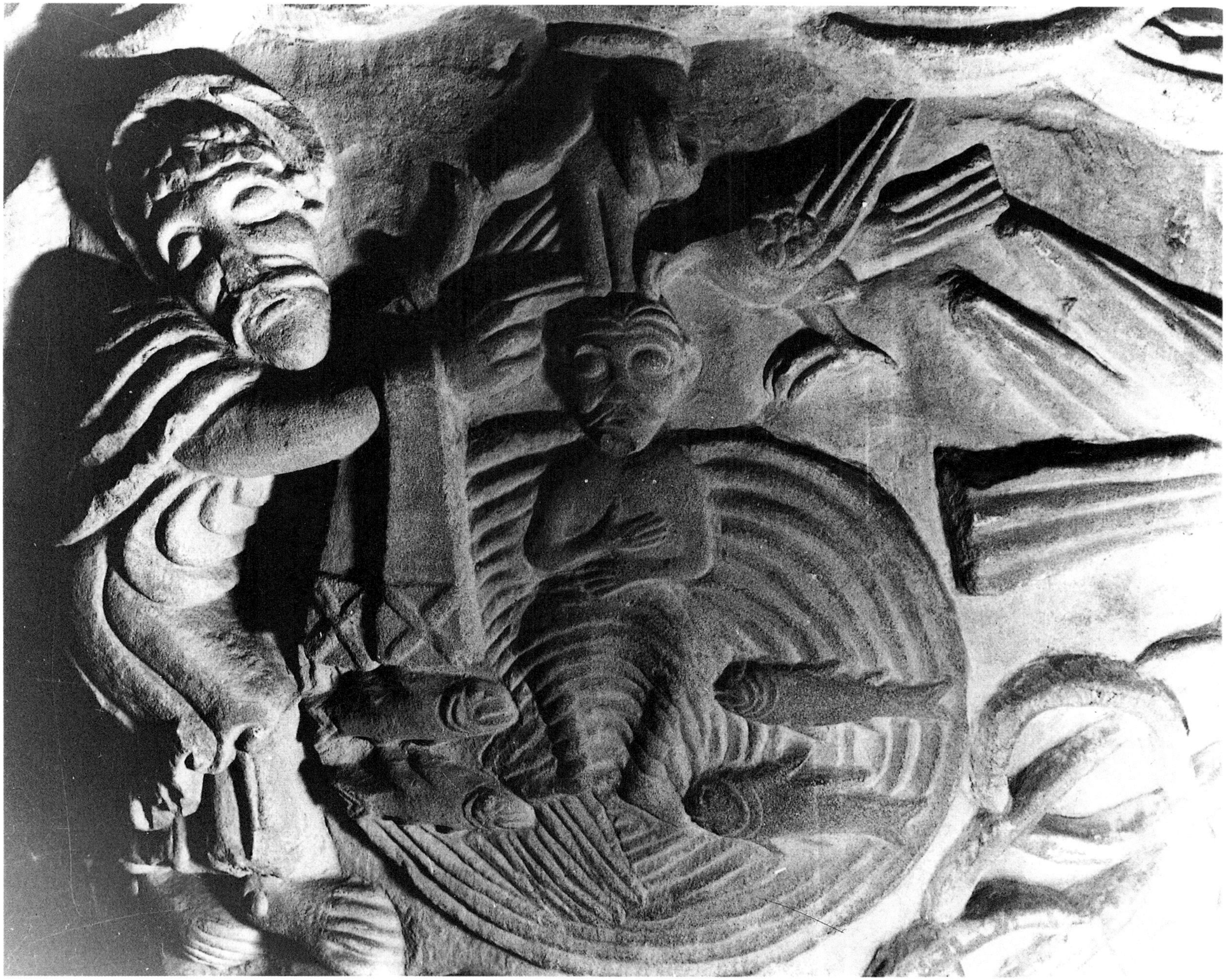

117 Font at Castle Frome, Herefordshire

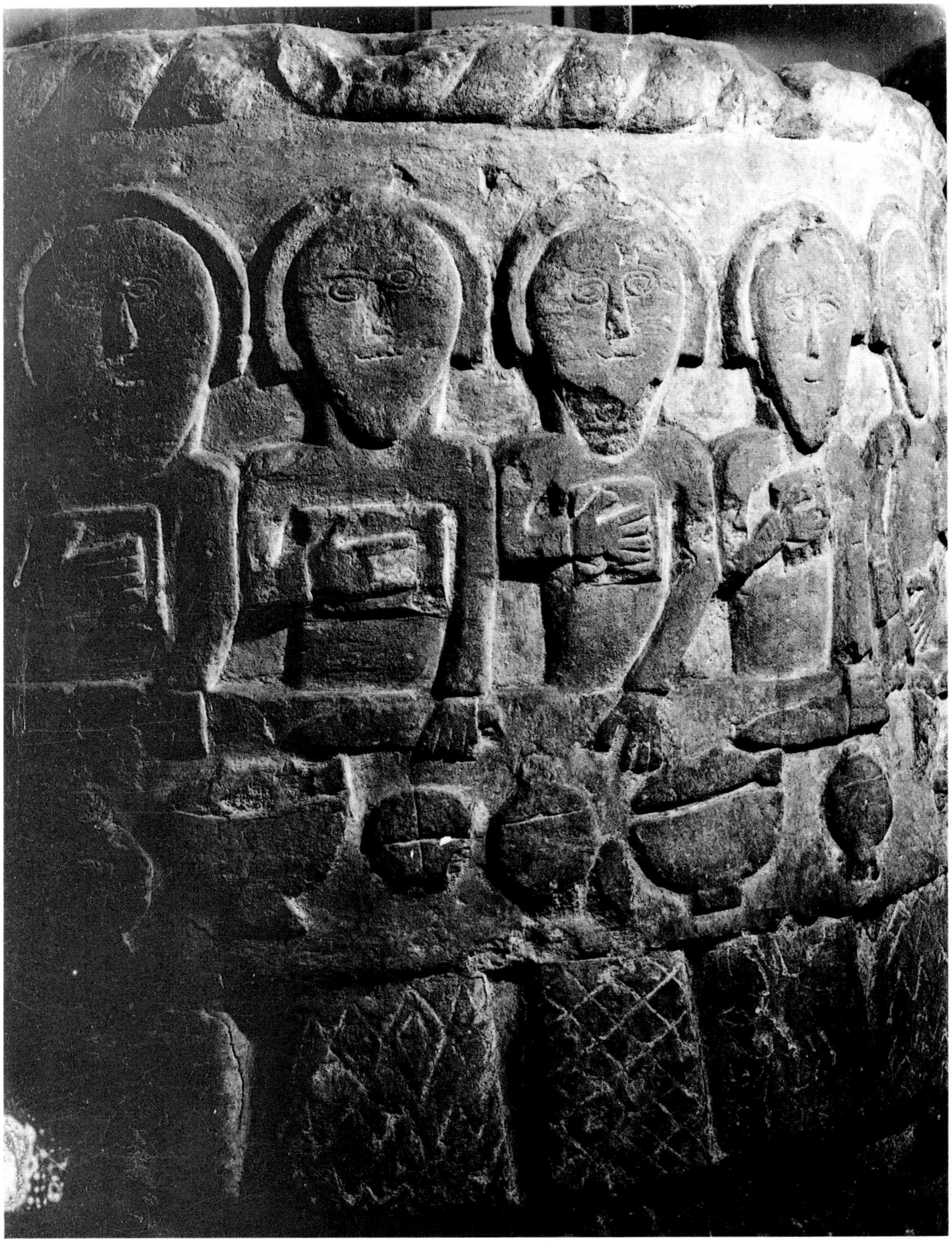

118 Font at North Grimstone, Yorkshire

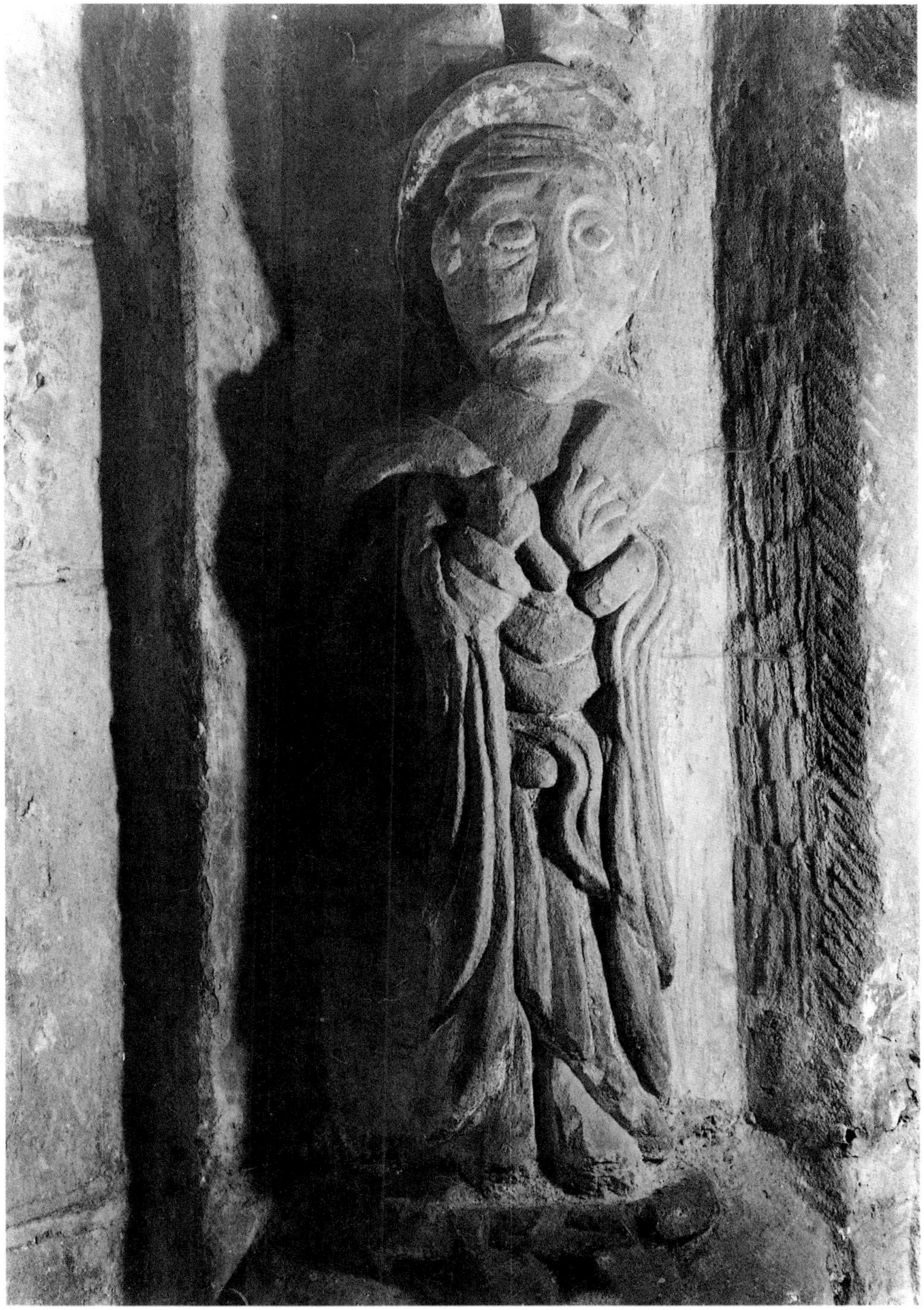

119 Norman figure on chancel arch, Kilpeck, Herefordshire

List of Photographs

In 1985 John Piper generously deposited over 5,000 negatives in the Tate Gallery Archive. All the negatives have been contacted and sorted topographically by English and Welsh counties, Scotland and other European countries and individually numbered. With John Piper's help most of the locations have been identified.

Copyright remains the property of John Piper (and his family) and all requests to publish will have to be agreed in writing prior to prints being released.

Applications to view the photographs should be made in writing to the Tate Gallery Archive. All applicants should be either working on a post-graduate thesis, a book, a television or radio programme, an exhibition or film.

Images identified by a Tate Archive number in brackets have been reproduced from negatives deposited in the Archive; the others have been made from old prints, for which negatives have yet to be found.

1 Weymouth Pier, Dorset [76.1.6]
Architectural Review January 1938

2 Beach huts [188.2.7]
Architectural Review January 1938

3 Beach Object, Construction by John Piper, 1937 [186.1.4]
The Painter's Object, 1937

4 Coastguard Station, Rye Harbour, East Sussex, 1977 [251.7.2]

5 J. P. Seddon's University College of Wales, Aberystwyth, Dyfed [54.1.2]

6 Canal Basin, Stourport, Worcestershire

7 A harbour light at Ramsgate, Kent [141.1.5]
Architectural Review January 1938

8 Farm buildings, Trefasser, Dyfed [419.2.1]

9 From Strumble Head, looking towards St Davids, Dyfed [113.1.10]

10 Harwich, low light and high light, Essex [13/19.3.4]
Shell guide to Essex, 1968

11 Tower house at Littlestone, Romney Marsh, Kent

12 Martello tower at Camber [244.1.6]

13 Dryslewyn, near Llandeilo, Dyfed [368.6.1]

14 Houses at Portland, 1937 [241.1.8]

15 Portland Roads looking towards Weymouth, about 1970 [418.1.1]

16 Tryfan, Snowdonia, about 1950 [329.3.2]

17 The summit of Tryfan, Snowdonia, about 1950

18 Limekilns at Llandybie, Dyfed [77.2.1]
Shell Guide to South-West Wales, 1963

19 Quarryman's staircase, Corris, Gwynedd [101.1.2]

20 Hopfield at Horsmonden, Kent

21 Edlesborough, Buckinghamshire

22 Sheep in brussels sprouts, near Claverly, Worcestershire, about 1980

23 Backwater of the Thames, Lechlade, Gloucestershire, 1936 [266.3.7]

24 Ladie's Bridge on the Kennet and Avon Canal, Wilcot, Wiltshire [61.3.10]

25 Keystone of gateway to Fonthill Abbey, Wiltshire [63.1.4]
Shell Guide to Wiltshire, 1968

26 A back garden at Adderbury, Oxfordshire, 1937 [419.1.9]
Shell Guide to Oxfordshire, 1938

27 Barn at Combwich, on the Parrett near Bridgwater, Somerset about 1938 [267.1.1]

28 Stebbing, Essex
Shell Guide to Essex, 1968

29 Model Village, Milton Abbas, Dorset [268.3.3]

30 South Creake, Norfolk [83.5.3]

31 Avoncroft Museum of Buildings, Bromsgrove, Warwickshire

32 Bishop Auckland, Durham [124.2.6]
Shell Guide to County Durham, 1980, end paper

33 Coal wagons at Middlesbrough, about 1938 [74.1.5]

34 Stoke on Trent, 1953

35 Bar in the Royal Oak, Cerne Abbas, 1936

36 Slate quarry, Blaenau Ffestiniog, Gwynedd [311.4.4]
Shell Guide to Mid Western Wales, 1971

37 Sheffield [137.1.8]

38 Mine buildings at Redruth, Cornwall [434.2.2]

39 Deserted tin mine St Austell, Cornwall [412.1.1]

40 Infant School, [159.1.3]
Shell Guide to Norfolk, 1958

41 China clay tip, Nanpean, Cornwall [190.1.8]
Shell Guide to Cornwall, 1964

42 The kitchen of an Oxford College, about 1936 [274.1.4]

43 Wisteria at Bretforton, Worcestershire [82.3.1]

44 The Library, Hafod House, Dyfed, 1939 [176.1.7]

45 Model made by Joy Mills of John Piper's design for the Festival Gardens, Battersea Park, 1951 [277.2.3]

46 Wheatfield, Oxfordshire

47 Stables of destroyed manor house, Wheatfield, Oxfordshire 1968 [74.2.5]
Architectural Review, September 1947

48 Kirby Hall, Northamptonshire [317.2.1]

49 Model by John Piper of set for John Cranko's ballet 'Harlequin in April', 1954 [278.7.7]

50 Ruined house near Stamford, Northamptonshire

51 Smallholme Tower, near Kelso, 1975

52 Ettington Park, Warwickshire
Shell Guide to Warwickshire, 1979

53 Screen at Ettington Park, Warwickshire
Shell Guide to Warwickshire, 1979

54 Harlaxton Manor, Lincolnshire, 1978 [1.1.6]

55 Harlaxton Manor, Lincolnshire, 1965 [42.1.4]

56 William Kent's eyecatcher at Rousham, Oxfordshire, about 1938 [266.7.8]
Shell Guide to Oxfordshire, 1938

57 Blenheim Palace, Oxfordshire, 1978

58 Bodiam Castle, East Sussex, 1977 [120.2.5]

59 Bishop's Palace, St David's, Dyfed

60 Ivied figure at Wotton, Surrey [197.2.8]

61 Staircase feature at Coleshill, Berkshire [270.2.6]

62 Doddington Bastle House, Cumbria, 1975

63 Preston on the Weald Moors, Shropshire [203.1.1]

64 Palladian Bridge at Stowe, Buckinghamshire
Murray's Guide to Buckinghamshire, 1948

65 William Kent's rill at Rousham, Oxfordshire, 1975

66 Temple of the British Worthies, Stowe, Buckinghamshire, 1950s [136.3.2]

67 Congreve Memorial, Stowe, Buckinghamshire

68 Turf maze at Somerton, near Northleach, Oxfordshire, 1930s [426.1.2]

69 Caerlaverock, Dumfriesshire [418.1.5]

70 The Arch of Hadrian, Shugborough, Staffordshire [214.1.9]
Shell Guide to Staffordshire, 1978

71 Hamstead Marshall, Buckinghamshire, 1960s

72 East Barsham manor house, Norfolk
Shell Guide to Norfolk, 1958

73 The Root-house, Badminton, Wiltshire, about 1974 [418.1.6]

74 Horton Tower, Dorset [420.1.4]
Shell Guide to Dorset, 1966

75 In the park at Castle Howard, Yorkshire [61.4.5]

76 Rievaulx Abbey, Yorkshire

77 Sculptured stone, Llanwnda, Dyfed [299.1.12]
Shell Guide to South-West Wales, 1963

78 St Edrens, Dyfed [169.1.2]
Shell Guide to South-West Wales, 1963

79 Bawsey, Norfolk [114.1.9]

80 West front of Durham Cathedral [102.1.3 & 102.1.4]

81 Detail of South door, Stoke-by-Nayland, Suffolk [132.1.2]
Sell Guide to Suffolk, 1976

82 Glass at Cherington, Warwickshire

83 Ruined chapel, Trecarrel, Cornwall, 1941

84 Screen at Dennington, Suffolk [196.1.5]

85 Kederminster pew, Langley Marish, Buckinghamshire [154.1.2]
Murray's Guide to Buckinghamshire, 1948

86 Foot of the Tower at Lavenham, Suffolk [48.1.9]

87 St George Reforne, Portland, Dorset, about 1970

88 Baptist Chapel, Llangloffan, Dyfed
Shell Guide to South-West Wales, 1963

89 St Govans Chapel, Pembrokeshire, 1970 [29.1.4]

90 Interior at Worthen, Shropshire, 1939

91 Fortheringhay, Northamptonshire [415.1.1]

92 Spire of Fleet, Lincolnshire
Architectural Review, November 1940

93 Fountain at Alton Towers, Staffordshire [78.2.4]

94 Tower of Chewton Mendip, Somerset

95 Tower at Tardebigge, Hereford and Worcester, about 1950 [366.7.6]
Shell Guide to Worcestershire, 1964

96 Kirkham Priory, Yorkshire, about 1950

97 Walpole St Peter, Norfolk

98 Interior, Launceston, Cornwall

99 Tower of Hamsey, Sussex, 1939

100 Harvest festival

101 Interior of Warminghurst, West Sussex [71.1.1]

102 Window at Gipping, Suffolk, 1968 [434.3.4]

103 Hougham, Lincolnshire [279.1.11]

104 The 'marble church', Bedelwyddan, Flintshire
Shell Guide to North Wales, 1971

105 Monument at Sparsholt, Oxfordshire [30.1.3]

106 Doorway at Tugford, Shropshire
Shell Guide to Shropshire, 1951

107 Nave floor, Whitchurch, Buckinghamshire [396.1.1]
Murray's Guide to Buckinghamshire, 1948

108 Harvest festival at Charlbury, Oxfordshire [425.1.4]
Shell Guide to Oxfordshire, 1938

109 Cast iron tracery at Longnor, Shropshire
Shell Guide to Shropshire, 1951

110 Tower at Thundrige, Hertfordshire

111 Rhosycaerau, near Fishguard, Dyfed, 1970

112 Howard monument, Rudbaxton, near Haverfordwest, Dyfed
Shell Guide to South-West Wales, 1963

113 Chapel at Pembrey, Dyfed
Shell Guide to South-West Wales, 1963

114 Font at Cowlam, Yorkshire [21.1.1]

115 Font at Toller Fratrum, Dorset [108.1.5]

116 Font at Hook Norton, Oxfordshire
Architectural Review, October 1936

117 Font at Castle Frome, Herefordshire
Architectural Review, October 1936

118 Font at North Grimstone, Yorkshire

119 Norman figure on chancel arch, Kilpeck, Herefordshire [50.3.3]
Shell Guide to Herefordshire, 1955